Anthropocene Mobilities

Anthropocene Mobilities

Sustainable Travel and Caring for the Commons

Peter Cox

BLOOMSBURY ACADEMIC
LONDON • NEW YORK • OXFORD • NEW DELHI • SYDNEY

BLOOMSBURY ACADEMIC
Bloomsbury Publishing Plc
50 Bedford Square, London, WC1B 3DP, UK
1385 Broadway, New York, NY 10018, USA
29 Earlsfort Terrace, Dublin 2, Ireland

BLOOMSBURY, BLOOMSBURY ACADEMIC and the Diana logo are trademarks of
Bloomsbury Publishing Plc

First published in Great Britain 2025

Copyright © Peter Cox, 2025

Peter Cox has asserted his right under the Copyright, Designs and Patents Act, 1988, to be
identified as Author of this work.

For legal purposes the Acknowledgements on p. viii–ix constitute an extension of this
copyright page.

Cover design by Grace Ridge
Cover images © Andi Purnomo and alphabetMN via Getty Images

Bloomsbury Publishing Plc does not have any control over, or responsibility for, any
third-party websites referred to or in this book. All internet addresses given in this
book were correct at the time of going to press. The author and publisher regret any
inconvenience caused if addresses have changed or sites have ceased to exist,
but can accept no responsibility for any such changes.

A catalogue record for this book is available from the British Library.

Library of Congress Cataloging-in-Publication Data

ISBN: HB: 978-1-3504-6474-2
PB: 978-1-3504-6478-0
ePDF: 978-1-3504-6476-6
eBook: 978-1-3504-6475-9

Typeset by Newgen KnowledgeWorks Pvt. Ltd., Chennai, India
Printed and bound in Great Britain

For product safety related questions contact
productsafety@bloomsbury.com.

To find out more about our authors and books visit www.bloomsbury.com
and sign up for our newsletters.

Contents

Acknowledgements and thanks | viii

Introduction | 1

1 Setting the scene | 9
   Why Anthropocene mobilities? | 12
   Genesis and process | 13
   Situational analysis: Where are we? | 16
   Who is the 'we'? | 17
   Bodies in movement | 19
   Moving and being moved | 24
   Democracy and the mundane | 26
   Conclusions | 30

2 Anthropocene citizenship | 33
   Introduction: Anthropocene as context | 33
   EcoJustice in the Anthropocene | 36
   Defining the Anthropocene | 37
   Emancipatory politics in the Anthropocene | 40
   Contributory discourses for Anthropocene citizenship | 42
   Directions for Anthropocene citizenship | 47
   Citizenship, democracy and the more-than-human | 50
   Non-domination | 52
   Citizenship as encounter | 53
   Conclusions | 55

3 Being-in-the-world: Care and commoning | 57
   Introduction | 57
   Relationality and dialogue | 58
   Resonance | 59
   Care | 65

Non-domination and thinking through care   69
Care and relationality   70
Being cared for   71
The commons and commoning   73
Commoning and the more-than-human   76
Commoning and democracy   77
Commoning and care   78
Commoning as critique: Mobilities   79
Commoning, scarcity and plenitude in mobility   80
Uncontrollability   82
Uncontrollability and uncertainty   84
Uncontrollability, instrumentalism and traditions of resistance   85
Transformative action   86
Conclusion: Care and commoning for Anthropocene citizenship   87

4   Pedagogies and mobilities: Learning and perception   89
Introduction   89
The traveller as assemblage   91
Extraordinary and mundane travels   92
Wild pedagogies of mobility   93
Bodies in movement   95
Modes of perception: Meeting the world around us   97
Feeling the travelscape   102
Motor traffic shapes the world   104
Conclusions   108

5   Human scale movement: Walking, wheeling, cycling   111
Introduction   111
Human scale speeds and travel   112
Walking as a way of being-in-the-world   115
Repetition   118
The sensory journey: Perception and care   119
Exclusive space and the commons   123
Walking, wheeling and cycling in a motoring world   125
Wheeling   127
Being-in-the-world as a cyclist   128
Technologies of cycle travel   132
Travel technologies and alienated labour   133

Encounters care and commoning 135
Human scale limits as virtues 136
Mobility, leisure, aesthetics and knowledge production 139
Conclusions 140

6 Passengers and drivers 143
Introduction 143
Passenger sensations 145
Categories of passenger 146
    Families, strangers and degrees of trust 146
    Dependent and compulsory passengers 148
Passenger transport as public space 150
Waiting spaces 153
Interior spaces 155
Understanding encounters 156
Aeromobilities 158
Driving in a system of automobility 159
Motoring as citizenship 161
Anthropocenic motoring? 165
Conclusions 166

7 Coda: Towards Anthropocene mobilities 167
Introduction 167
Sufficiency 168
Anthropocene mobility as an abolitionist project 170
Non-car natives 171
The ambiguity of vulnerability 172
Infrastructures 173
Conclusions: Frugal abundance 175

References 177
Index 195

Acknowledgements and thanks

The language of *Anthropocene Mobilities* has been used elsewhere, particularly for a special issue of *Mobilities* in 2019 (issue 14(3)) arising from a 2016 conference. The special issue used the heading to focus on the intersection of critical climate migration studies and thinking about the Anthropocene (Baldwin et al. 2019). This approach is further developed in Mimi Sheller's *Advanced Introduction to Mobilities* (2022). As befits her pioneering work in conceptualizing mobility as a paradigm shift in the social sciences, Sheller considers how the mobilities paradigm can be used to think through the implications of the Anthropocene concept. Consequently, her analysis of *Anthropocene Mobilities* takes a geohistorical perspective that allows her to link these insights to her extensive work on mobility justice and to mobile commoning.

My scope here is much more limited and is indebted to the work of the Rachel Carson Center in Munich in its explorations of the cultural implications of the Anthropocene (Möller et al. 2014). The focus of this book is on literal mobility and everyday movement, the travel patterns of the past, present and, potentially, future. Although grounded in a mobilities perspective, its title might even be Anthropocene Travels, but my concern is to go beyond the limits of transport and travel studies, to remain rooted in social theory (compare Chester and Allenby 2021).

Much of the initial work for this book was enabled by a Landhaus Fellowship at the Rachel Carson Center at LMU Munich in 2023, which built on earlier work there under a Leverhulme International Academic Fellowship in 2014/15. Special thanks must go to the director of the RCC Christof Mauch for his steering, explanations and encouragement to expand my interest from too tight a focus on cycling. My fellow Landhaus Fellows, Moremi, Loretta, Roberta, Craig, Nye, Mona, Nandita, Alex and Fred at Hermannsdorf all provided valuable input. Thanks must also go to Tom and Michela of the Critical Pathways to Sustainability research group at Utrecht University for inviting me to talk and to lead workshops in November 2023, supplying valuable feedback on the core ideas. I have also benefited enormously from a Visiting Fellowship at TEMA-T, Linköping University, in 2024 where the book was finished. The whole team under Harald Rohracher gave me considerable support in the final stages and yet another opportunity to spend time alternating field work with rewriting and editing. I must also thank colleagues past and present of the Department of Social and Political Science at the University of Chester who have supported my research over the years, especially Paul Taylor. This book is dedicated to Rosie, the expert on wheelchair travel.

Introduction

The realities of climate breakdown and the advent of the Anthropocene challenge us collectively to identify and understand both the actions and the thinking that have led to multiple crises. An ever-growing body of evidence and analysis points to the scale and scope of these problems and to their uneven distribution (Gupta et al. 2024). These studies also highlight ways that damage can be mitigated through reduction in harmful activities and point towards the adaptations required to cope better with changes already 'locked-in' by actions to date. The need to change unsustainable, high-carbon, high-energy and high-consumption practices and to move beyond fossil fuel dependence is widely acknowledged. Even the previously cautious IPCC (International Panel on Climate Change) in its most recent *Sixth Report* (2021) together with its numerous annexes not only identifies the impacts on climate from a range of sectors of human action but also begins the process of outlining potential policy and practice changes to alleviate the most profound impacts.

Transport and travel will be profoundly affected by fossil fuel phase down. The *Lancet Planetary Health–Earth Commission Report* suggests that a globally fair share of motor travel, ensuring that everyone globally can have an equal share without exceeding the boundaries for global sustainability, might be as low as 4,500 km per person per annum (Gupta et al. 2024). Solutions to the unsustainability of current personal transport practices are largely clear and uncontested. Electrification of vehicle fleets, lower speeds, more and better public transport and increases in walking and cycling for short journeys are key solutions that have been proposed for decades (see, e.g. Banister 2005). Discussions on policy measures to achieve these goals, however, often remain largely abstract. Traffic flows, modelled on fluid dynamics and accessibility indices related to urban densities and economic profiles, can be hard to relate to everyday life. But travel is something we all do. It is a mundane reality. And, however we move around, whatever mode of transport we might employ, movement is an experience. Walking, driving, riding and various ways of being a passenger all offer different experiences and possibilities. Each is also dependent on the spaces and environments through which it travels.

This book explores the implications of personal travel practices through the lens of human experience – the bodily and emotional interactions that different ways of travel create. It questions the currently dominant travel practices by the hypermobile (by global standards) whose everyday travel is unthinkingly part of a pattern of high-energy individualized transport system enabled by an era (now ending) of cheap fossil fuels. It challenges this system of automobility for its consumption of space and violence towards other humans and the more-than-human world, and above all for the ways in which it separates us from each other and from the world in which we live, and it proposes ways in which changed mobility practices can contribute to more equitable and inclusive outcomes. It is interested in how the sensory experiences of travel foster different values and in how these values build (or undermine) social understandings and sensitivities appropriate to future flourishing in the era of climate instabilities triggered by burning fossil fuels.

There are those who might object that this is an address to a relatively small (by global standards) and select group of persons who are in a sufficiently privileged position to make changes to their personal travel patterns and that it might be insufficiently sensitive to the inequalities of power, income and distribution of mobility, or to the transport of goods on which contemporary life depends. However, my concern is not to provide yet another set of arguments as to why we should change and what priorities need to be set in mobility transformations. The text is really interested in what happens in acts of personal travel, how different ways of travel foster different ways of relating to the world and whether these ways of relating to the world help or hinder us in our collective search to find ways of living within the planetary boundaries necessary for a good future. It argues that we can learn skills and insights into how to live less destructively (to become more fitting Anthropocene citizens) through everyday travel practices of walking and cycling. The book is thus a way of providing an alternative discourse to instrumentalized approaches aimed at applicability to policy and intervention.

The scale of impact of the Anthropocene as an era in which we recognize human action as the most significant force acting to shape the planetary biogeochemistry goes significantly beyond specific issues of climate change. A danger of over-concentration on low carbon futures and solutions is that the fundamental values and systems of resource use and consumption central to the bigger picture of the Anthropocene go unexamined. Approaching transport policy changes from the other end – from the experience of travellers and non-travellers – enables a broader critique to be developed: one that attends to values created by mobilities. Consequently, this book challenges the choices we make about travel and explores what they do to our individual and collective relationships with other humans and with the natural world. By concentrating on how travel experiences shape our understandings of and our relationships to the world, it asks how these experiences shape values and provide resources to enable us to live together as less destructive planet-dwellers. Conversely, it also necessarily confronts ways that some mobility practices can actively prevent development of appropriate qualities and values for responsible living.

The chapters of this book split the problem of thinking about these issues into two parts. The first explores ideas and ways of thinking that can help us to comprehend the qualities and values that might be needed to thrive, not just survive, in a post-fossil-fuel era. These orientations also need to be capable of preparing us to cope with the uncertainties of climate breakdown. The second part of the book explores in more detail what happens when we travel. It looks at a range of ways of existing routine and regular travel possibilities to see how they reinforce or challenge our complicity not just in climate breakdown but in the problematic broader relations to the world of which we are part.

The first chapter sets out the scope of the problems and outlines the approach taken throughout the work. The search for less environmentally toxic and destructive patterns of movement is only one part of a search for sustainable mobilities. Ecojustice and mobility justice perspectives highlight the inseparability of environmental and social concerns. As a means to knit these together, Chapter 2 develops the concept of Anthropocene citizenship as a way to think about living- and being-in-the-world shaped by uncertainty.

The effect of sustainable practices not tied to a wider critique of the social and economic structures that gave rise to the crisis of unsustainability can only be, at best, ameliorative. Anthropocene perspectives, reacting to the complete transformation of resource and energy use since the 1950s, often known as the 'great acceleration' (Steffen et al. 2015), highlight the need to do more than find novel ways to extend the lifespan of current trajectories of resource use and unsustainable mobility practices.

Chapter 3 turns to Hartmut Rosa's concept of resonance to provide a critique of the causative structures of the alienation that produce a disregard for the world around and to simultaneously articulate concern for its remedy. The chapter pays particular attention to its grounding in a relational understanding of the world. Resonance is a way of exploring the quality of relationship and the effects it has on us as people. If we are to understand the experience of travel, we need to have a way of comprehending the ways in which we relate to and interact with the world, both human and more-than-human. This enables individual life experiences to be linked to a structural critique of modernity. It provides a logical basis to connect a study of the world of senses and of who we are that is doing the sensing to a broader political project. Challenging individualist narratives of the self, relational models of being have the advantage of providing a way to understand not just human-human relationships but also relationships with the more-than-human, that which is often bundled together as 'the environment' or 'nature'.

Implicit in Rosa's affirmation of resonance as a means to explore ways of being-in-the-world that challenge the dominant destructive patterns of modernity are qualities of care and processes of commoning. Care and commoning can be used as values and measures with which to examine the experiential and consequential element of travel. Put simply, they allow us to ask whether any particular practice makes us care more, or care less, about other people and the world about, and to ask whether our practices enclose, shutting others out, or whether they allow for greater shared opportunity.

A corollary of resonance is that creating moments and situations that can deeply affect how we see ourselves and the world does not involve a predictable linear process of change. We cannot entirely control how experiences change us, even though we can work with them and their outcomes. Consequently, Rosa has elaborated on the idea of uncontrollability. Uncontrollability is not merely descriptive of not knowing what is going to happen, nor is it simply being out of control. It has political consequences as a mode of critique. It refutes the will for certainty, control and domination built into the expectations of many of the systems and institutions of modernity as described by scholars from Max Weber at the beginning of the twentieth century to George Ritzer at its end (Radkau 2009, Ritzer 1993; 2021). On a practical level, reconciliation with uncontrollability is also vital to develop flexible and responsive resilience measures in the face of instabilities unlocked by climate change. Living in the Anthropocene demands that we create institutions and practices that can cope with the uncertainty inherent in this new geologic era. For mobility, thinking about the consequences of uncontrollability gives us a further criterion to analyse how any given practice contributes (or not) to Anthropocene mobilities; does it contribute to the illusion of control, or is it conscious of the limits of our human capacity?

Drawing from existing travel practices, the fourth chapter returns to the theme of experience. How do we perceive the world? What are the multiple dimensions of perception that we bring to bear in our engagement with others, whether people or places? Physical sensations are only part of the equation: emotional and imaginative perceptions and responses also shape the way that we experience the world of human and more-than-human. Only when we have a model of perception that allows us to talk about the sensory worlds of travel can we turn to exploring how different ways of travel engender different experiences of being-in-the-world.

Transport studies conventionally distinguish travel by 'mode', usually vehicle type and/or as individual or passenger transport. This is an obvious categorization for traffic planners, reliant on easily identifiable criteria (although vehicles that do not fit into clear categories are problematic – see Cox and van de Walle 2007). Notably, walking and cycling have often been almost invisible in planning based on this kind of journey analysis. Foregrounding experience requires a different set of distinctions. To this end, I approach the issue of travel by distinguishing its level of dependence on energy inputs. Walking and cycling don't require any external energy source. At the other end of the scale, motoring and flight depend on the high energy density of fuel oils or on the storage capacity of high-energy-density battery systems, which in turn also require new extractive regimes. Higher speeds of travel necessitate separation of the traveller from the external environment. Passenger vehicle travel is clearly distinct from travel alone, regardless of speed, and the level of crowding on a service is also influential. Passengering takes a range of forms. Design of passenger service vehicles and service provision is all about the manipulation of experience. Further affecting experience is the degree of agency of passenger or driver. Is the service scheduled or on demand? Part of the history of scheduled travel is the history of the spaces provided for waiting, from bus shelters to airport terminals. Does travel rely on shared availability or on private vehicle ownership? In either case, to what extent is the vehicle accessible or in easy proximity (time or distance)?

But before addressing driving or passenger experiences it is essential to consider the fundamentals of everyday mobility – not reliant on external power, not limited by the implications of energy use, only self-limited by the availability of bodily energy. Travel experiences are mediated by a complex interweaving of degrees of bodily exertion, of sociability, of speed and sensation, of exposure and enclosure, of waiting and connecting. Each combination and journey is capable of creating unique sensations and interactions. Chapter 5 connects experiences of walking, wheeling and cycling to the qualities and values for a good Anthropocene citizenship, thinking through the engagements they create with the world around and with our bodies. The caveat to any discussion of non-motorized travel in a situation of the hegemonic domination and prioritization of private motoring that is taken for granted is that our perceptions are inevitably influenced by that context. Nevertheless, we have sufficient knowledge taken from actions taken in car-free spaces on how walking, wheeling and cycling can contribute to or impede the development of values forming Anthropocene citizenship.

After this focus on walking and cycling, I move on to consider travel reliant on external power. What ways of being-in-the-world does driving or being a car passenger create, and how does the dominance of motoring affect those beyond the car travellers? Drawing on the widespread analyses of automobility and its discontents, a core question is what an Anthropocenic driving might look like. Are there ways to envisage e-motoring that avoid the powerful role of automobility as a core element of the reproduction of capital and an essential component of accelerating economic growth? In response to these problems, I suggest that we need to consider how our travel, which inevitably creates encounters with others, allows us to respond and which values it embeds.

Transitions to mobility habits appropriate to the challenges of the Anthropocene, what the book calls Anthropocene mobilities, are not just about individual decision-making. There are roles for collective authorities. The final chapter therefore concludes the study by thinking briefly about the ways in which mobility practices that develop the skills and values for responsive Anthropocene citizenship might be institutionalized. In other words, what might we do collectively to support these actions? Here the book connects a little with the world of transport policy, not as planning but as a means to support and nurture the transformation of values and responsibilities outlined in Chapter 3. Considering mobility as a function of citizenship creates grounds for making demands of those institutions that habitually consider their participants as citizens. Anthropocene citizenship may move emphasis from rights to responsibilities and shift attention from national constraints to the planetary scale, but the institutional structures still remain as providers of the infrastructures that make actions and choices possible. Consequently, infrastructure providers (in their own role as Anthropocene citizens) have a responsibility to provide settings that enable transformations of travel behaviour. Concomitant with the actions taken by individuals, therefore, are the actions of institutions already being taken to fulfil their inter-institutional obligations (recognized in treaties and policy frameworks) of good citizenship in the Anthropocene. These considerations also bring us back to the relationships of institutions of governance and those governed, finally returning us to the renewal of democracy central implicit in reasserting citizenship. By shifting the focus from travel as a rather abstract concept to its physical reality as everyday experience, the book looks to add a new perspective to thinking through the issues of sustainable mobility.

1

Setting the scene

This is a book about living and moving in the Anthropocene. It is an attempt to think through things that are already happening. It is not a blueprint for actions in an unspecified future but a way to address real and very present issues that confront us in the new geological era *already* brought about by high-energy, carbon-fuelled lifestyles. More precisely, it is a way of thinking through ways that we live and move today and how they can assist in building values and habits of action required for the profoundly altered times that we face.

The book examines what an Anthropocene citizenship might entail in terms of everyday mobilities. It does not presume technologies yet to be developed nor does it rely on changes anticipated at some future date. It explores resources of action and activity that we already have. Its primary focus is on movement, the ways we move around, everyday experiences of mobility often taken for granted. It considers how the ways we move teach us about the world: how they build relationships and values, and the kinds of relations and values that they teach. It presents a critique of the value implications of currently dominant mobility practices: the social, political and economic structures and physical infrastructures that support them and how these ill-prepare us for responsible citizenship. Finally, it looks at ways that we might adopt and develop approaches that provide less destructive ways of living. But to do this it first has to consider our situation and the values that are fostered under current arrangements.

Its focus on mobility practices is linked to a series of observations. First, that in 2019, travel practices were responsible for 23 per cent of the global emissions that contribute to climate destabilization, as reported in the *IPCC 6th Report* (Jaramillo et al. 2022). Seventy per cent of these emissions come from surface transport (Böhm et al. 2023). In the UK, surface transport is the highest emitting sector of all activity at 22 per cent of emissions (CCC 2020). These emissions remain stubbornly persistent: the overall volume of output has remained relatively level since 1990 (CCC 2022). Efficiency gains in vehicle engines have been nullified by increases in vehicle mass (which requires more energy to move) and increased distances travelled. Consequently, under any plan to change our emissions profiles we cannot avoid significant changes to current travel practices in which private motoring prevails as a default mode of travel. Pollutants arising from mass car use cause further significant damage to air quality, human health and disruption to ecosystems (Paterson 2007). However efficient the combustion, these impacts are largely unaffected; changing the engine type in the current vehicle fleet will not address many of the problems of particulates. Mass car use pollutes physical space, requiring significant land to be set aside for parking and travel, adding to urban sprawl, thus feeding its own dependency. Physical spaces of car use colonize and enclose travel spaces to the exclusion of other modes of travel, rendered vulnerable and endangered by motor vehicles (Böhm et al. 2006; Seiler 2008). Moreover, current high-energy, high-speed travel practices (not just driving) have negative effects on perceptions of time, commodifying travel time as a negative value, something to be minimized, ideally erased (Whitelegg 1997). Yet movement is something we all engage in and depend on and so we have to find ways to move that allow us to live with lower impacts. We are tied into global networks of the mobility of goods and services that we are unable to control. We undertake personal journeys over which we do have some kind of agency. They may be tied to larger structural issues such as the relationship of housing to employment and the local availability of services ranging from shops to education, but the web of obligations is at least partly spun by life choices that we take.

Moving around is fundamental to human activity. We cannot avoid or do without it. Even if we ourselves stay within the confines of our own homes, we rely on the movement of others to supply basic needs and services. So, the choices of mode of travel and the amount of travel that different modes facilitate are crucial to finding more sustainable social arrangements. The corollary of the increased distances that current dominant modes take for granted is the exclusionary spatial arrangements that follow from expectations of travel. Assumptions that everybody can drive, for example, allow separation of essential goods and services from areas of housing, and thus make that housing unusable (or severely problematic) for those unable (or unwilling) to drive. It puts many leisure possibilities beyond the immediate reach of the non-driver. Put simply, this creates dependency.

The more a society facilitates driving, the more it makes it almost essential to drive for the basic functions of social and economic life. Yet it does not have to be this way. Exploring the experiences of different forms of travel allows us to think through what it might mean to develop habits that encourage responsible living, that is, of ways of living that minimize our destruction of the physical and social worlds around us. To travel responsibly in the Anthropocene era requires us to think differently about travel: how it shapes our experiences and expectations of the world around us.

The emphasis throughout the book is on the need for prioritization and promotion of walking and cycling, as recommended in the AR6, the specialist contribution on transport within the IPCC 6th Report on climate change (Jaramillo et al. 2022) and in numerous governmental vision documents such as *The Pan-European Masterplan for Cycling Promotion* (PEP 2021). But this book is *not* primarily an argument as to *why* they should be adopted. International agreements and scientific analyses of the predicaments of climate change and other measures of unsustainability have already established rationales both as to why changes need to be made and recommendations as to how to proceed (see, e.g. Banister 2005; Pooley et al. 2013). Rather, I want to consider how ways of travelling (travel modes) shape the way we see and encounter the world.

The book examines how active mobilities provide relationships between humans and humans and between humans and the more-than-human world that differ from those experienced when we travel as drivers or public transport passengers, and further, how these experiential effects have political implications if we desire to build values more appropriate for living in the Anthropocene. To do so requires thinking about how to relate to each other and to delve into the values and relationships that are fostered by different ways of moving. Specifically, we can ask if there are qualities in the mundane actions of walking and cycling that provide insights into developing more responsible habits.

Traditionally, ideas of citizenship have been used to negotiate relationships between self and society. Though citizenship is a troubled and contested concept, I suggest that a concept of *Anthropocene citizenship* is useful as a way to focus on and to build values, especially those of care and commoning. It can therefore be a useful way to develop the qualities required for a significant rethink of people and planet.

I argue that thinking through the ideas of care and commoning, which in turn develop feminist and decolonial perspectives on relationality, provide a framework to think through what an Anthropocene citizenship might mean and to consider how different modes of travel support or hinder its development. Care and commons are interlinked ideas that will be explained and referred to through the course of the explorations, not as magic talismans but as signposts to highlight the importance of different ways of thinking. Care and commoning provide values and ways of understanding to help us recognize the scale of changes needed to develop less destructive patterns of activity. Further, they furnish ways to begin the transitions and transformations required, heightening the possibility of resonance, another idea explored in relation to mobility. A final factor is required to guard against the hubris that any image of future mobility provides a perfect blueprint for what needs to be done. To this end I also draw on what Hartmut Rosa has described as uncontrollability, a recognition of the limits of human design and planning (elaborated in Chapter 3).

Why Anthropocene mobilities?

Why use the language of Anthropocene mobilities, not just sustainable mobilities or walking and cycling for sustainability? Because I want to indicate that the game has changed. It is no longer possible to fool ourselves that we can keep on going in the same paths, but just with lower carbon emissions. In championing sustainability, particularly when working for more sustainable mobilities, we perhaps need to pause and ask what is being sustained. Advocacy policies to protect and promote walking and cycling as primary mobility modes have achieved huge successes in the past thirty years. Working in the language of sustainable mobilities, they have changed the international agenda and those involved can be rightly pleased with the changes made.

Meanwhile, much of the rhetoric, especially in relation to cycling, places more walking and cycling as ways to maintain productivist, accumulative economies. They act as a fix for the worst excesses of capitalism. Justin Spinney (2021) put it brutally clearly that cycling has been weaponized for growth. Rather than asking how we can make current practices more sustainable, let's start by thinking about where we are today, and what we can do to build a tomorrow that is less transgressive of boundaries that maintain conditions of habitability. To do this requires thinking about how we live with each other. Behind all the declarations of rights and the constitutions that reflect them, the basic impulse for concepts of citizenship is a desire to make public how we can manage to live together: to develop 'the ethical and moral sense which is necessary to build community' (Cayley 2005 loc 1443). Put simply, citizenship supplies the *hausordnung*, or 'house rules' for a group of people that are shared so we don't have to argue all the time.

My argument is that recognizing our location in the Anthropocene and the destructive capacities that we have already unleashed allows us to think about the qualities and values that might be needed to be less destructive planet-dwellers.

High-energy, high-carbon consumption is profoundly maldistributed. Moreover, its distribution does not necessarily map conveniently onto economic inequalities. Nevertheless, we are forced to acknowledge that the beneficiaries and practitioners of high-energy travel, including everyday motoring, are currently consumers of far more resources than needed for sufficiency, simultaneously responsible for the majority of the destructive forms of pollution, whether in the form of atmospheric chemistry effects of greenhouse gases or the accumulation of evermore materials such as microplastics (including microparticles from tyre degradation and other vehicular micropollutants). Given the degree of overshoot of planetary boundaries already visible, then a citizenship for the Anthropocene for those among the globally wealthy and highly mobile must also be a citizenship for degrowth, a lessening of resource use and pollution production by those who use more than could be considered a globally fair share. This analysis has been described as Earth-system justice, an approach that 'recognises unequal responsibility for, and unequal exposure to, Earth-system changes, and also recognises unequal capacity to respond and unequal access to resources' (Gupta et al. 2024: 1). Earth-system justice requires that those who have most responsibility for Earth-system changes also have most responsibility to act. The argument here is that the destructiveness of hyper-mobile lifestyles has become almost invisible, normalized and justified as necessity. To (re-)learn to live responsibly requires us to foster those things that develop an ethic of care: that embrace commoning and that recognize the destructive implications of the obsession with control.

Genesis and process

To arrive at the connection between values needed for Anthropocene citizenship and the practical considerations of how we get about in our day-to-day lives has involved a constant series of digressions into philosophies of self and the world around that is not-self. It intrudes into questions of subjectivity, of the relationships of human and more-than-human life. The study also engages theories of citizenship, the Anthropocene and concepts from mobilities and practice theory. Some of these apparent digressions will appear through the text and the oddly wide-ranging references serve to reflect the indebtedness I have to the significant spectrum of readings that have been necessary for a career as an interdisciplinary social scientist with a prior background in philosophy and religious studies (Cox 2010).

Although I write this from an academic perspective, I am also a concerned citizen, one whose life and actions have been tangled up in a range of activities to express my concerns and explore possibilities for living less destructively. It is some forty years since I was first prompted to read writings of Martin Buber, pioneer of a philosophy of dialogue. A slow process of thinking through the implications of his work has accompanied my own thinking and writing ever since. His writing introduced me to the primacy of relational, rather than identitarian understandings of the self; this relationality underpins the thinking and writing throughout the book.

In the 1920s, Buber proposed that, rather than starting with an individuated self and exploring how it relates to the world about, one should consider dialogic relationship as fundamental (Buber 1937 [1923]; 1961 [1929]). There is no 'I' or pre-existent 'self' outside of our relationships. It is in the ways that we relate to that-which-is-not-our-self that our self and our personhood is understood and expressed. The self only becomes itself in relation. Of course, there is the complication of how we consider the dissolution of boundaries implied by more-than-human thinking, while still maintaining the distinction of that-which-is-not-the-self so that there can be relationality. However, many of these complications are founded and resolved in the limitations of the language of the self, the other, the I and the not-I of both alterity and unity, as will be developed through the discussions.

This relational account of selfhood is fundamental to the way that ideas are explored in this study. It doesn't imply a slavish adherence to Buber's writing but acknowledges an intellectual debt and takes his ideas as a stepping stone that enables exploration of new directions for how we can understand being-in-the-world (Mendes-Flohr 2018). There are clear connections to be found in many of the key writers whose ideas are explored here. For example, despite his lack of direct reference to Buber, Bakhtin similarly took a dialogic relationality as a grounding for his analyses of language and interaction (Matveev 2018). Richard Sennett's core ideas on the uses of disorder, a critique of control that mirrors Rosa's proposals on uncontrollability, were developed through conversation with Erikson, whose personalist vision was in turn derived from Buber (see Sennett 2021 [1970]). Hartmut Rosa, whose work on both resonance (2019) and uncontrollability (2020) is pivotal for my thought on Anthropocene mobilities, is clear and open in his references and indebtedness to Buber. Relational thinking is a recurrent theme among numerous writers and activists struggling to articulate what might constitute a 'good life' in the Anthropocene, understood as a creative resource for addressing the existential and practical crises we face in light of climate destabilization and increasing inequalities, local and global. I will argue that relational thinking, that I am not me without you, rather than identitarian models that seek to establish an individual's core identity provides tools with which to build more appropriate ways of being and living sustainably.

Relationality is constitutive. Put another way, 'I' is the singular of 'We', 'we' is not simply the plural of 'I'. What we call the self extends beyond our relations to other humans to encompass our relations with other beings: living and non-living, creatures and environments for which following after Maller (2018; 2021) and Dobson (2021) I use the shorthand of the more-than-human. 'The idea of the "more-than-human" world … attempts to challenge the anthropocentric view of "nature" as other. Humans and non-humans are entangled together in ways that cofabricate worlds, spaces, and encounters' (Dobson 2021: 7). To think through and respond to the problems we face does not demand a new belief system. Nor does it entail wholesale acceptance of a predetermined (or rediscovered) political or analytical framework. Instead, I want to take the reader on a journey through some problems and the implications that arise from taking seriously the issues that we now face in relation to climate, environment and human action, despite our frequent attempts to delay or avoid confronting them. Nevertheless, there are political implications.

To take seriously the imperative of unsustainable overconsumption requires a serious critique of existing forms of capital accumulation and, beyond them, to the capitalist mode of production itself, dependent as it is on ever-increasing growth (Rosa 2013). Likewise, productivist socialisms that depend on maximizing production even when owned as a form of common wealth provide little cause for optimism (Esteva 2023). Any political economic ideology dependent on increasing growth, and on the classical forms of what is called development that accompany it, is difficult to reconcile with a need to reduce energy throughputs, especially those dependent on carbon technologies and other forms of material extractivism. The focus for attention and action to build less destructive and exploitative ways of living together on the planet therefore falls particularly on the lifestyles and mobilities of those with the highest carbon footprints and greatest material consumption. The book is thus intended to be a commentary, observing and seeing afresh the problems and the possibilities that low-energy, low-carbon ways of doing mobility provide. I want to do more than propose active mobilities as travel alternatives; I want to explore how alternatives to the dominant and default of high-energy travel provide ways of seeing and ways of being-in-the-world that are lost under a system of automobility.

Situational analysis: Where are we?

Let's start with the bad news. The climate crisis cannot be 'solved'. It is, as Naomi Klein (2014) has stated, a system crisis not a symptom crisis. In a brilliant but shocking study Collings outlines the scale of the problem:

> Climate change is not just a crisis for the biosphere; it is a crisis for our very significance and purpose as human beings. …
>
> Climate change … threatens to transform our entire world if we stick to our current habits, founded as they are on the extravagant use of fossil fuels. Our way of living threatens itself. No previous generation of human beings has ever confronted that possibility – at least not on the planetary scale. …
>
> Climate change is different. Nowadays, our everyday lives are the source of the problem: everything we depend upon to live as we do – the energy we use to get around, to heat or cool our homes, to power the industry that produces the goods we use – is also pumping enough greenhouse gases into the atmosphere that eventually our climate will be transformed. … we in the developed nations are the equivalent of slaveholders, resting easy on the fierce subordination of the world's ecosystems. (Collings 2014: 12, 15, 16)

Nor does climate change indicate that we are moving from one stable condition to another, as is often assumed in descriptions of our transition from the Holocene to the Anthropocene. The Holocene is where we come from, the geologic era in which all human life has hitherto been lived. The Anthropocene is an era whose parameters we do not and cannot fully know. Whether we take its commencement from the beginning of human agriculture, from European expansionism and empire building, the Industrial Revolution or from the atomic age is immaterial for its reality, though it may have implications for the political responses we generate. The physical source energy transitions of European production regimes, from coal to oil and to nuclear energies, have been inextricably entangled with European colonial expansionism, sequestering land and resources at the expense of indigenous lives. Increasing energy-dense fuel sources were integral to transport innovations, and the use of high-energy-density battery systems for a new generation of electric vehicles still relies on the expansion of extractivist regimes, where the beneficiaries of lithium and rare earth metals live far from the sources of their mining and the pollution it incurs. The use of these resources and the actions of the societies they have enabled are what have brought about the Anthropocene. As a historical reality it is not something that can be unmade. What the Anthropocene indicates is that in climate terms we are moving from an era of relative stability to a situation characterized by instability. Shortly before his death, Bruno Latour (2022: 47) put it much more bluntly: 'The covid-19 pandemic merely foreshadows a new situation from which you will never emerge.'

The Anthropocene designates an era in which humans have become a telluric force: altering earth systems. But power does not indicate control or mastery. The planetary systems we have destabilized are not under our command. Nor, despite the great hopes of modernity, are we even in a position to exert directional control over those planetary processes. We have the power to kill but not to restore life – this is the full impact of the irreversibility of the Anthropocene. Human action may undermine the conditions for the continuation of human civilization as we know it, but planetary life will continue. Our capacity to know exceeds our capacity to do. We can dissect the frog to understand how all its biological systems work, but we cannot then reassemble it so that it can hop off the table. We live facing greater uncertainty and unpredictability as a consequence of a trajectory of climate impact and environmental destruction that we inherit and which we currently address only half-heartedly.

Who is the 'we'?

The generalized implications of the Anthropocene understanding of climate destabilization, environmental degradation and resource depletion are that its consequences are blind to the social and economic standing of different groups of humans. Existing inequalities ensure that its impacts are differentially experienced. Those with greater resources to devote to resilience measures will suffer less immediate disruptions but the climate destabilization is a constant. This generalized condition should not be confused with the specific collective agency of destruction in these discussions. This agency is comprised of those (of us) who are privileged beneficiaries of high carbon lifestyles and (carbon) capital accumulation: those who, willingly or not, are also the inheritors of centuries of colonial processes in which both earth and labour have been treated as commodities for exploitation or impediments to extractivism.

The agents of destruction are a global minority, separated by an *abyssal* divide from the majority world (Santos 2018; Santos and Meneses 2019). However enlightened, progressive, green or radical we consider ourselves to be, the expectations of over-consuming citizens are shaped by relative privilege on a global scale. When we think in terms of planetary boundaries and the problems of overshoot, overconsumption and hypermobility are not limited to particular nations or to a global 1 per cent. This is not to deny the very real and intersecting injustices of gender, race, social and economic class *within* societies. Citizenship is far from equal. Regardless of the complex and intersecting inequalities at play in any given situation, there is a fundamental difference between those who face questions of basic everyday survival and those who face exclusions from particular zones within lifeworlds of basic security. Within the overconsuming world, social and economic inequalities do not correlate to the inherited realities of carbon class privilege and exclusion.

The 'we' I refer to throughout this book is the collective positionality of those whose carbon class privilege makes high-energy lifestyles normal and expected. The lifestyles and livelihoods of those with the highest carbon footprints are those that require the most substantial modification. Sadly, the situation is not one in which we might have the luxury to demand action from those at the very highest level of carbon consumption and wait our turn as action requirements trickle down towards (slightly) lesser users. Whether we like it or not, the abyssal divide places an onus for change on all higher energy carbon class citizens.

Nor should the irreversibility of the realities of the Anthropocene lull us into an anti-politics. The contemporary divorce between *power*, the capacity to make things happen, and *politics*, the capacity to make choices about what is desirable, should not blind us to the difference between earth-system processes and human social, economic and political systems (Baumann 2013). While we (as concerned citizens) may have no power over the earth-system processes that we (collectively as inheritors of the industrial wealth derived from colonial histories) have set in motion, by, for example, raising atmospheric carbon concentration beyond 420 ppm (parts per million), we do have power to change the politics of our current and future actions and the further contributions made to atmospheric carbon levels. Systems of society, economy and politics remain entirely products of human action. Zygmunt Baumann (2013) connected the problems of current democratic political systems to the challenges facing contemporary action for Anthropocene and climate politics – both hinge on the disconnect between power and politics. Noting the deficits of current political processes and regimes that downplay or ignore the biophysical reality of climate change, and confronting those challenges, is a call for more, not less democracy (compare Lummis 1996).

The need for action and to develop capacity to take action regardless of the political structures at play is the reason that I approach the problem through the lens of citizenship, that is, through the securities and political social and economic responsibilities and obligations that arise through collective identifications. Politico-economic arrangements and social practices are entrenched but they are not unalterable. Social action needs to be engaged in order to ensure policy makers and actors respond to the climate emergency. Conversely, as Leinfelder (2013, 13) argues, 'politics alone will not be able to institute the changes necessary to create a sustainable society'. Politics and policy recommendation for sustainable transport are plentiful. The aim here is to extend that discussion into the cultural and social realm by thinking about how mobility practices form us as human social beings, relating with each other and with the more-than-human world.

The existential challenge we face is how to live responsibly in the Anthropocene. Transformations are already underway and our choice is to be agents of change or victims of change. To use a phrase that has galvanized writers over the past century and a half, 'What is to be done?' Bringing this into the present, we can ask 'What would it mean to be good citizens of the Anthropocene?' Or, if 'good' is too normative and 'citizen' is too problematic at this point in the discussion, let us rephrase the question: 'What would it take to live together as less-destructive planet-dwellers?' Or, even more specifically, 'How do the resources that we have in terms of the everyday ways in which we move around enable us to live together as less-destructive planet-dwellers, and how do other mobility practices prevent this?'

Bodies in movement

The first step to thinking about mobility habits in the Anthropocene is to think about the moving body. To do so needs a cognitive shift from understanding mobility through the big picture of transport and infrastructure provisions and to refocus on details of actual journeys made. It is to ask what our various everyday practices of movement have to teach us about the world around and how they define our interactions with it. 'The body comes to know itself, through its environmental interactions', argues Ariel Salleh (2017 [1997]: 291).

My own consideration of these environmental interactions originated in thinking through the practices of one such (self-)discipline that allows the body to come to know itself, namely cycling (Cox 2018, 2019). In the simple act of riding, for whatever purpose, no matter how fast or slow, how utilitarian or mundane, riders interact with their surroundings. Cycling takes place in space, usually public space, so other persons also form an important element of our environmental interactions. The rider encounters the atmospheric elements and interacts with the earth through the various forms of built environments of travel, from trails to streetscapes. The bodily competencies and skills initially required in learning to ride, and which are then developed through use, are ways in which we learn about our bodies in their interactions with these external environments. Through movement we come to know what we are capable of, what our bodies' limits are, how it feels to use muscles. If we ride over a life-course, we also become aware of our age-related changing capacities. But before cycling comes walking.

Walking is the basis of all movement on land. Walking relates distance to time in an immediate and human fashion. Traditional settlement patterns are shaped by both access to resources and to the walkable distances between all the elements needed for life and livelihoods (the basis on which the fifteen-minute city is being rethought). Walking, supplemented by animal traction and water navigation, has dominated historic human mobility.[1]

Wheeling and cycling are relative newcomers. Sleds and wheeled carts for those unable to walk, propelled by hand (or with a stick), can be seen in the fifteenth-century paintings of Pieter Breughel. Fully manumotive carriages and cycles appear as designs and experiments in nineteenth-century literature. Personal wheeled travel, propelled by coasting (the 1817 Laufmaschine of Karl Von Drais) and later through directly driven wheels (after Michaux in 1863), enabled the traverse of greater distances, and the carriage of loads over those distances, than could be managed by walking alone (Herlihy 2004). Although there are interactions specific to each mode of self-propelled human mobility, whether arising from mechanical differences or from cultural expectations, it is their commonality in contrast to motorized transport that I want to emphasize. One might also digress into other modes of travel that harness natural elements of wind or that employ animal traction. Each provides fantastic opportunities for reflection on more-than-human mobility relations but necessarily remain beyond the scope of this study of today's mundane mobilities in the Global North.

Ways of moving provide ways of knowing and ways of seeing. Each mode of travel makes requirements of the human body, such as the speed of decision-making required and the degree of contact it provides with the world beyond the traveller. Variations in these requirements generate varieties of ways of seeing

---

[1] It is worth reflecting on the scope of human mobility and trade as far back as the early Bronze Age as evidenced by the sources of metals compared with find locations. A separate study would need to be conducted about the skills and experiences of water travel.

and knowing. The body is both a part of and apart from that environment with which it interacts. The histories and ways of imagining these interactions provide the substance through which we can begin to comprehend the ways in which we come to know our-self; as agent, as (relational) subject and as participants in socio-political regimes that reach far beyond the bounds of individual agency. The choices we make about movement, the interactions brought about, and the structures and infrastructures that make choices feasible or possible are shaped by our situations and, we must also acknowledge that the choices that we make to comply or to resist dominant practices shape those situations and make alternative actions less or more possible.

As one begins to examine the ways of knowing and seeing the world around (human and more-than-human) that emerge from non-motorized forms of travel, common factors and perspectives begin to emerge. Chapter 3 focuses in particular on three themes that I have found increasingly valuable as a means to articulate and develop ideas about qualities that non-motorized travel gives access to. Care and commoning together with uncontrollability have important value as both lessons for and as tools to build the capacities needed for responsible Anthropocene living. All are features that can be learned in human-powered mobility. Identifying care, commoning and uncontrollability as three ways to analyse the experiences and parameters of active modes of travel, together with resonance as a way to describe their potential to overcome alienation, is designed to draw attention to the ways that mobility modes provide ways of seeing and knowing. They will also highlight a fundamental divide between those modes of travel that rely on human power, however augmented, and those in which external motor power entirely supplants human energy in the travel process. Using these factors as lenses to analyse the impact and effect of mobility modes allows insight into the ways that qualities of experience and relationality are fostered or destroyed by different ways of everyday movement.

Schivelbusch's (1977) groundbreaking work on train travel showed how the growth of mass rail travel in the nineteenth century produced a new 'gaze': a way of seeing the world as a passenger. Over the course of time, the world of passengers became increasingly separated from the landscapes through which they travelled: physically through enclosed carriages and cognitively by the speed of travel. The experience of railway travel transformed human relations with the world (Presner 2007). A fascinating collection of essays, *The World beyond the Windshield* (Mauch and Zeller 2008), similarly explores how car travel produces different views and encounters specific to the particularities of vehicles and the roads on which they travel. Both are designed and manipulated by their respective engineers to produce specific sensations. It is notable that building routes specifically for car travel has frequently been dictated more by ideological narratives about movement than by rational assessment of the requirements of travel. The history of motorways, for example, is less one of the rational production of efficient mobility (as might be supposed) and more one of ideological projection by the states that finance them (Zeller 2006; Moraglio, 2017; Merriman 2007). To extend this form of analysis, I want to look at how human-powered modes of travel present very specific ways of seeing and modes of encounter with the world beyond the traveller, and how these affect travellers themselves. It is both relevant and notable that in many European and North American locations the creation of many cycling-specific infrastructures is largely coincident with the repurposing of redundant transport infrastructure (especially rail). This in itself designates cycle travel as a non-essential mode, requiring only the surplus of travel space, contrasted with the essential movement imputed to motorized mobilities (Egan and Caulfield 2024).

Separating physical travel from muscular effort is a significant step. It changes the relationship between energy and movement. Outsourcing the power required for travel from that available within the traveller shifts movement into a realm of the symbolic. No longer is terrain a direct signifier of the energy required for movement. Even with animal traction, the exhaustion of the animals in the traces is directly connected with terrain, speed and the duration of time. When all that is required to overcome the effects of terrain and atmosphere in a mechanically driven vehicle is an increase in the power (through greater fuel provision and consumption), then the correlation between topography, energy and the traveller is shattered. Travel is no longer limited by or respondent to bodily energy resources. As a corollary of this separation that transforms acts of travel, we see a new space appear for lives no longer dominated by physical activity. In the mid-1990s, Alberto Melucci wrote,

> Inhabiting a space lived principally on the symbolic plane, the relationship with our bodies tends to be sundered. The body thus loses its spatial skills and its ability to test its own limits. We must then resort to physical exercise and to hobbies to relearn the elementary skills needed to move in physical space, to measure distances in terms of our own physiques, to handle objects. (Melucci 1996: 17–18)

Bodily activity has ceased being a necessary normal requirement of daily life but exists as a separate activity of physical exercise to be undertaken as isolated act.

It is relegated or transferred to a sphere of leisure and dissociated from practical utility or necessity.

Digitalization has further transformed our relationships with our bodies and the spaces in which we live, as well as most obviously our interpersonal communications in the decades since Melucci's observation. Personal cognitive assessment of physical spaces is now as likely to be mediated through digital networks, relied upon as primary sources of information, as it is through physical appreciation of travel spaces. Most people are now familiar with using mobile phones as first resort navigation devices, not the physical experience to space that is mediated through fixed-scale maps. On a fixed-scale paper map, the bigger the space between points on the sheet or page, the farther away it is and the longer the time it will take to get there. Map sheets or books tend to replicate their fixed scales, allowing us, with practice, to visualize distance and time simply from a glance at the map itself. Digital mapping, with instantaneous zoom capacity, sunders any sense of fixed scale that can be correlated with time and physical experience. Even though street views can give us insight into the visual appearances of spaces, and specific journey times can be predicted with a relatively high degree of accuracy, the broader context is lost. Travelling those distances is further disconnected from (bodily) energy requirements.

These thoughts are as pertinent as ever when considered in relation to the bodily skills of walking and cycling. Digitization suggests that today we might recognize lives lived predominantly on the virtual plane as having the same alienation from the physical world. Restoring physical (bodily) movement and energy as a focus for mobility thinking shifts the physical exercise of bodily movement from the realm of leisure (and therefore of surplus and dispensability) to that of necessity, a basic part of everyday (re)production. It takes consideration of walking and cycling from the realm of physical exercise and hobbies (i.e. for a world defined in terms of leisure) back into the ordinary mundanity of daily life.

To prioritize walking and cycling is not to endorse a neo-primitivist rejection of all motorized mobility technologies. It is to recognize that one of the major stumbling blocks for sustainability in mobilities is simply the sheer volume of movement. As transport geographer John Whitelegg (2016) powerfully argues, the best way to more sustainable mobility is simply to have less of it. Mobility reduction remains important, and in the trilogy of reduce, reuse, recycle, the order is crucial. This should not require us to stay at home in self-induced lockdown, nor is it to treat all mobility as somehow sinful. It is, however, a call to re-evaluate the distances we move and that we *expect to move,* and thus the ways of moving (modes) that might be possible or appropriate (Sheller 2022). Normalizing high-speed, long-distance travel makes us dependent on it.

Thinking towards longer term changes, and with respect to the political imagination of mobility transitions, experiences of pandemic lockdowns showed how rapid redeployment of mobility spaces could facilitate easier and safer walking and cycling (Cox 2023; Rérat and Orthar 2024). They also prompted rethinking of local provision of goods and services to reflect homeworking. Fifteen-minute city initiatives were commenced well before the Covid-19 pandemic but rapidly revealed during lockdowns to offer crucial coping mechanisms (Rérat, Haldiman and Widmar 2022). The localization on which the fifteen-minute city or twenty-minute neighbourhood concept is constructed, in which all core services should be available within a limited travel time of the majority of residents, has in-built resiliencies. These are not just capacities that can cope with climate change or pandemic containment but allow continued accessibility via non-motorized transport without reduction of the quality of life.[2] Crucially, localization that enables the goods and services needed for everyday life to be accessible to walking and cycling also changes the incentives and imperatives of everyday travel and the need for high-energy travel modes. Facilities that allow us to cope with periods of crisis have important social equality implications.

Moving and being moved

To extend the thinking further, I want to develop the idea that practices have a pedagogic role: *doing* teaches us *how* to do, and its inverse, how *not* to do. We learn what is possible and what is not possible, what works and what doesn't work. Some actions serve to bring us closer to the world around us. They work to make us sensitive to the world about and, consequently, through their effects on us, make us *care*-ful about those surroundings (Paulsen et al. 2022). We discover how to 'fit' into the world. Some practices serve to distance us from the world around. They work to make us insensitive, that is, to *care*-less.

A responsible citizenship in the Anthropocene will require us to foster and to make habitual those practices that make us more aware of our impacts and, by corollary, to problematize and minimize those actions that serve to 'offshore' the

---

[2] Working with planning organizations based in large cities, it is noticeable how assumptions made are frequently insensitive to the degree to which smaller settlements and suburbs have become derived of the provision of basic services, or how larger housing areas have been constructed without possibility of non-car access to those services.

impacts and consequences of our actions (Urry 2014). Maintaining systems of human and material exploitation has always relied on hiding the consequences and costs from sight and from accounting measures. Offshoring, out of sight, out of mind, works in both spatial and temporal dimensions. Consequences of actions taken today may be felt most destructively only in other geographical locations from where their benefits accrue. Or consequences can be projected forward in time, where they will only be experienced in years to come, just as we today continue to inherit legacies of actions taken in the historic past. Only now are we realizing how locked in we are to the accelerating resource use and pollution trajectories that have been long built into mobility infrastructures through decades of investment in motor-oriented traffic development. Responsible citizenship requires us to engage with practices that highlight and help us to learn how to perform those values we wish to inculcate: to refuse the outsourcing and offshoring of negative consequences. Everyday mobility practices and expectations of mobility are crucial not only in terms of carbon footprints, but for the structural implications they have for the societies we build.

One of the fascinating dimensions of this investigation into the ways that doing assist us to learn is the linguistic connections that arise when thinking about movement in the English language. To 'move' is to act, either on oneself or another. It is to set in motion. To 'be moved' requires the agency of another. Being moved, I am set in motion by the force of something other than myself. But we use the language of being moved in reference not only to physical travel but also to emotional impact. Interestingly, this is one of the few areas in which we conventionally acknowledge the agency of the more-than-human. 'That which moves us' (emotionally, but also physically if actions such as crying and laughing are involved) may be things seen or heard. The power of nature or of music to move us, to set emotions in motion, is not controversial. Acknowledging the power of the not-human or the more-than-human to move us begins to open a wide-ranging discussion not just of the power or force of nature but also the attention as and attitudes that render us susceptible to these forces. These capacities extend to movement, physical and spatial. Mobility practices move us emotionally as well as physically. They can both isolate and create encounter. They can induce joy and terror. The sensory worlds of the walker, cyclist, motorcyclist, car passenger and driver, bus and rail passenger and flyer are all very different. Neither are these sensory worlds fixed, they are not essentialized characteristics invariably peculiar to each mode. People experience modes of travel differently, their experiences correlating with social positions and personal histories that they bring with them to travel. All these discussions also contribute to the ways in which we might begin to conceptualize and describe a mobility citizenship for the Anthropocene.

It is worth noting that to explore the world of the sensory and the aesthetic should not be considered a retreat from the political (Kompridis 2014). Rather, one of the central themes I want to explore, and one underlying the understanding of the pedagogical role of mobilities, is that material encounter with the world has power to transform. Taking sensory and aesthetic dimensions of life seriously challenges the scope of the political. Thinking of the agency of the more-than-human we need to consider not only its direct effects on individual humans but also to acknowledge more-than-human agency in the formation of human societies: we need also consider where and how the agency of the more-than-human is acknowledged and recognized. Citizenship, as explained in the next chapter, provides an obvious location for human recognition and of recognition of the more-than-human. Consequently, exploring the world of the sensory and the aesthetic also asks questions of our commitments to and framing of democracy – Who has a voice in the discussion and how are voices recognized?

Democracy and the mundane

Today, democracy is often used as no more than a shorthand cipher for a voting system through which governments legitimize their roles as rule-makers and regulators and justify priorities for the provisioning and distribution of social goods for their citizens. Democratic voting systems usually fragment into party systems designed to reflect sectoral interests of specific groups: social, political and/or economic, sometimes allied with cultural or religious identities. Yet it has not always been this way. Edward Carpenter's epic poem *Towards Democracy*, written in Britain in the last years of the nineteenth century (more than two decades before general male franchise and over thirty years before the same rights were accorded to women) provides a vivid and poetic expression of democracy as a spirit of liberation (Carpenter 1896). Carpenter depicts democracy as a spirit moving over the land to banish oppressions, awaken new life and bring hope to the oppressed. This spirit is vitally linked to empowerment and autonomy (in the sense of self-efficacy), a dream of attaining the capacity to make decisions for oneself, to participate fully in the shaping of future prospects. It signals a break from subjection to the patriarchal and colonial masters of a ruling class claiming exclusive rights to decide what is in the nation's (and therefore implicitly the whole populace's) best interests. This spirit of democracy restates that whoever we are, we matter. Whatever we do matters. It matters not only to ourselves and our immediate contacts, but in a bigger scheme of things. Democracy is a spirit that pervades all of life's processes, not simply the chance to elect a government.

A century after Carpenter, a collection of essays *Democratizing Democracy* was issued as the first volume of a larger project: *Reinventing Social Emancipation* (Santos 2007). In it, Santos and Avritzar (2007) argue that liberal democracy has confined democracy to the political realm and thus to the field of state intervention. The struggle to democratize democracy, however, requires us to consider that 'in capitalist societies there are six large forms of power: patriarchy, exploitation, unequal differentiation of identity, fetishism of commodities, domination and unequal exchange. These correspond to six main structure-agency time-spaces: household-place, workplace, community-place, market-place, citizen-place, and world-place' (Santos and Avritzar 2007: lxii). How might each of these be transformed by democratization, the authors ask? What would each place look like if allowed to be shaped and transformed by thinking and working for democratization (in that sense of participation and self-efficacy)? Adopting these multiple challenges prompts us to imagine how the realm of the everyday and the mundane becomes a space and a means to extend participation and to affirm the legitimacy of all involved. Simultaneously, the current problematic exclusions created by power relations are also highlighted. Who and what is made not to count, or to count for nothing, by today's arrangements of (democratically justified) political power? Radical visions of citizenship are tied to radical visions of democracy.

Nancy Fraser (1990) also argues that for meaningful dialogue, political democracy requires substantive social equality. Mobility spaces cannot perform a dialogical communicative space without substantive equality between diverse users of those spaces. When travel spaces act as commons, they provide spaces for such dialogues. Enclosures and annexations that exclude some users and reserve exclusive access for other classes of users undermine their capacity to do so. Travel spaces are locations for political dialogue and negotiation.

Dialogic interactions initially made possible by common travel are tainted by the power inequalities between ways of moving. The physical inequality of powerful and massive motor vehicles and unprotected fleshly bodies in the same travel space makes dialogue between travellers difficult, if not impossible. The sheer scale of difference between a one-tonne vehicle and a pedestrian or cyclist creates a threat of violence that is only intensified when speed differentials are added.

The history of pedestrian and cycling activism has been a history of the creation of subaltern counterpolitics. Associations speak against exclusion and unequal treatment, but also provide spaces for their own internal discussions and creative visions of travel worlds arranged otherwise (Cox 2024). Remaining excluded from the dominant discourse and physically dominated in public spaces, other viewpoints can be raised in those 'hidden' spaces of conversation and assembly, silent as far as the dominant mobility discourses are concerned. These are not necessarily pure spaces – they have their own problems of inequalities and different classes of users. Yet the scale of difference of internal power relations is rarely sufficient to be greater than the broader distinctions against which they are confronted. What I am concerned about here, however, is not the details of oppositional or counter-politics but to recognize that people do continue to walk and to cycle, despite the difficulties that may be placed in their way (Dunlap et al. 2020). By better understanding the experiences of those travellers and comprehending how they contribute to the continued travel, we may begin to see how such experiences can help reinforce values for a new era.

If we want to understand the potential for everyday walking and cycling, we can start by acknowledging those who walk and cycle, and who manage to thrive without driving in a car-dominated world. Being granted the capacity to participate, to have a voice, is to have one's agency in the construction of society recognized. It is (potentially at least) to be a peer or even an equal partner to all others granted that status. An Anthropocene citizenship will need to take account of these multiple and often silenced voices.

The extension of who or what might be granted citizenship status or accorded rights equivalent to those arising from recognition as citizenship is a live question. Granting of some form of legal rights to nature as part of initiatives to rewrite constitutions in recovery from exploitative and extractive regimes is radically important (Kothari et al. 2019). However circumscribed, propositions to grant a form of citizenship to the earth have profound consequences. For the argument here, however, it is important that consideration is given to everyday, ordinary activities. These are the spaces in which sustainable practices are embedded as mundane habits. To discover what it means to be Anthropocene citizens, and to work out how to live as such, it is vital that this is not seen to require extraordinary or heroic actions. Rather, it is 'daily practices that allow us to cultivate interexistence' (Escobar 2020: 28). These may, as Mimi Sheller (2023) observes, demand substantial challenges to find ways that do not reproduce high carbon dependencies and the colonialities on which they depend. 'Only by walking and dwelling in common with those who have lived outside or resisted the energy cultures of contemporary carbon form might we find pathways to alternative futures through the ongoing communing of relational worlds of care' (Sheller 2021: 6). This emphasis on praxis, connecting ideas with actions, that has driven the desire to write this book was stressed by David Abram in his book *Spell of the Sensuous*:

> It may be that the new 'environmental ethic' toward which so many environmental philosophers aspire – an ethic that would lead us to respect and heed not only the lives of our fellow humans but also the life and well-being of the rest of nature – will come into existence not primarily through the logical elucidation of new philosophical principles and legislative strictures, but through a renewed attentiveness to this perceptual dimension that underlies all our logics, through a rejuvenation of our carnal, sensorial empathy with the living land that sustains us. (Abram 1997: 50)

Diversity is fundamentally characteristic of everyday life. Recognizing and valuing diversity is vital for any serious examination of ordinary lived experience. The specificities and details of the microlevel cannot be reduced to generalities or to universalized modes of analysis or action. We need to examine the detail of situations and be sensitive to the variety of needs of different participants. Simplified universal solutions are not sufficient. Specific actions and experiences are grounded in local realities and personal perspectives that need comprehending alongside the structural elements of class and gender (for example). Hence the political analyses and action built to address this everyday search for ways to live responsibly is often characterized as a 'pluriversal' politics (Escobar 2020; Kothari et al. 2019; Esteva 2023). That is, it does not stem from the assumption of a universal political ideology but emerges from the specificities of local realities and how they diversely enable us to respond to shared core values. Pluriversal politics are also mutable, necessarily adapting to changing circumstances and relationships. Shared critique and constructions of broader political projects are not to be dismissed, but the idea that one can produce and enact a universal political analytic that engages equally and fairly with the diversity of historical experiences and legacies of dominant, even hegemonic political regimes is to reproduce the very hegemonic structures that underpin the inequalities with which one is trying to deal. This is a core argument to emerge from the discussions of the World Social Forum (see Sen et al. 2004). In Santos's terminology, 'counter hegemonic globalizations' seek to challenge the hegemony of globalization but also challenge the idea that current hegemonic forms of globalization can be replaced by another hegemonic form (Santos

2006). In other words, these politics are not just those of counter globalization but simultaneously those of counter hegemony. Counter hegemonic politics shifts the locus of political action from the formal field of the politics of the state, and obsessions with the seizure and holding of power, to think instead how power relations pervade all aspects of our lived existence. In this manner it also revitalizes the classic feminist insistence that the personal is political (Hanish 1970, compare Mackay 2015). All this feeds the analytic presented here in respect to learning and building critical awareness through everyday experience. Again, it must be emphasized that the translation is not automatic but must be built.

Conclusions

So far, this background contextualization has outlined the broad territory of thought and highlighted some of the issues explored in the rest of this book. To begin the journey of ideas that enable a radical rethink and new perspectives on mobility habits, the first step is to explore in more detail what I mean by Anthropocene citizenship. What is it about the Anthropocene era that might cause us to rethink ideas of citizenship and how might they be reconfigured? Is citizenship with its connotations of rights and nationality too problematic an idea to be used in the face of planetary climate change? How might it be reconciled with increasing recognition of and sensitivity towards the realization that humans are not the only ones that matter? Can citizenship be a meaningful tool to think through the rights of animals and environments? The next chapter begins the discussion by exploring what resources the idea of citizenship provides for understanding our predicament and how we might formulate ideas of a good citizenship. These are questions that need to be dealt with. However, they should not distract us from the central task: to analyse how travel practices cultivate or destroy the sensibilities required for living responsibly in the Anthropocene. To make that analysis however, we need a second stage. This is provided in Chapter Three through an examination of care and commoning, located within a broader context of Hartmut Rosa's work on *Resonance*, especially in its implications for recognizing the uncontrollability of the world. In particular, his emphasis on uncontrollability presents a challenge to presumptions about instrumentalism in the assessment of agency and efficacy.

Only with this theoretical framework in place can the study then address the central theme of how various modes of movement shape the ways we experience the world. To do so we also have to consider how perception and experience are constructed so that we can comprehend the ways in which mundane, everyday journeys can alert us to values that we need for Anthropocene citizenship. The obvious place to start is on foot. From there we go on to think about wheeled travel, especially cycling. Next, we have to consider car travel and the politics of the Anthropocene. Travel and mobility are inseparable from energy use, and we have to think about the embeddedness of energy systems in modes of travel and their vehicles. Our current mobility practices are not only dominated by the private car but to understand these patterns we need to examine far more than vehicles and their use. Rather, the car is simply part of an interlocking 'system' of automobility that, for the whole of the twentieth century, has been inseparable from the reproduction and proliferation of carbon capitalism (Urry 2011). What might Anthropocenic car travel look like if it is at all possible? What existing technologies provide appropriate resources for thinking through the issues of travel sufficiency, rather than the constant expansion of possibility linked as it is to the reproduction of privilege. Finally, we take a brief look at how future reconfigurations of mobility prioritizing walking and cycling might be used to develop low carbon mobilities and what is needed to scale up the immediacy of localized configurations of travel.

2

Anthropocene citizenship

Introduction: Anthropocene as context

'Anthropocene' denotes the arrival of a geological epoch in which human activity is the most significant factor in shaping planetary systems (Crutzen and Stoermer 2000; Trischler 2016; Steffen et al. 2016; Binczyk 2019; Paulsen 2022). Human civilization includes all our agriculture, industry, cultures, philosophies, science and politics that emerged during the previous, unusually climatically stable, period: the Holocene. The productive and accumulative processes that define modern civilizations supplied surplus wealth invested in education, arts and culture, and thus greater economic investment in opportunity building. But this accumulation was (and remains) inseparable from the histories of exploitation and colonization pursued by those civilizations that defined themselves as modern (Douthwaite 1992). The mechanisms through which wealth was acquired for a limited few delivered their bounty at the cost of the impoverishment and structural disadvantaging of the many, through practices of widespread enslavement and other forms of unfree dominations (Lessenich 2019).

This Western history of economic expansionism based on a variety of forms of colonialism, domestic and imperial, had unintended consequences. The capacity for global expansion depended on harnessing ever greater densities of material and energy resources. The constantly accelerating expansion of material extraction and production, coupled with the 'waste' by-products of processing, manufacture and use, outstripped the planetary capacity to replace and absorb them (Brand and Wissen 2021). To illustrate, the era of climate change is heralded by rising levels of a range of gases released by human activities, including most familiarly carbon dioxide (CO_2). These build up in the atmosphere and, as they do so, produce a rise of global temperatures, resulting in destabilization of weather patterns. The impacts of these fall most damagingly on those with the least resources available to deal with them. The benefits of high carbon economies, however, are almost exclusively transmitted to those whose economies and political systems are designed around the colonial imperative, whether focussed internally, externally or both.

The Anthropocene designation marks the conceptualization of a new era of geologic time in which human activity has greater impact than any other force in shaping earth history (Möllers and Crutzen 2014). Simultaneously, it provides a cultural concept that both requires and enables reconsideration of the relations between our human species and the planetary context in which human story is played out (Möllers et al. 2014). Human activity is now visible as a primary element in the formation of the conditions for the reproduction of all life, human and other-than-human, in the very make-up of the atmosphere and in the soils and earth. It is visible in the increased level of atmospheric CO_2. It is visible in the deposition of materials that neither accumulate normally through earth processes, nor break down through organic decomposition. They range from radionucleotides to plastics and those substances now referred to as 'forever chemicals'. What then does this mean for human self-understandings? Western thought, and all of the cultural forms it has produced, has been predicated on a meaningful distinctiveness of (certain) humans from other creatures and from the material world, between culture and nature. This breakdown of an external other is a central characteristic of the Anthropocene.

Helmuth Trischler, director of research at the Deutsches Museum (The Science Museum in Munich) and co-director of the Rachel Carson Center, argues that these two perspectives on the Anthropocene, as both a geological and a cultural term, are 'inextricably interwoven and can only be fully understood by stressing the linkages between the geological and the cultural layers of the concept' (Trischler 2016: 32). However, it can be difficult to switch between the two different time frames: geologic time, and the time constraints of human lives and cultures. The Anthropocene 'designates a state of the planet in which key natural systems are coupled with social systems at a global level, thus influencing Earth system as a whole, thereby turning the human species into a global geophysical force that put the future habitability of the Earth into question' (Arias-Maldonado 2020: 98). The implications of this new perspective are profound. Perhaps the most significant of all the implications is that the Anthropocene dissolves the nature/culture boundary on which so much of our fundamental political tradition is founded. This means that many of the concepts we conventionally use to navigate our political thinking now need redefining in light of these realities (Hickman et al. 2019).

The Anthropocene is a catalyst for political change, but its scale is such that the existing analytical categories and philosophical concepts we use to envision and construct these changes may need 'bold reinterpretation' (Bińczyk 2019). Citizenship, I argue, is one of these. No longer tethered to the boundaries of the nation state, or even limited to the species boundary of humans alone, the Anthropocene poses new questions concerning how we live together. What might be the 'house rules' needed for dwelling less destructively and more inclusively reconciling humans and non-humans alike? Our lives as Anthropocene citizens are characterized not in abstract declarations but in the everyday mundane experiences of living on a shared planet. Common dwelling defines our shared interest, not the infinite divisions and demarcations commonly used to define our identities and belonging. In short, as Arias-Maldonado (2020, 109) puts it, 'the Anthropocene is … not a political artefact that pursues political ends on behalf of particular interests'.

The Anthropocene cannot be ignored. Postcolonial theorist Dipesh Chakrabarty's influential 2009 paper *The Climate of History: Four Theses* outlined the dilemmas for social and political theory. He structured the problem in terms of four sequential propositions:

> 1: Anthropogenic explanations of climate change spell the collapse of the age-old humanist distinction between natural history and human history …
>
> 2: The idea of the Anthropocene, the new geological epoch when humans exist as a geological force, severely qualifies humanist histories of modernity/globalization …
>
> 3: The geological hypothesis regarding the Anthropocene requires us to put global histories of capital in conversation with the species history of humans …
>
> 4: The cross-hatching of species history and the history of capital is a process of probing the limits of historical understanding. (Chakrabarty 2009: 201, 207, 212, 220)

He was criticized for arguing that 'the whole crisis cannot be reduced to a story of capitalism' (Chakrabarty 2009: 220) and accused of overlooking profound differences in privilege and exclusions. Chakrabarty responded to those who suggested that his setting of the issues pays too little regard to issues of injustice and inequalities in a later paper:

> Political thought has so far been humancentric, holding constant the 'world' outside of human concerns or treating its eruptions into the time of human history as intrusions from an 'outside.' This 'outside' no longer exists. What is

'just' for humans over one period of time may imperil our existence over another. Besides, Earth system science has revealed how critically entangled human lives are with the geo-bio-chemical processes of the planet. Our concerns for justice cannot any longer be about humans alone, but we don't yet know how to extend these concerns to the universe of nonhumans (that is, not just a few species). (Chakrabarty 2018: 29–30)

The consequences of this reorientation of the critical imagination prompted by recognition of the Anthropocene are what we must deal with in working to envisage Anthropocene mobilities.

EcoJustice in the Anthropocene

The term 'ecojustice' was specifically coined by those working to address the issues raised by new insights into these interwoven problems. It indicates the need to extend and fuse *economic* and *ecological* justice (Sölle and Cloyes 1984; 2001). Current in activist networks since the 1990s, the term was foreshadowed by the integrated approach to these issues outlined at the World Council of Churches meeting in Canberra in 1983. Its commission on Justice, Peace and the Integrity of Creation gave equal weight to the inseparable elements necessary for common planet-dwelling (see, e.g., Sölle and Cloyes 1984).[1] Only more recently has the term 'ecojustice' and its underlying commitment to the fusion of radical political and environmental politics become recognized in academic analyses that often derive from those distant from the activist networks themselves.[2]

If, as Sheller (2018, 2021) rightly argues, mobility justice needs to be at the heart of Anthropocene mobilities, then ecojustice gives us a framework to locate these issues at the heart of the Anthropocene dialogues that embrace the human and more-than-human. Citizenship has been the conventional mechanism to think through the rights and obligations necessary for living together and with ideas of justice as a basis of law. Bringing these concerns together we can ask what citizenship might look like through the lens of the Anthropocene. What might the Anthropocene mean for the political and cultural concept of citizenship?

---

[1] The term 'creation' need not imply any external creator but can simply be used to acknowledge that which is brought about by the creative forces of evolution and natural selection, highlighting the agency of the non-human world. In this form it usefully avoids the difficulties of using the term 'nature' to refer to the more-than-human.

[2] Oddly a number of otherwise perceptive left political analyses operating outside of those activist networks also fail to recognize the inseparability of social and environmental justice frameworks in the history of eco-activism (e.g. Fraser 2023).

How might rights and duties appear in light of humans as not just social and political beings but as a telluric force? How can competing rights and demands for recognition, usually the content of citizenship claims, be made sense of in this time lapse separation that shifts scales between human historic and geologic time? Is the conventional framing of citizenship in terms of the liberal model of the autonomous subject appropriate or even viable in light of Anthropocene realities, or does a reframing of the political subject allow different thinking on ecojustice issues? To approach these questions, I will first identify some outlines of the Anthropocene as an operating concept and then proceed to examine some of the approaches to citizenship that have shaped the debates so far on what Anthropocene citizenship might entail.

Defining the Anthropocene

As a geologic concept, the Anthropocene is used to mark the emergence of human activity as the dominant force in shaping a functionally and stratigraphically distinct era. It is not a situation that can be unmade. At precisely what point and through which key activities and their markers this occurs will continue to be a matter of debate. Precisely which human activities, structures and systems of organization are held as key demonstrates the intertwined identity of the geological and cultural ideas.

As a cultural concept, the inseparability of human and environment implicit in the geologic concept challenges the boundary setting and dichotomization that has underpinned Western intellectual thought. Jedediah Purdey (2015) suggests that, intellectually, the Anthropocene marks a third fundamental revolution in the ways that Western philosophies understand ourselves and our world. Previous upheavals demonstrated that neither politics nor economics could credibly be thought of as 'natural', that is, as fixed and predictable processes based on immutable laws. The Anthropocene now destabilizes our working assumptions of 'nature' and 'the natural world'. It is a recognition of our move from the relatively stable state and conditions of the Holocene into an era of unpredictability. It is an era in which we are no longer 'living in a stable environment that simply serves as a stage and resource for our actions, but we are all actors in a comprehensive drama in which humans and the nonhuman world equally take part' (Renn 2018: 3).

There is a paradox at the heart of this debate. All planetary systems are involved, and there is no escaping the implications of the multiple crises we face in this novel era, including anthropogenic climate change. At the same time, two factors need to be borne in mind, both of which having pressing concerns for how we might conceive of current and future citizenship. These have been explored in a series of debates following on from Chakrabarty's influential paper. First, causation is not evenly distributed. The greatest impacts have been made in the course of specific historical and technological trajectories pursued in the context of expansive and extractive colonialism that has fuelled industrial production systems and political economies. Second, though none can escape its effects, those effects are profoundly maldistributed, impacting most on those with least resources to mobilize for adaptation and resilience. Yet, at the same time, as Cohen and Colebrook (2016: 7) argue:

> One of the features of what has come to be known as the Anthropocene is that very few want to own up to being the guilty party: as soon as the Anthropocene was declared as a way of uniting humans once again, objections started pouring in. Why would 'we' want to sully the entirety of humanity by placing it as the author or agent of this late-modern event? So many declare, against the Anthropocene: 'Not in my name!': the Anthropocene is really the Capitalocene, the Corporatocene, or is better figured as a critical zone rather than one grand evil mess that includes all of humanity.

If we are the beneficiaries of fossil-fuelled transport systems, then we must acknowledge our complicity in the Anthropocene.

One response to recognition of human capacity is to double down on modernist conceptions of agency and the desire for control. Advocates of ecomodernist citizenship advocate not harmonization with nature, but further separation via technological innovation to shrink our ecological footprint, that is, the effect that human societies have on planetary systems. However, even its supporters also note the contradiction at the heart of this approach. It requires both a humanist commitment to 'ensure that people everywhere are included in the democratic governance of our planetary future' while also demanding institutional change and 'a central role to publicly funded innovation in steering technological change towards socially desirable objectives' (Symons and Karlsson 2018: 700; 690). Even assuming benevolence and voluntary action by governments to these ideals, the assumption that the human has the primacy and privilege to control and subdue earth processes for the furtherance of the human species (or at least a small part of it that exercises those privileges) is awkward. Who will decide which ecosystems and which species will be sacrificed for the furtherance of this vision or is it really assumed that such dramatic interventions can be met without cost?

A more problematic issue for Anthropocene citizenship is that this project demands a techno-optimism that seems ill-warranted. Clive Hamilton (2020: 117) dismisses this optimistic, even cornucopian vision, noting that current trajectories of climate breakdown suggest the Anthropocene as more of a rupture, marking the 'collapse of the great dream of the modern age, of humans using their unique capacities to take control of their environments and create their future'. The link between aspiration and its incapacity to deliver is clear: a 'loss of faith in the systems built by modern humankind is a repudiation of techno-optimism because the extreme danger of techno-industrialism has brought us here. We are inescapably enmeshed in the Earth System so that our power is always countered by a more powerful Earth' (Hamilton 2020: 118).

The Anthropocene designation acknowledges the exceptionalism of human agency in its capacity to change ecosystems. The scale and nature of many of these changes are irreversible. There is no longer a 'natural state' to which things can be returned (Dzwonkowska 2021). Yet this very exceptionalism poses the challenge of meeting the responsibilities that come with power. Furthermore, just as 'we appear to have taken control over nature and have become the principal force of its transformation, we also appear ill equipped, and perhaps unable, to govern a world under the influence of these changes' (Hamilton et al. 2015: 10).

Recognizing the influence that has been wrought by human activity it is tempting to assume that the knowledge of our capacities and effects implies an imminent response to become the agent of salvation. The cornucopian assumptions of eco-modernism are relatively easy to dismiss, but other more grounded political analyses can easily elide understanding the problems with an automatic consequential shift to action. Responding to those who assume that with knowledge of the destructive forces we have unleashed will come an almost automatic reaction to rectify these behaviours, Claire Colebrook takes a more eco-pessimistic stance. She poses the question: 'What would the present begin to look like if we refused both the claim for humanity as global agent and humanity as proper potentiality?' (Colebrook 2016: 88). Such a view need not be grounded in despair nor imply throwing up one's hands in horror and accelerating the demise by doubling down on destructive action (though both may be widely observed in reactions to the Anthropocene). Colebrook's broader perspective recognizes that current framings of the dilemma of the Anthropocene from which argument proceeds might themselves be problematic.

It seems that we have two options: either the Anthropocene is an effect of man in general, or it can be attributed to capitalism (or corporations, or colonialism, or patriarchy), in which case man can emerge as an innocent animal – as a new humanity to come. But what if one were to refuse both these options by suggesting that man is neither the global culprit, nor the global victim, and that there are many living beings on this planet who live, dwell, struggle and survive with no sense of humanity in general? (Colebrook 2016: 88)

Placed in a more positive way, these observations might be reframed as a way of asking what concepts and ways of thinking about the human and human action might be appropriate to such a context. In this manner, citizenship as an expression of belonging, of incumbent duties and responsibilities, as well as of incurred rights, can give some useful answers. However, it will also mean challenges to existing frames of reference and to established discourses. Again, Hamilton and his colleagues (2015, 4) indicate the scale of the challenge: 'The idea of the human, of the social contract, of what nature, history, society and politics are all about – in other words, all of the essential ideas on which these disciplines have been constructed – ask to be rethought.' Humility rather than hubris might be in order as a guiding principle.

An implication of Hamilton's observations is that so many of our concepts of change and of future thinking in Western society are implicitly tied to a linear and teleological narrative that imagines time progressing towards a meaningful end, often propelled by some ultimate external agency, whether divinity, history, technology or simply time itself. How we might begin to operate without assuming these external forces is a bigger question that needs to be explored later. For the moment the problem needs recognition as part of the framework in which we must build responses.

Emancipatory politics in the Anthropocene

If the corollary of the Anthropocene's dissolution of boundaries serves to remove the 'other', in other words, that which is external, it follows that the 'other' of emancipation, that is, the possibility of political salvation, is also rendered problematic. What might emancipation look like if we are forced to re-envision it, not as an escape from our material and political limits into an abstract realm of freedom, but as finding our proper place *within* the limits of the planetary systems? Anthropocene mobility planning will need to consider what levels and volumes of travel might be compatible with staying inside limits, not just what might be desirable. The eternal (but often denied) compromise of liberal democracy is that the freedom and emancipation offered have only ever existed within the limits of constrained choice (Escobar 2007).

Ecological emancipation is not to be found or imagined in the escape from the boundedness of the biophysical world into a limitless future, but in recognizing that there is no such thing as life outside the ecosystem we inhabit, or beyond its limitations. Being human involves accepting limits (Gorringe 1999). A bounded and finite existence requires us to reimagine emancipation not as a liberation from constraints but in finding our place and role within the planetary household (ecologic) community. Lest this appear bleak, we should remember that the rapid expansion of possibilities provided by the expansion of industrial modernity was premised on colonization and dispossession by enclosure. The extractivism on which the technological revolutions and industrial development of the West relied was made possible by sequestrating resources and by physical enslaved labour and oppression of populations and peoples who were not counted as citizens of the imperial powers (Bhambra and Holmwood 2021). Citizenship has always been deployed by nation states (even in their formation as an escape from absolute rule) as a mechanism of exclusion as well as recognition (James 1938; Mies 1986). As much as it includes identifying some people as citizens, it also demands the exclusion of others as the cost of ensuring the privileges of its subjects.

Total liberation as an absolute value is an enticing but ultimately meaningless fable: one can never be liberated from obligation (Lou 2019). Political visions of total freedom and autonomy could only ever apply to the colonial patriarch who outsources and offshores all the necessary labour of social reproduction. These observations likewise imply that we need to think about how autonomy is defined within the contexts of the Anthropocene and of a relational self. A realistic ecopessimism should not dull us into inaction, nor lull us into a nostalgia of desire to restore pasts that no longer exist and possibly never did (MacCormack 2020). Without downplaying the seriousness of the tasks facing us there is room for a melancholy hope. As part of this, I want to endorse an idea of citizenship as a way of living together in transformed conditions, recognizing interdependence and addressing inequalities. This requires delinking citizenship from its narrow confinement to the nation state and to the exclusively human.

This is the space in which to question the desire that seeks to identify a singular agent of salvation and specific means of redemption from our collective troubles, and as a corollary, a desire that seeks clearly identifiable enemies to be vanquished. Reductive simplification of the problem and its solutions is tempting but fails to address the complexity and multi-levelled dimensions of diverse politics and histories. Nor does the comfort of clear ideological solutions necessarily assist in the practical identification of actions and tasks to be undertaken in the necessary short term.

The more direct task is to acknowledge our individual and collective complicity in bringing about the conditions of destabilization (even if only through an unasked-for inheritance). Understanding our connections to the problems, and continued benefit from destructive processes, it then makes sense to ask what modes of living might be more appropriate for the challenge of the Anthropocene and to find less destructive ways of living. Those who are beneficiaries of high energy and high resource use, capital accumulation and its command of carbon in constructing the nations often referred to as the Global North need to recognize *our* conditions of privilege, and the ways in which these privileges are woven, often invisibly, into our lives and livelihoods. The motivation for this book is not to promote a vague hope of a salvation from a condition that cannot be solved, but to identify and celebrate existing paths of action that do not further accelerate climate destabilization. Given our complicity in climate change, how might we begin to find ways in which to be more responsive citizens of the Anthropocene?

Contributory discourses for Anthropocene citizenship

The historic linkage of citizenship and state might appear to be fundamental, and thus an impassable barrier to its reconceptualization beyond the nation state. Yet if we work from some basic implications of that relationship, we can consider how citizenship has been constructed as that which confers access to resources, to identity, to belonging and as a basis for the development of civic virtue. All of these, in some very different ways, have been visible resources in the emergence of debates towards Anthropocene citizenship.

The emergence of environmental and ecological concerns in international politics, expressed most visibly in the 1972 United Nations Conference in Stockholm, shifted perspectives in perhaps unforeseen and unacknowledged ways (Friends of the Earth 1972; Ward and Dubos 1972). Environmental problems, framed in terms of pollution and resource depletion, it was rapidly recognized, could no longer be credibly considered only within territorial boundaries of nation states. Subsequent studies, especially in atmospheric pollution (and, in particular, concerns with atmospheric CO_2 concentrations), required reconfiguring problems to a planetary scale. Ideas of planetary environmental and ecological citizenship were constructed by destabilizing the nation state as the basic unit of political community and acknowledging the global links of trade in access to physical resources. The negative downside of focus on the global scale and interlinked-ness of problems was the erroneous assumption made by some commentators that only global scale thought and action (characterized by universal solutions) was required in response. Despite the intentions of many involved in these negotiations, local responses and community-led actions, especially those taking place outside the Global North, were often sidelined and disempowered (see Agarwal and Narain 1991).

Examining how environmental issues affected ideas about citizenship, Dobson (2003) identifies two main strands of thought, corresponding to broader responses to awareness of the problems (see Naess 1973; Bookchin 1973, 1980; Dryzek 2013). *Environmental citizenship* is a version of liberal citizenship which extends the discourse and practice of rights claiming (beyond civil political and economic) into the environmental context. *Ecological citizenship*, in contrast, is formed around the language of virtue. Ecological citizenship is not territorially bounded – since the community in which it engages is global – hence it can also be read as a form of cosmopolitanism (Beck 2016). Global in identity it may be, but it is also grounded in the local, in specific experience rather than as the attribute of an abstract liberal subject. In a planetary context, citizenship obligations are unreciprocated and unilateral. If the Anthropocene further draws attention to the effect of human action across time as well as geography, then it also further reshapes obligation and rights, civic virtue extends from the public into the private spheres.

Although the demands of different forms of citizenship might appear to pull in competing directions and provide contradictory narratives it is worth being reminded that citizenship is inherently multilevel (Maas 2013). Historically, nonstate communities or jurisdictions also conferred rights and status with attendant obligations. These can be contentious, even construed as threats to the nation state. Yet their coexistence, even if uneasy, is manageable. For example, religious traditions provide transnational communities that offer forms of citizenship coexistent with more formal, nationally bounded state citizenships. Sociological approaches to religion conventionally understand it through categories of belief, ritual and identity, corresponding to the social relations of individual choice-making liberal subjects. Thus, the narrative of secularization makes sense as a way of explaining the spread of Enlightenment modernity to cast off the shackles of religion. However, to understand religious communities instead as collective participation in a relational form of citizenship (a concept equally rooted in the modern) can help comprehension in both directions: from both inside and outside faith perspectives.[3] It also helps explain why secularization theory has proven so problematic. However, there remains a need to be alert to the powerful danger of exclusionary boundary setting that is equally pernicious in nation states and religious communities. Both can foster on fundamental(ist) identities and the alienated 'othering' of those who do not conform to membership criteria.

Seeking a pragmatic exploration of practical citizenship and citizenship building in light of emergent Anthropocene discourses, Fremaux (2017) recognizes the fundamental problem of citizenship's exclusions and hints at the (re)habilitation of 'denizen' as an organizing concept, the denizen being someone who not simply inhabits a space but is part of its active creation. By implication, this would extend Dobson's ecological citizenship in a particular direction. Although as yet underdeveloped, this direction points towards a pragmatic means to stay within a firmly humanist, republican tradition. Fremaux's vision of Anthropocene citizenship rejects the liberal attachment to rights and allows for a rebuilding of a sense of common obligation across boundaries. Yet we are also forced to confront the limitations of humanist perspectives on political subjectivity in their capacity to address the realities of the Anthropocene identified earlier.

While Dobson's ecological citizenship is deterritorialized (in the sense that it does not refer to the arbitrary boundaries of nation states), this is not the same as globalized. We cannot simply dismiss the historic centrality of place in the construction of citizenship and the concomitant inclusions and exclusions that have arisen from its territorialities. Nevertheless, we need also consider how place functions within the identifications of citizenship as it constructs the citizen. As Tim Ingold (2000) has extensively shown in his consideration of *dwelling*, place provides possibilities for identity and belonging. It meets the very real human need for a meaningful citizenship to provide connections and a means for social integration. In territorially bounded citizenship, the citizen is formed and affirmed as subject through the recognition by the governing entity. Belonging and identification are fostered by citizenship of the territorial state. In Walter Mignolo's (2017: 14) eloquent summation, 'if the State became the legal

---

[3] Having noted the role of religions as conferring a form of citizenship it is perhaps worth noting the early role of faith-based activist networks of concern in publicly highlighting the problems of climate change. For example, the Church of Scotland's report *With scorching heat and drought?* (Pullinger, ed.) came out in 1989. John Houghton's *Global warming: the complete briefing*, later to become a standard Cambridge University Press textbook, was first published by an independent Christian publisher in 1994.

form of governance, the nation became the sensing, the feeling that connects people of the "same nation," the nationals, the citizens'. In examining the sensing, feeling process unlocked by different modes of travel, I want to consider how mundane, habitual practices can connect people to planet, particularly to the specific locations through which people travel, in short, to explore how Anthropocene citizenship can be experienced as denizenship.

The challenge posed by the Anthropocene is not answered solely by finding how we might foster a global ecological citizenship but also requires us to recognize and act upon the historic colonial legacies that have shaped citizenship in nations benefitting from their position as former colonial powers and their allies (Kanji 2017). In the Anthropocene, our conceptions of citizenship and its qualifications are further challenged by the status of the nonhuman and the more-than-human. To put the discussion another way, the bios, specifically the Anthropos, is now implicated in the geos (Rose and Novas 2005). Our human story is no longer just a human story: there are other actors involved. The agency of planetary systems in shaping future political and social relations, and even the territorialities on which conventional expectations of citizenship are based cannot be ignored. We should also be careful, however, to distinguish between chemical inevitability arising from rising atmospheric carbon levels and political inevitability. There is no determinate politics arising from determinate geobiochemical processes. No political vision or policy direction necessarily arises automatically from recognition of the certainties of atmospheric physics. Our responses must still be formed and fought for. Our politics arises from our capacity to make moral or value judgements on the factual observations we can make. They reflect the values we give to the relationships we build with others: other persons and the more-than-human others. In this context, recent developments in thinking through the conceptual world of the posthuman may provide resources through which citizenship can continue to have meaning and traction.

As we look for maps and for ways to navigate the terrain of the posthuman in the Anthropocene, Rosi Braidotti's work is especially helpful. Her article, *Four theses on Posthuman Feminism* (2017), starts with the argument that Western feminism is historically bound to Enlightenment humanism in its claims for equality. It was constructed around claims for equality and thus modern concepts of citizenship have been central to it. Nevertheless, she argues that, as assumptions of commonality (of interest and identity) have come under fire in feminist theory, so responses and adaptations have provided new directions for its development. She affirms that feminism is not a humanism and is antihumanist to the extent that it rejects methodological nationalism in its affirmation of postcolonialism (Braidotti 2017). Contemporary ecofeminisms (and posthuman feminisms) draw from philosophical antihumanisms that delink the human agent from a universalistic positionality. They join with activist narratives from radical environmental/ecological movements that share an antihumanist or, as Braidotti alternatively calls it, a radical neohumanism. Through this move, Braidotti allows us to set aside the claim that representation is a vital part of citizenship. Rather, it is the existence of the state that historically allowed citizens to see themselves as citizens. In the context of the Anthropocene, a planetary scale of our civic identity can provide a ground for a new interpretation of citizenship. Recognition of the commonality of more-than-human sharing in this belonging extends it to denizenship.

Developed further in *Posthuman Feminism* (2022), Braidotti's argument transforms cosmopolitan perspectives on citizenship. Beck's cosmopolitan analysis already presents a powerful critique of methodological nationalism (Beck and Grande 2010; Culver et al. 2011; Beck 2016). Rather than the liberal presumption of the theoretical equality of all and thus their equal claim on rights, Braidotti (2022: 4) builds implicitly on cosmopolitan critiques to observe that the very status of what it means to be human is 'shot through with power relations organising access to privileges and entitlements'. Even in the context of the formative struggles of the late eighteenth century, she pertinently reminds us, the universal citizenship proclaimed by revolutionary subjects was still reserved for a relatively privileged male elite, exclusive of women and persons of colour (compare Mies 1986).

The context of the Anthropocene, Braidotti argues, forces us to reconsider subjectivity. It is therefore fruitful for thinking through the issues of Anthropocene citizenship. Relinquishing 'both the liberal vision of autonomous individual, as well as the socialist ideal of a privileged revolutionary subject', Braidotti (2022, 6) reframes the problem of the political subject away from one of recognition to one centred on an ethics of affirmation, grounded in praxis. Knowledge generation is an essential part of this praxis, becoming aware of the entanglements of the human and more-than-human. Posthuman feminist perspectives therefore provide an unexpected means through which to rehabilitate citizenship in the Anthropocene, albeit in a different frame from previous emphases on bounded territoriality, rights and equalities. Most importantly, Braidotti argues, this moves us from the politics of a reparative project to a transformative one.

Directions for Anthropocene citizenship

Anthropocene citizenship necessarily has to be conceived very differently from national, ethnic or religious citizenship, defined as these are by their boundaries and exclusions. If, as already noted, Anthropocene thinking renders the external obsolete it then requires that we disrupt the role of boundaries established to define and assert citizenship as an exclusive property of select groups. Rather, the Anthropocene breakdown of externalities points towards citizenship as a common property of all planet-dwellers. Citizenship of the planet pre-exists the nation state. Anthropocene citizenship is a concept that enables us to supersede nation state citizenship.

What courses of action might we seek in order to realize Anthropocene citizenship as a praxis? One very valuable direction suggested by Renshaw (2021) is to take emotions more seriously; cultivation of a relational and aesthetic sensibility becomes crucial in forming Anthropocene citizenship as 'quiet' citizenship. By quiet, Renshaw does not mean passive or inert (although this is not to denigrate passivity or stillness as important values in themselves). The idea of quiet citizenship can draw attention to a set of value transformations that shift citizenship away from a stance that makes declarations and demands, towards a position that stresses accommodation and affirms qualities of emotion and the capacity to be affected (Bohlin 2020; Atkinson 2018). Anthropocene citizenship is the shared quality of planetary denizens. As Fox and Aldred (2019: 122) suggest, a posthuman ethics can be based on a new sense of interconnectedness.

Subjectivity is not a given but produced in a flow of relations with multiple others. To make this possible, however, requires openness to a flow of relations and acceptance that these will inevitably be transformative. We will be changed, be moved when we open ourselves to this possibility. Not the primary agents of such changes brought about by other-relations, we are not in control of them. This can be a fearful proposition. To develop an attitude of care requires a sense of empathy, the capacity to identify with others. Consequently, values matter in order to determine our attitudes towards those outside of our necessary and immediate relations of obligation. Developing those capacities demands not only adding qualities of attentiveness but also minimizing or even abandoning those actions that hinder their development. To embrace responsiveness and create an ethics of care (as described in the next chapters) is not to add yet another dimension to the already globally privileged. It is to recognize that this ethics requires us to voluntarily surrender aspects of that privilege so that we can act *care*-fully.

What we see in this care- and values-based approach is a refocussing of citizenship away from rights-based claims that ultimately only amount to ego-fulfilment (Nayer 2012). Citizenship is recast as a journey of growth into finding one's place within a net of relations. Of course, this does not remove or dismiss the capacities to recognize and address inequalities and injustices, nor does it flatten everything into a single undifferentiated mass in which every status is predetermined and unchangeable. It presents a re-imagining of issues for thinking about citizenship and what it entails.

Dedeoglu and Ekmekcioglu (2020) draw on prior discussions in environmental ethics to explore the implications of citizenship beyond a nature-culture distinction. They highlight especially Curtin's (1999) critique of dominant views of citizenship as being rooted in Western culture, state formation, colonialism and sexism. Wary of this tainted legacy, meaningful ecological citizenship and therefore a means to realize citizenship in the Anthropocene requires incorporation of ecological communities stretching beyond the human. Therefore, they argue in line with Curtin (1999: 16) for 'a global practice of localized care' to define a new role for citizenship. This provides, as we shall see in Chapter 5, a way to think about walking and cycling as everyday travel disciplines. The corollary of changing everyday travel modes is a significant reduction in everyday driving (which can also change the dynamic of road space, as was seen during pandemic lockdowns). If overall travel is not to grow, then substitution by non-motorized modes is required. Walking and cycling are not an augmentation to driving trips. The norms of growth are so firmly embedded that it is difficult to think of change in any other than an additive mode, that is, any novel action is simply 'added on' to otherwise unchanged patterns. A degrowth in motor mobilities suitable for Anthropocene citizenship implies not just taking occasional non-car journeys, but subtracting many or most of the mundane journeys where other modes are possible.

A further, closely related implication of this approach of care and one, incidentally, which appears centrally in support communities for radical ecological activism is to consider how we as humans deal with the emotional recognition of our own destructive capacities highlighted in the Anthropocene dilemma. In two articles that bridge academic and activist perspectives, Lesley Head (2015, 2018) produces a long list of required qualities that could well serve as guidelines for Anthropocene citizenship. Citizens of the Anthropocene need, she explains, to learn to acknowledge their grief, live in uncertainty without stress and understand how they are embedded in the earth. Practically speaking, they need to become good at sharing; capable of living in diverse families and communities and to develop a different orientation to time and its 'use', compared with the Moderns. Finally, Head identifies the importance of changing relationships to materials and the need to be able to live with shifting patterns of both abundance and scarcity. These qualities will appear later in discussion of everyday mobilities as a means to demonstrate the relation between mundane practices and Anthropocene citizenship.

One caveat should be held up to the whole of this discussion of Anthropocene citizenship. Historically, discussion of citizenship has been conducted almost entirely from the perspective of the dominant Western male subject. Ensuring that this exclusive bias is not replicated in thinking about Anthropocene citizenship and in the ways that mobility practices might foster different sensibilities requires vigilance and sensitivity. It also requires attention to inclusion of the agency of the more-than-human. However, the mobility practices that need addressing are still those of humans, and specifically high-energy mobilities.

If citizenship is a product of the modern Western constitutional state, then it is within that context, and to that context a redrawing of the boundaries and the obligations of citizenship need addressing. While the posthuman draws our attention to the continuity of life and agency beyond the anthropocentric gaze of existing politics, it is to human agency in mobility practices that calls for action needed to be addressed (Häkli 2018). As Hamilton (2020: 118) argues, 'our task is not to deny our extraordinary power and attempt to abandon it but to work out how to use our power responsibly'. Agency is still valid, and citizenship remains a significant location in which agency is realized. That agency extends beyond the human is clear, but we always live with an existential inability to fully know another's position and experience. We can only collectively act in our own capacity in solidarity with others. Though the structural agency of natural forces is powerful and inescapable, it does not take away from the responsibility for our human agency.

As a summary for the cultivation of Anthropocene citizenship in line with the directions pointed to above, it is perhaps worth turning back a century to an observation from Bakhtin that seems to summarize both the sense of connection that contributes to Anthropocene citizenship and much of the discussion of care and commoning in the next chapter. 'Lovelessness, indifference, will never be able to generate sufficient power to slow down and linger intently over an object, to hold and sculpt every detail and particular in it, however minute. Only love is capable of being aesthetically productive; only in correlation with the loved is fullness of the manifold possible' (Bakhtin 1993 [1919–21]: 64). We have the resources and capacities to live differently: they do not require acquisition of previously non-existent qualities; they do demand us to nurture ways of being with each other in the world and of loving each other and the world that have been repressed.

Citizenship, democracy and the more-than-human

One of the challenges facing politics today is how to reconfigure the scope of politics, and in particular democratic politics, to restore visions beyond those that have typified its recent narrowing of focus. As Kompridis (2014, xviii) argues, 'If [politics] is about what we are able to see and hear and about what we are unable to see and hear, then *democratic* politics is about letting what could not be seen and heard *be* seen and heard by cultivating new ways of seeing and hearing.' To address this gap, he suggests, we need to pay particular attention to the problem of voice and voicelessness. Who has the capacity to speak? Which voices count and which are excluded? And to extend this into the realm of the posthuman, we can consider how we might address the voices of those with whom we share the planet, but have not historically been included in our category of citizens. Can our imagination of democratic politics be expanded to think in terms of the rights of nature, whatever that might mean in our rethought concept of citizenship (Tabios Hillebrecht and Berros 2017)?

Recent growth in discussion of the rights of nature would seem on the surface to be an obvious corollary of citizenship. By themselves, these rights do not constitute an expression of Anthropocene citizenship in the manner I am exploring here, given that it does not imply a rethinking of citizenship itself. To accord legal rights to nature, even in the formation of a constitutional recognition, is not necessarily a barrier to 'increased resource extraction with detrimental social-environmental effects', as Laastad (2020: 401) notes. Indeed, as Tănăsescu (2022: 148) argues, the very focus on rights 'risks propagating liberal orthodoxy' and 'growth-fuelled development' unless it is carefully identified what rights are accorded for (hence the usefulness of the concept of the integrity of creation discussed above). The same argument was used from an environmental ethics perspective by Mick Smith (2001). He identified axiological extensionism (of which rights-based arguments applied to animals or nature as a whole are examples) as a problem of liberal modernity. While arguments remain framed in these terms, it is almost impossible to criticize the prior framework from which they stem. This is not to denigrate the vital role of the animal rights movement, either in its search for animal liberation or working to give legal protection against animal and planetary exploitation. The legal personhood of animals and ecosystems is a vital part of the struggle. Smith recognizes that asserting rights is necessary within the philosophic norms in which we currently operate, but that an ethic of care renders exclusive rights claims redundant. This theme of care will be expanded in the next chapter.

While for practical terms we can accord legal rights to the non-human as a first stage, however inadequate, a further difficulty is how to avoid the interpretation of nature and animal rights in a paternalist and patriarchal frame. One response to this latter problem is to be found through practical exploration of the problems encountered in academic reflection on processes of interviewing as a research method.

> Qualitative researchers using humanist theories of the subject typically equate words spoken by participants in interviews and then transcribed into words in interview transcripts as data. In humanist qualitative inquiry, the assumption is that voice is produced by a unique, essentialist subject. Mazzei (2013, 732)

So far so straightforward. Yet working from a relational (not essentialist) subject raises significant problems of this interpretation. Even within its own terms of reference there are difficulties. The very process of interviewing, even with a vocal respondent, is an intervention that creates a dynamic interaction (Bonham and Bacchi 2013). To assume that an interview can reveal or arrive at a truth is to presume an essential singular pre-existent reality that can be uncovered. Rather, as we consistently recreate our selves and identities through our interactions, we need to think more carefully about the assumptions that we bring to the problem of giving voice to participants in research. Further, the simple process of asking respondents to give voice can be an exercise in the removal of power. Although Demart (2022) makes this critique in relation to research, pointing out how academic research can reproduce relationships of coloniality, the same can be said about the elicitation of political voices in democratic institutions.

Voting in a representative democracy necessarily involves simplification and compromise, requiring voters to decide which issues take priority and which can be held in abeyance. Even participatory political discussions reach artificial compromise, not a perfect expression of citizen voices (Gret and Sintomer 2005; Santos 2007). Ultimately, representation assumes essentialist forms of identity and such colonialist forms of political theory still need to be challenged (Disch, Van de Sande and Urbinati 2019; Shilliam 2021).

Taking an explicitly posthumanist feminist perspective, Mazzei (2013) queries conventional assumptions of qualitative research to examine the problem of subjectivity. Developing the argument that subjectivity is produced in a network of interaction (rather than being the possession of an individual subject), she observes that 'voice' cannot be thought as existing separately from the milieu in which it exists, it cannot be thought as emanating 'from' an individual person. There is no separate, individual person, no participant in an interview study to which a single voice can be linked – 'all are entangled'. Further, and this is crucial, 'material and human agencies are mutually and emergently productive [or constitutive] of one another' (Mazzei 2013: 734). Mazzei thus brings in the role of more-than-human as a constitutive part of human voice: in her phrasing, 'a voice without organs'. Democracy can be revitalized as a way of thinking about radical inclusion.

Non-domination

One guide to resolving these difficulties of finding voice without projecting one's own assumptions onto those assumed to be without voice is to engage and observe as far as possible a strategy of non-domination. The non-domination I am thinking of here is that indebted to an anarchist tradition, rather than a neo-republican one. Anarchist analyses, whether coming from a secular (Eisenstadt 2013) or religious/mystic tradition (Sölle 2001), are less restricted by the constraint of the nation state, the form that dominates and structures non-domination in neo-republicanism (Kinna and Pritchard 2019). For Anthropocene citizenship, the limitations of nation state base thinking are clearly obvious. Eisenstadt highlights non-domination and the care of the self as key principles for thinking about the values that we reproduce in our actions. The perspective he opens up is that transformative actions are not justified by their utility in meeting a specific end goal or target. Actions can have value, even virtue, in and of themselves. They are done because they are needed to be done and are in line with the underlying value of non-domination. The implication of this action without calculation of its utility value is explored further in relation to uncontrollability, again in the next chapter.

From the outside, these concerns may look worryingly abstract and an artificial problem of academic overthinking. What they have in common is that they are all attempts to work with the consequences of moving from a strictly realist or representational perspective without losing sight or touch of material realities. What does that mean for our encounters with the world? Even in common language we are familiar with the capacity of things and situations to speak to us. This even applies to abstract entities. Simone Weil (2021 [1951]) wrote of the 'living silence' of the church, reflecting on its power to move (emotionally) the observant and its capacity to inspire action not through words and letters but through its abstract existence as an historical body, expressed in architecture and art. She was not speaking of the actuality of the institution but its symbolic presence and material instantiation. The inability to speak verbally can be more meaningful than speech. Might we consider whether (and how) the more-than-human presents us with a similarly living silence? The earth speaks, but not in a human voice or one that can be reduced to human tongue. It may be linguistically silent but is in full voice. To listen to it, we need to attune.

To listen and attune will require setting aside those actions that make listening and attuning difficult, if not impossible. If we can listen and we find that 'that which has no voice' has the capacity to shape and transform our actions, then what political responses might we make in response to that agency? If the granting of rights is but the first step in the development of a working notion of citizenship, deriving its substance in relation to the modern state, then what would constitute a second step for the Anthropocene context? One might still counterargue that to attribute agency and voice to the more-than-human is to be guilty of sentimentality and projection. Yet facing the very real crises of the Anthropocene then considering the rights of nature as more than just a noble or abstract expression might provide a way into an ethic of care if we can shift the discursive frame in which we understand rights not in isolation but as a property of citizenship.

Citizenship as encounter

One final problem in discussions of citizenship stemming from liberal perspectives is their frequent focus on the individual subjects or, conversely, as collective responsibilities in which personal experience is subsumed within an undifferentiated collective. We need to consider how we understand selfhood and personhood in relation to the individualized subject even when that individuality only proceeds from the relations through which it is constituted. This is especially pertinent since the perceptual and sensory awarenesses on which the focus on mobility experiences rests is only encountered through individual participation, even though the interpretative frames through which meaning and comprehension is given to those experiences are collectively produced. As sociologist and psychologist Alberto Melucci wrote, it is

> impossible to imagine forms of resistance or opposition to the contemporary manifestations of power which do not involve individual experience. I however, do not think that it is possible to postulate a kind of an 'uncontaminated' natural core or essence … We only exist within culture and within society, but since we still, at the same time, belong to nature and carry within ourselves and inner nature, the problem is where to draw the borderline. This is a cultural problem, no longer something involving a 'fact' of nature. (Melucci 1996: 152)

We are sensing and perceiving selves. Our own experiences, rooted in physicality, help to define our personal separation from others. In trying to share these experiences, we form bonds between participants. 'There is always a part of the bodily experience which is not translated into language. Feelings, emotions, sensations, and movements are not entirely communicable to others because they also represent the deepest and most intimate parts of human experience' (Melucci 1996: 151). At the same time as we recognize the individual experience, and our own unique interpretations of those physical sensations, we also recognize the importance of sharing and simultaneous experience.

To travel alone is one form of experience, travelling with others provides another. There are other more obvious forms of experience sharing. For example, we constantly, almost incessantly, share online images. Why? Not simply to sate a desire for narcissistic self-projection but to affirm shared experiences and to allow others at least a glimpse to those perceptual events and feelings when they are not with us to share at first hand. FOMO, 'fear of missing out', may be an egotistical driver for instantaneous digital communication, but its flipside is also the other-directed 'fear of not being able to share' (FONBATS perhaps?), a fear of being trapped within our own experiential world to which no one else has access.

Beasly and Bacchi (2012) deliberately question how to link perceptual worlds of these enfleshed body experiences – the worlds of physical sensation – to concepts of citizenship. Their starting point is to review Elizabeth Grosz's account as one that typifies feminist body theory. 'Bodies in Grosz's account are neither consistently "other" than minds/selves/subjects nor consistently at one with them. There is no stable mind/body split or unity' (Beasly and Bacchi 2012: 103). However, they are uneasy at the abstract and individualistic focus that reduces the political impact of such discussion. To remedy this, they proposed a much stronger emphasis on the social in these 'fleshly imaginings'. The lack of exploration of the social in body theory, they argue, is a clear parallel to the absence of actual bodies in thinking about citizenship.

To provide a stronger ground upon which to build an analysis of contemporary citizenship would require bringing both ways of thinking, on sociality and fleshly bodies, through a concentration on 'social flesh'. The combination, though complex, might provide: 'an ethico-political starting point for thinking critically about politics, interconnection and sociality' (Beasly and Bacchi 2012: 107). Such a perspective is invaluable in working out the implications and matters of concern of an Anthropocene citizenship. Anthropocene citizenship is therefore about social flesh, embodied and physical while recognizing that the cognitive isolation often correlated with concentration on the sensory and perceptual needs to be challenged by interconnected sociality. Fleshly imaginings are central to the experience of travel and thus knit together these various strands of arguments.

Conclusions

Despite these many difficulties, the concept of citizenship still has much to offer. A critique of citizenship, both as it is and as it historically has been, opens up the way to rethinking citizenship as it could be. Usefully it provides a means to engage with a wide variety of debates about what it means to be-in-the-world as a human in the Anthropocene. Expanding the horizons of citizenship further allows us to think about the implications of other beings' rights to their being-ness and how we relate to each other. In practical terms we can then move forward in thinking about what it might mean to be a responsive citizen and specifically what this means in the limited terms of this study: to move about in the world. Before looking at the central problem of mobility habits and their implications, we need to think about relationality and encounter. This requires thinking through the issues of the perceiving, relational self in order to develop the discussion of care and commoning.

3

Being-in-the-world: Care and commoning

Introduction

This chapter takes us from the Anthropocene as context for the search for an appropriately reimagined citizenship onto an examination of ideas that can give shape to a positive and what I will call a *responsive* citizenship. Responsive is used here because I want to indicate both responsibility, our sense of connection to a given situation, and respons-*ability*, that is, developing the capacity to act in response to a situation. Sequentially, this chapter explores care and commoning as important themes that emerge in dialogues concerning how to act and think in relation to the complex and multiple challenges posed by the Anthropocene (Nikolaeva et al. 2019). It places them within a framework provided by Hartmut Rosa's writings on a sociology of 'being-in-the-world', further exploring the implications of the relational self, derived from Buber, as briefly outlined in Chapter 1. This allows us to think through the implications of experience while safeguarding against the hubris of imagining that we can determine perfect solutions to the problems we face.

Care and commoning are two themes that have come to the fore in the search for principles and values appropriate in an era of degrowth (Schmelzer et al. 2022). They are part of a myriad of values and alternative orientations towards the world and each other gathered in what has been termed a pluriversal politics (Escobar 2020). The interweaving of many different paths from a variety of local, emplaced traditions has together been dubbed a global tapestry of alternatives (https://globaltapestryofalternatives.org). 'Pluriverse' highlights the rejection of universal solutions in favour of multiple ways of thinking about the good life that respect local traditions within a broad frame of respect and care. Finally, this chapter returns to Rosa's insistence on uncontrollability as part of resonance and links it to issues of power and control in other traditions of resistance to situations of dominance. Together, these ideas provide the tools through which we can interrogate the experiences and practices of everyday travel.

Relationality and dialogue

Relationality is at the heart of human life. We are fleshy and social beings, but our sociality is not limited to encounters with other humans. We are embedded and entangled in relationship with the worlds around us, worlds of both material and imagination, that we are part of the making of. Through histories of farming and agriculture, through forestry and quarrying, through building and the constructions of infrastructure, streets, pavements, workplaces and leisure spaces and through our travels in these built worlds, everything we meet and encounter is part of our social lives, our networks of interactions. These physical worlds around us are complemented by worlds of story, of history and of imagination. Virtual worlds give context and meaning to the physical worlds.

As noted earlier, Buber argued that the individual self does not exist outside of its relationality. It is not fruitful to think about the 'I' as if it exists independent of the relationships it is part of. Relationality is a dialogue and interaction between the self and the other. The self does not exist without the other, but the other is not subsumed into the self. Bakhtin's early work on dialogic relationality similarly develops this model, particularly with respect to the world beyond the human but he proceeds without the language of the divine that shapes Buber's work (and that can become problematic for some readers). We need to keep the dialogic dimension at the forefront of this analysis so as not to become immersed in an ego-driven projection of the self, concentrating solely on the agency of the I-end of the interaction. Consequently, types and quality of relationality are crucial.

Buber suggests we can distinguish two primary forms of relation: the I exists either as I-It or I-Thou.[1] 'The primary connection of man with the world of It', Buber (1923: 55) writes, 'is comprised in *experiencing*'. The 'experiencing I' of I-It observes and interprets the world, understanding its separation from that world. The I-Thou relationship, by contrast, resists objectification. The I-Thou relation is fully entered, intense and involves the whole of our being and being-ness.

---

[1]	I retain the 'Thou' of the R. G. Smith translation to lift the 'other' of the relationship from the familiarity and ordinariness of you and to retain a sense of radical alterity even within the identification with the other in the I-Thou.

The I of this relationship becomes aware of its one-ness, 'sharing in being' and 'co-existing' with the Thou of the I-Thou (Buber 1923: 66). In the I-Thou there exists no 'other', nothing outside the relation, despite the continued radical alterity of the Thou. To understand how ones moves between these modes of relation is also to understand how the 'I' is constantly reconstituted.

Buber's refutation of any self beyond its constitutive interrelationships places intense importance on lived, concrete experience but recognizes two very different dimensions of experience. First, the objectified, knowledge-creating experience (I-It), and second, that which dissolves the boundaries of objective reality of things and ideas, a knowing that is approached through feeling rather than knowing about (I-Thou). The I-Thou is not merely informational but transformational. Although we must use theory to explain and communicate it, experience is central but not reducible to an objective collection of happenings and events participated in. When we consider forms of perception in the next chapter, these will necessarily be framed in terms of the I-It but analysed as the origin of possibility of I-Thou.

The conditions of possibility inherent in this transformative relationality are clearer when we turn to explore Rosa's concept of resonance, which does much to rework dialogic relationality in the contemporary context. Where Buber's analysis of dialogue arises from reflection on the implications of an ecstatic mysticism rooted in religious tradition, Rosa's work on resonance needs no such basis. Yet in dealing with reaction to and against alienation, it articulates sensibilities often associated with or explained through religious explorations of experience.

Resonance

Drawing on a background of dialogic relationality, Rosa develops his concept of resonance, elaborating and exploring multiple dimensions of relationship to expand on Buber's simple binary of forms. Resonance is a way of thinking about being-in-the-world. How do we relate to what is about us? What are the potential consequences of that relating? For Rosa, as O'Brien (2020: 383) neatly summarizes, resonance is

> an intense and profound experience, in which we are gripped, touched, and transformed; where our relation to the world opens up; in which, we do not simply go through something, but possess agency where we can effect that which

affects us in turn. As an experience, it is more primal than communication, needing to be articulated, but often being tricky to do so, and yet is more than an emotion, and is not limited to a particular emotional state.

In this idea of resonant experience, Rosa is describing something very close to Buber's description of the I-Thou. To comprehend such moments of resonance, we first need to clarify exactly what Rosa means by the invocation of this new and unfamiliar terminology. Rosa's own explanation and justification is full and expansive, but he provides an invaluable summary (Box 3.1) in a response given to a seminar on his work.

Box 3.1 Resonance

Resonance is not definable in terms of a certain range of experiences or a substantive area of application, for it denotes a specific form of relationship. Thus, the core claim of resonance theory is this: A relationship can be defined as resonant if it fulfils the following four criteria: (1) Af←fection: A subject (or an entity more general, … feels 'called upon' and is touched, moved or gripped by something or someone 'out there', as part of the world he or she encounters. (2) E→motion or Self-Efficacy: The subject responds to this affection in a self-efficacious mode of reaching out and touching or influencing the object or entity encountered. (3) Transformation: In this dynamic, two-way process of encounter, both sides – self and world – are transformed to some extent. Hence, resonance is not about the affirmation of identity, but rather about its transformation. (4) Uncontrollability [Unverfügbarkeit]: Finally, resonance in this sense is essentially open ended, that is, uncontrollable and unpredictable in two respects: First it is constitutionally impossible to predict its occurrence, and secondly, if it happens, it is absolutely impossible to predict or control the outcome or result of the ensuing transformation. One might add as a fifth element the necessity of mutually accommodating resonant spaces, that is, of the appropriate temporal, spatial, social, physical and psychical conditions. But in my view, this should be treated as a necessary precondition rather than an element or resonance. Thus, the concept of resonance only gains shape and precision when understood as a specific mode of connection.

Source: Rosa (2020: 398).

The first two elements in his description of resonance (Af←fection and E→motion) concern the interactions of the participants. The arrows Rosa inserts into the two terms emotion and affection indicate the bidirectionality of this interaction. Encounter is not one way. It is not simply a projection of the experiencing subject, nor does the experiencing subject simply absorb information from a fixed externality. The interplay of these two directions of information and awareness has a transformative effect. Stressing this transformative dimension as the third element of resonance allows Rosa to highlight the way in which both elements are changed and reconstructed by resonant interaction. This means that identity is not a fixed object that can be essentialized, but something constantly refashioned – a process of identization, to use Melucci's (1995) term.

The fourth element, translated to English as uncontrollability, is perhaps the least obvious. I will argue that it is particularly crucial for building the political project of resistance to dominant destructive and exploitative systems, the purpose of an Anthropocene citizenship. For further exploration and its links to other forms of resistance to the more destructive tendencies of modernity, it will be returned to in more detail later in this chapter. Rosa's suggestion of a fifth element in this excerpt, that of resonant spaces, is the one that I apply here to spaces of mobility. It gives us an opportunity to think how different mobility modes create 'temporal, spatial, social, physical and psychical conditions' that make resonant experiences possible.

Rosa describes resonance, this affecting and energizing relationality, as operating in three interconnected, often simultaneous, dimensions or axes. These axes describe the worlds of people, ideas and things respectively, that is, the social, the mental and the physical. In his study of the implications of Rosa's work, Susen (2020) gives examples of the areas of life that these three dimensions describe. First, as 'family, friendship and politics' in which the normative world of sociality 'obtains a voice'; second, 'as religion, nature, art and history' in which the transcendent 'obtains a voice'; and third, 'objects, work, school, sport and consumption' in which 'the objective world of things obtains a voice' (Susen 2020: 316). In these sites and moments of resonance, therefore, the worlds of the more-than-human 'obtain a voice'. They are 'speaking' as part of the dialogic interaction of af←fection and e→motion. This should recall the practical problems of citizenship, democracy and the more-than-human in research highlighted in the previous chapter. Recognizing that resonance is not just a concern of interhuman interactions encourages us to see the interconnectedness of the human and the more-than-human. When we think about the different forms of mobility for their capacity to open or close possibilities for responsive Anthropocene citizenship, we can use the possibilities of resonance as an evaluative criterion.

Rosa's analysis of this relational self is inseparable from his prior analysis of the deadening impact of the alienation brought about by accelerated and accelerating modernity. In O'Brien's (2020: 384) summary of the implications of this work,

> Modernity ... is a resonance killer, and because resonance is a basic human need, this means that modernity is pathological and pathogenic. ... In the shifting, competitive landscape of accelerated modernity, reification becomes the dominant relation to the world, involving an objectification of the world and of our own selves, to make them controllable, in response to competitive pressure. The result is a replacement of a dialogic relationship to the world with relationships of control and mastery.

While deeply critical of modernity, Rosa is at pains to explain that he is not anti-modernist: 'While I do claim that modernization is a "resonance killer", I insist that modernity is not just that: It also is constituted by a growing desire and sensibility for resonance' (Rosa 2020: 412). This ambiguity is a dilemma central to the contemporary situation. Recognition of the Anthropocene has only occurred now when it is effectively too late to undo the impacts of human organization and exploitation on planetary regulatory systems. Yet with this recognition also comes a capacity to respond and a desire to imagine the possibility of doing and being-in-the-world differently. Self-awareness and self-criticism are not necessarily correlative with nor consequential upon recognition of the Anthropocene. Yet both are visible in collective resistances that form in opposition to, for example, climate crisis (as they have previously done in reaction to other clear existential crises).

In interview, Rosa elaborates on this problem to make the claim 'that modern subjects, as all human beings, seek resonance relationships. In the capitalist society, the yearning for such relationships is transformed into a desire for commodities' (Corrêa et al. 2021: 126). The problem is that commodity desire is a product of the very alienation that it seeks to cure and it is thus incapable of solving the problem and may well exacerbate it instead. Mobility, of course, is only one such commodity. In its growth, possibility, desire and consumption are systematically interlocked. Thinking about resonance is a way to confront that circular problem of commodity desire and alienation by addressing the alienation itself.

> What I wanted to do is to define a good life in a way that is independent of the logic of growth, increase, acceleration etc. Because I realized that even those philosophers who want to move beyond the GDP as a yardstick for the quality of life still think that having more choices, options, capabilities etc is better than having less. ... Thus, I formulated the idea that the quality of life is not defined

by the resources at hand but by the quality of our relationships to the world. (Corrêa et al. 2021: 126)

Resonance provides us with a way of thinking about being-in-the-world and of living well that is no longer tied to the growth imperative. Rosa does not simply demand quality over quantity but identifies mechanisms for understanding our being-in-the-world.

Like Escobar, Nandy and other authors who write from a post-colonial and post-developmental perspective, Rosa maintains a critical view of modernity while retaining a commitment to its emancipatory project (Nandy 1983; Mohanty 1995; Escobar 2020; Esteva 2023; Ziai 2023). These authors recognize that emancipatory politics requires rethinking if it is to avoid repeating the colonial, extractive, patriarchal, exploitative (the list of negatives could go on) formulae that the current freedoms of some have been built on (compare Sheller 2023). There is no meta-narrative of progress that can be relied on, no certainty that History (with a capital H) will vindicate the analysis that best observes and exposes the contradictions of dominant social worlds and economic systems. Hence again we see a shift of the language of emancipation from its association with the pursuit of a singular ideological project to an embrace of a pluriverse of alternatives in the formulation of political solutions (see also Cox 2025).

In the general formulation of emancipation, however, the stress on the rights and freedoms of the subject, argues Rosa, 'is only one side of a resonant form of being-in-the-world: To be self-determined is not enough. Resonance always starts with receptivity: With openness to the call of something out there. It does not start with the subject. In fact, resonance, to some extent, always involves an element of heteronomy' (Corrêa et al. 2017: 127). Here one can usefully recall Carpenter's image of Democracy, the spirit that sweeps over the earth calling out to its promise of freedom and potential to those whose lives are otherwise determined by their entrapment in systems of oppression. Citizenship, as a modern concept (following the same logic) is important for its stress on belonging and for its fostering of solidarity and identification, but it cannot assist us in the Anthropocene unless reformulated around more than rights and self-determination. It is the connection to other citizens and affirmation of our shared position as denizens that reveals the capacity of freedom as connection within a web of interrelations and inter-responsibilities.

Resonance is only possible in a disposition in which you renounce your self chosen and given rules and aims and listen – in which you make yourself essentially vulnerable. You answer the call of something without knowing where

> it leads you to. ... the one-sided conception of autonomy has itself become a
> motor of acceleration and hence alienation. (Corrêa et al. 2017: 127)

That Rosa's response constitutes a political project is clear" 'We cannot "engineer" resonance, but we can work on the preconditions which make resonance more or less likely. ... what I dream of is a world which is built on institutions that enable resonance between citizens, between society and nature, between past, present and future generations, and so on' (Corrêa et al. 2021: 128). By examining how different mobility practices make different forms of resonance less or more possible, how they open or foreclose dialogic interaction, we begin to see how institutions that enable resonance might be built.

Mobility habits are built on repetitive sedimentation. Social practices, as Shove, Pantzar and Watson (2012) demonstrate, are constructed, with elements of materials, competencies and meanings. They are not just the sum of what people do, but actively recruit or are dissuasive for new participants by their provision of conditions of participation (for an example of how these relate to transport, see Watson 2012, Cox 2019). Mobility habits are enabled by the constructions of the social practices they participate in. How institutions of transport and mobility enable (and conversely, dis-able) resonance is considered in the next chapter.

All citizenships demand certain actions and behaviours in return for the recognitions that they present. An Anthropocene citizenship requires that we learn or relearn more sympathetic and empathetic ways of relating to the physical and social world. Conversely, we need to unlearn and to stop reinforcing those ways of being that are destructive to empathy and sympathy. A first step in thinking about ways of relating is not to think of empathy and care as innate qualities for individual possession (or not), that present us with pre-set or pre-given dispositions to the world, but as processes of learning. Education is a process of both individuation and integration, discovering our own individual capacities and uniqueness while simultaneously realizing our fundamental sociality wherein individuated, deeply personal perception and insight exists only in its interactions with others. Hence the centrality of care as an idea for thinking about Anthropocene citizenship. Moreover, the two-way dialogic interaction suggests that modes of travel, as core means by which we encounter the world that is not-self, might have their own pedagogies. They teach us about the world in particular ways. Modes of travel teach us values and skills in ways unique to the forms of experience they engender and the interactions they foster.

Care

An ethics of care derived from recent feminist analysis is logical correlation of a relational self (Robinson 2011: 4). An ethic of care is an ethic of relationality. Put simply, in an ethics of care, morality is not grounded in a priori rules or principles but in practice, in the responses to the contingencies of the situation. The quality of relations is what matters. One certainly operates with principles, and a relational and situational ethic has to be grounded in a commitment to a shared notion of the good life or of forms of virtue. An ethics of care, therefore, approaches relationship by prioritizing attentiveness and mutual respect: being with, caring about and caring for. It is 'an ethics that tries to let the other be, to preserve its voice, but nevertheless seeks to reach out and touch it and let it transform itself' (Rosa, 2020b: 410). It therefore involves a stress on non-domination, an important and recurrent aspect that recurs in several different contexts in working out how to make choices in practical action.

Care is political. Kathleen Lynch's study, *Care and Capitalism*, points out not only how care is inseparable from thinking about issues of power and how it is used, but that political systems have different relations to care. She concludes that neoliberal capitalism is fundamentally hostile to care. A politics grounded in love, care and solidarity need another basis (Lynch 2022). Moreover, she further argues that this political grounding of care and the re-orientation that follows expand the realm of care beyond human-human relations into the broader realm of the human relations to the non-human.

What we care about and what we choose not to care about are choices that imply an elective valuation of peoples, situations, relationships. Loretta Lou (2020) uses the term 'unnoticing' to explain how people cope with difficult situations of environmental degradation. Unnoticing allows us to think through how people can actively set aside consideration of situations that are too problematic and too challenging to deal with. This is not the same as not-caring. It is a strategic coping mechanism. When we think about care and not-caring we need to recognize that they do not exist in a simple binary: the necessary setting aside of noticing may not be not-caring but a caring self-defence mechanism that allows other struggles to go on without an individual or community being overwhelmed. However, much of the unrecognition of our own complicity in tacit support of structures of injustice arises not from being overwhelmed but simply through a refusal to look and a fear of the challenges that active consideration of the implications of the Anthropocene might bring. Engaging with the scale of transformations required will need reckoning with our own mobility practices dependent on fossil fuel mobility and other high-energy travel. These are uncomfortable propositions and cannot be taken lightly. Yet in the big picture, there is only so much unnoticing that the polycrises we face can tolerate. Some consideration has to be given when our unnoticing of the contradictions between our political imagination and our own mobility habits becomes denial. When we have the capacity to act and we fail to do so, there has to be culpability. Mimi Sheller (2022), for example, provides an eloquent and moving study of how her own reflection on academic flying has brought about personal action from not noticing, to unnoticing and ultimately to a change in practice.

Relations of care are constructed by relations of power, argues Robinson (2011) in her application of a feminist ethics of care to politics and international relations. Relations of care do not just arise as a response to pre-existent needs and responsibilities. Power relations permeate all interactions; therefore, part of the task of an ethics of care is to consider how relations become those of domination, oppression, injustice, inequality or paternalism. Every form of oppression maintains its position through both its active proponents and the tacit complicity of those who recognize but do not resist. This moves the ethics of care away from a simple moral exercise into a political one. Applied to mobility practices, it poses serious questions about the everyday transport choices we make, but also raises question of whether care is selective. Different transport choices might result from the prioritization of different objects of care. There is no perfect universal solution, but to make non-domination an objective of our travel impels us to think about the implications of our travel choices.

Care comes first in the considerations of values for Anthropocene citizenship because it outlines a fundamental value for orientation towards the other, a discussion further elaborated in Chapter 6. In its basic form, an ethics of care is driven by feelings of responsibility for the other of the relation. That is, it takes a normative, moralistic approach. However, as just noted, work developing feminist perspectives on the ethics of care challenges the shortcomings of a normative moral position and much of the recent discussion on an ethics of care draws from two separate but interrelated sources, one in feminist ethics and the other in environmental ethics (Taylor 2005).

Mick Smith (2001) concludes the value and necessity of an ethics of care from a discussion of environmental ethics. Dominant, legalistic models of environmental representation, he argues, are not adequate as a basis of our relation to the more-than-human world. That is, if current models of law have proved an inadequate basis for social justice, then their extension is no guarantee of environmental justice. Nor, he continues, can 'nature' in an abstract fashion be used as a basis upon which to draw moral conclusions (compare Latour 1999). The decision to seek to address ecojustice (economic and ecological justice) should rather be grounded in deliberately and purposively identifying matters of moral concern – that is, in an ethic of care. It is not grounded in utility or justified by the gains that might be made from protection of particular persons, species or ecosystems, or a search for equality but from a basis in community. It requires recognition of others as our kin (Haraway 2016).

María Puig de la Bellacasa's (2011; 2012; 2017) work on care has fundamentally transformed the way that care can be thought about, bringing together both feminist analyses of power and the struggle of environmental ethics to come to terms with the issues of thinking about and through more-than-human relationships. She argues 'that "thinking with care" is a vital requisite of collective thinking in interdependent worlds, but also one that necessitates a thick vision of caring' (Puig de la Bellacasa 2012: 197). A thick vision is one that moves beyond surface perception and outward visibilities into active participation. Caring, she insists, is an orientation of knowledge – a way of relating to the world, a way of being-in-the-world.

In the same manner that Rosa's work gives us novel ways to think about being-in-the-world as humans with humans, Puig de la Bellacasa uses care as a way of thinking about human interrelations with more-than-human world. Rejecting normative moralistic visions of care (i.e. that certain persons have a duty to care because of their position in society), she suggests that 'caring is more than an affective-ethical state: it involves material engagement in labours to sustain interdependent worlds, labours that are often associated with exploitation and domination. In this sense, the meanings of caring are not straightforward. Interdependency is not a contract but a condition' (Puig de la Bellacasa 2012: 198). Care provides the first step in a process of confirmation of relationality and provides an orientation towards dialogic relations. It is hard to care for something you do not know. Conversely, it is easy to care for those people and places whom you come to know and love. But these responses are far from automatic. They require work and commitment to render them substantial. For us to come to know and love things, we need to encounter them on a regular basis. Everyday travel habits are an obvious arena of regular encounter.

An ethic of care applied to everyday mobilities suggests that practices that distance us from the consequences of those actions are less likely to produce either resonance or relations of care than those that connect us with their consequences. What we care about is worth defending, and caring demands action. If we are disconnected from our social and physical selves it is easier not to care. We can reconnect this with the idea of resonance. Resonance implies that we are moved by the resonant experience, there is a form of transformation that comes about because of the way we experience the world in those moments of resonance (Af←fect, E→motion and Transformation). Care and thinking through care provide a way to structure that response.

If resonance is a positive experience, as Rosa argues, then caring about is a product of that experience, its opposite would be indifference. If caring is anything it is not being left indifferent to a situation. Matters of care are those that provoke a response: to do, to act, to respond. Care is the necessary response to the recognition of networks of agency, where we are caught up in our connections to others, whether human or more-than-human (Latour 2022). Resonance is not a precondition of care, although resonance will likely produce responses of care. Care requires doing and intervening. Walking, wheeling and cycling under our own motive power, for example, bring us into immediate relationships of encounter between our physical and emotional selves, with material technologies, and with physical space and its human and more-than-human inhabitants, and the relationships between as we shall see. Conversely, high-speed, enclosed travel makes any encounter with the world beyond the interior of the travel space impossible, other than as visual imagery.

To examine everyday movement for Anthropocene citizenship through an ethics of care is a way to explore what a non-dominating embodied co-existence might look like. An example is found in Bohlin's work on living with objects. Bohlin (2020: 96) argues that for developing an ethic of care, 'one of the most pressing issues could well be right under our noses, embedded in the seemingly trivial quotidian practices of living with domestic belongings'. By engaging with everyday processes through a lens of care Bohlin (2020: 111) argues how 'subtle and unspoken forms of responsive, receptive and caring ways of being with things … resonates with calls for a post-anthropocentric ethics of care that extends responsibility towards nonhuman things and processes'. To explain her rationale for this relationship to everyday objects, she cites Olsen and Pétursdóttir (2016: 40) on the need for an ethics grounded in 'curiosity and openness to things' being, how they affect us upon encounter, and which, importantly, takes seriously how they persist, gather and outlive us'. These are precisely the qualities that, I argue, the encounters generated by walking and cycling can alert us to. Our interactions with the spaces through which we travel echo Bohlin's findings on close bodily involvement with everyday objects.

Non-domination and thinking through care

Non-domination has already been mentioned as a guiding value for consideration of relationships. Rosa's attempt to develop an ethics of resonance as a particular form of an ethics of care is distinguished by its commitment to the integrity of the other.

> This is an ethics that tries to let the other be, to preserve its voice, but nevertheless seeks to reach out and touch it and let it transform itself: The resonant subject does not try to transform the other, but it might try to open routes for self-transformation for the other. In this sense, the autonomy of the other is always respected: It is a consequence of accepted inaccessibility. I believe this sense of care for the other even extends beyond subjects: When we are in resonance with nature, or a piece of art, for example, we try to preserve it carefully: We will not step on rare flowers or touch a painting just to get a cool selfie for Instagram. However, this ethics of care and resonance does not stem from critical reflection, but from a resonant disposition towards the other, from a sense of 'responsive empathy'. (Rosa2020b: 410)

Care for the integrity of the others is a particularly useful way of thinking in relation to the other of 'nature', that is, the more-than-human, acknowledging both its 'otherness' and our connectedness with it. It is tempting here to use the language of creation (as previously discussed) to describe that which creates itself, as a distinction from that which is fully brought about by human action. Interestingly, this stress on the *integrity* of that which is not self is a phrase that has been used in activist circles since the 1980s in the connected work on Justice, Peace and the Integrity of Creation, and continues in, for example, *Laudato Si* (Pope Francis 2015). To recognize the integrity of the non-human demands that we act with respect towards it, not by dominating or destroying it.

These institutional examples in which a care ethic is used as a framing device alerts us to the ways in which it appears in discussions of sustainability. Though sustainability as a political concept has come under much scrutiny and criticism, it remains viable in policy terms and as practical political leverage. One of its most important contributions has been to interject the element of time into policy thinking and to create space for discussion of intergenerational justice. Fredengren and Åsberg (2020: 5) use the concept of intergenerational care to shift the analytic framework for assessing sustainability away from a stress on rights. Translating intergenerational justice into intergenerational care allows us to radicalize the concept of sustainability for the Anthropocene. What emerges from this translation is a framework that ensures what is being sustained are *not* the systems of economic and social reproduction that have caused the problems in the first place. Instead, a critique of (carbon) capital and its corollary, overconsumption emerges as not only obvious but necessary. Adding non-domination as a goal of sustainability interventions changes the way that they can be imagined.

A further consequence of taking a stress on non-domination is to challenge assumptions that power acquisition is the ultimate political goal. Again we are reminded of Rosa's insistence on the quality of relations, rather than mastery, as the aim of a politics of resonance. A corollary of this analysis is a need to question the way that action for change is evaluated. Success and failure are predominantly used as the ways to judge the validity of action. How efficacious is it, and in what ways? How is any goal served by the action? Exclusive focus on success reduces what we do to a simply instrumental calculus, judgeable by utilitarian criteria. Neither rational choice calculation nor cost-benefit analysis are adequate means to comprehend the unconditionality of care grounded in love. From the perspective of non-domination or care, any criteria based primarily on the achievement of final outcomes are problematic to say the least. Caring is not afraid of failure, only of failing to care. More useful is to think of action being grounded in fidelity to the vision and the values, ensuring that actions taken are consonant with the commitment to care and non-domination.

Care and relationality

One consequence of a relational understanding of the self is a capacity to step away from the liberal view in which the aim of interaction is to achieve morally autonomous rational individuation. This is not to deny personhood to the individual self, but to understand that personhood only exists within networks, webs of relationships. This means that to talk of ethics in terms of rights, whether positive or negative, or even as reciprocated in concomitant responsibilities, is to start from the wrong end of the problem. Instead, when woven into a web of interrelations, the solution to finding a basis for ethical reflection starts with compassion (Curtin 2022).

It is worth recalling that compassion is not a simple emotive sympathetic state but the capacity to suffer with, hence its intimate interrelationship with care. We encounter the more-than-human world neither as entirely other nor as part of an undifferentiated whole or oneness. The world is other, and we cannot grasp its otherness, but it is through our indivisible ties to and with its otherness that we realize who we are and become fully human in our relationality. As Curtin (2022) explains, this means we cannot or should not talk about rights in the classic liberal sense as the product of morally autonomous individuals, as these are secondary. Integrity of being might be a better phrase through which to express the ways we talk about the animal or ecosystem rights (not to be drawn too deeply into several decades of discussion in environmental ethics). It is in these discussions that we see the resolution of the problem of care and rights highlighted previously.

Responding with care to that which does not speak one's own language is not, or at least should not be, difficult. Elderly care, infant care, the care of the outlander all require similar attention. We observe and engage with how things grow and develop. Incommunicative humans do not lose our sympathy. Like the voiceless nature we recognize their capacity to love us, and in that interplay of affect and emotion we are called to respond. It is (or may be) easier for us to lose attention if our own egos are not being stoked with reciprocal gratitude, but to desire such gratitude is to desire that the other be indebted and therefore malleable – the first step of exploitative relations. This manipulative exploitation, as examples taken from religious observances and the use of power in religious settings demonstrate, exists prior to the advent of capitalism. However, it is a mechanism that capital exploits with the added twist of that relation being abstractly computed and measured through monetary relations.

Being cared for

There are limits and difficulties with thinking through care. Caring as an action is not always benign. It has the capacity, as noted above, to be manipulative. Sunaura Taylor (2022) argues from the perspective of feminist disability studies to trouble the 'easiness' with which care-for becomes patronizing. Acts of care risk creating an indebted subject. The cared-for can be deprived of agency and made dependent by the acts of care, however well-intentioned. Perspectives from the margins remain important in an ethics of care. The (re)assertion of rights (abstract) without a productive channel through which that declaration becomes operationalizable is just so much shouting into the void. Care depends, case by case, on the quality of relation in specific situations. Introducing disability perspectives into the discussion on care reinstates interdependency at the centre of relationships. Spotlighting interdependency as a function of mobilities illuminates the necessary connections between traveller, infrastructure and natural forces such as weather, especially in the context of climate breakdown.

We might clarify further by noting a distinction between autonomy and independence, the latter being associated with the illusion of a sovereign individual (the ideal liberal subject). The former is tangled and bound in webs of obligation and interdependence but still able to exert agency within the context of those relationships, social, ethical and political. The autonomy I refer to here is derived from *autogestion* –workers' organizing for self-management. It indicates a self-determination of lives against a background of eternal controls. It is freedom from being controlled, not the power to act without constraint (and consequence). Applied to mobility, it is the basis for Cass and Manderscheids's (2023) explorations of autono-mobilities, breaking free from the dependencies of automobilities. This background is constitutive. Autonomy exists against a similar background of control, of hegemonic systems that deny the capacity for choice and suggest that there is only one solution.

Understanding dependency/value relationships can also be informed by whether they exist within a productivist framework or not. Productivism as an underlying generator of value demands that only that which contributes to the whole, that which 'earns its keep', is valuable. In a productivist frame, care is a transaction that demands response or one that has utility value and is therefore tradeable. Removed from the demands of productivism, care shifts into the realm of the gratuitous. Care is restored to an act of giving. The gift, as Rosi Braidotti (2022) notes, is disconnected from a political economy of exchange regulated by lack and negativity. It therefore also connects us to the rejection of frameworks centred on scarcity (see also Esteva 2023). Gifts can be given whatever the economic preconditions. They are independent of conditions of scarcity or abundance. Thinking of care as a gift not a duty or transaction allows us to sidestep the distribution of resources. There is always the possibility to give care, even when resources are scarce (Soper 2020). Thus we move from a way of thinking based on scarcity as the base analytic to one of plenitude, based on human capacity not economic calculation. Love and the gift are closely related. Another way of looking at this is to note that care is a form of social reproduction, not production. As such it provides another level of challenge to capital production and accumulation and is thus, potentially at least, profoundly anticapitalist, as Lynch (2022) describes.

Thinking through care in this manner provides an approach to citizenship that allows us to develop more appropriate behaviours. Translating it into mobility practices and behaviours requires a little lateral thought. However, it should be possible to begin to comprehend how different modes of travel allow for different forms of caring. Who is being cared for, whose welfare does any given form of journeying promote? Who is marginalized by the travel choices made and whose travel is made more difficult? This brings us into consideration of the second of the two approaches that provide the theoretical foundations for examining mobilities for the Anthropocene.

The commons and commoning

A frequent starting point in any conversation of relationality might be 'what do we have in common'. The concept of the commons is not that far removed from what we recognize as unremarkable. The commons in a technical sense is defined as that which is held in common by the collected community, not for the exclusive use of particular persons or classes. It is destroyed by enclosure, fencing off, physically or legally. It is destroyed by regulation that determines only selected activities (and actors) as legitimate. Historically, of course, there have always been caveats to the use of commons and agreements and expectations, tacit or declared among commoners to ensure preservation and continuity of use. Nevertheless, commons and enclosure must be thought of together. Only with the threat of enclosure does one need to define commons in spaces, goods or ideas.

Enclosure is not a 'natural' or inevitable process of change, but an orchestrated exercise of power that claims exclusive control or limits the actions of others. It results in dispossession. Historically, commons are the spaces through which the majority of people made their living in subsistence; enclosure is the means by which that self-organized and shared living is destroyed, a process that took specific form in England in relation to land ownership claims. Enclosure became the mechanism of imperial and colonial property relations, delegitimizing the lives and livelihoods of those deemed as not equals. Today, thinking through the commons has become a means to reflect on the impacts of hyper-extractivism and extended forms of privatization (Brand and Wissen 2021). Usefully it also reflects a recognition of the continuity of these processes over time.

We live today in a human world dominated by enclosure. Privatization is only the latest form in a long history of both social and spatial enclosures. Spatial enclosure is more easily recognizable, enacted through the institution of private property and through physical exclusions, enforced by fear and threat. The enclosure of the social is perhaps less easily recognizable. Social enclosure is a corollary of spatial enclosure and exclusion. It is based on identity, the proclamation and fencing off of exclusive domains of belonging, of 'us' and 'them'. It arises when the collective self is conceptualized and defined outside of its relationships, when identity is fetishized as a possession. It is the fencing off of access to ways of being-in-the-world to exclude those who do not conform to specific markers of nation, creed and ethnicity, epitomized in nationalist forms of citizenship. Enclosure and exclusion intrude into the personal, subjective experience. Our relation to the fences that define social or physical space reaches into the emotional and affective realms, creating suspicions and fears often grounded in the anticipation of violence, physical or virtual, that may result from transgressing the boundaries that others have erected.

Historical processes of enclosure were essential to the establishment of private property and formed the basis of capital accumulation, legitimated through novel political-philosophical ideas and legal definition (Wood 2012). In the latter part of the twentieth century, these processes were given new impetus through mechanisms usually described as neo-liberalism. Enclosure provides an important interpretative idea for understanding both historical and contemporary economic and social reforms (Linebaugh 2014; Velicu and García-López 2018; Fraser 2022). It prompts reconsideration of what enclosures have destroyed (commons) and how that which has been destroyed might be reimagined and recreated (commoning). Contemporary struggles against dominant political processes responsible for destruction of social and material environments frequently draw explicitly or implicitly on commoning (Kothari 2019).

In the search for specifically economic models not defined in terms of contemporary forms of capital that require ever more enclosure and exclusion, it is not surprising that reconsideration has been given to both commons and shared economy as a means to draw attention to the processes of exclusion and deprivation. Velicu and García-López (2018) directly link the resurgence of interest with the intensification of enclosure by neo-liberal capital. The first wave of recent commons thinking, associated with the work of Elinor Ostrom, sought to affirm and devise institutional arrangements that would allow sustainable asset management. However, Velicu and García-López note that these approaches had several limitations. First, they relied over-heavily on rational choice theory, managerial solutions and perpetuated a nature-culture dualism. This is not unexpected since they operate within a general liberal individualist frame of thought. By contrast, focus on care and caring in the context of shared economies and practices offered a more radical alternative to productivist, extractivist and individualist orientations of capitalism (Villamayor-Tomas and García-López 2021). A second, perhaps even more important problem arising from over-emphasizing Ostrom's work as the starting point for recent analyses of commoning is pointed out by Clement et al. (2019); it overlooks the earlier important contribution of (eco)feminist and feminist political ecology analyses such as those from Mies and Shiva (1993) and Rochelau et al. (1996).

A further round of approaches to the commons/enclosure problem began by challenging the rational choice-making individual that underlies the idea of *homo economicus*. Consequently, attention has turned more strongly to commoning, the verb form signalling a need for action rather than commons simply being a pre-given object. As Nikolaeva and her colleagues (2019: 8) argue in their application of communing to mobilities, 'The notion of commoning, rather than commons, highlights active and collective processes of making commons.'

One of the leading proponents of this latter approach has been Peter Linebaugh who employs the term because 'I want to portray it [the commons] as an activity, not just an idea or material resource' (Linebaugh 2014; Linebaugh, cited in Ristau 2011). In a 2010 article, widely distributed online and reprinted as the first chapter in his 2014 historical overview, *Stop, Thief! The Commons, Enclosures, and Resistance*, Linebaugh lays out a series of principles of commoning. Importantly he makes a break with the economic management approaches by arguing that 'The activity of commoning is conducted *through* labor *with* other resources; it does not make a division between "labor" and "natural resources". On the contrary, it is labor which creates something as a resource, and it is by resources that the collectivity of labor comes to pass' (Linebaugh 2014: 13). Crucially, he further notes that 'Commons is antithetical to capital.' Indeed, enclosure, the act that destroys commons, is essential for the accumulation of capital. Consequently, actions aimed at commoning implicitly present a critique of capital. For this reason, they have figured centrally in explorations of degrowth thinking. In fact, as Schmelzer, Vetter and Vansintjan (2022: 159) argue, 'a degrowth economy should be rooted in the commoning initiatives that already exist in the multitude of alternative economies, and that the principles of commoning should be at the centre of organizing the entire society'. This rationale draws heavily on the centrality of commons as a feature of post-developmental critiques of expansionist capital (Escobar 2020). Paying attention to the idea of the commons has thus generated a wide literature, though much of this remains focused on commons as an object and location, rather than the processes of commoning (Clement et al. 2019).

In sum, the commons emerge in contemporary discourse as something to be produced through action, not a nostalgic object of preservationist concern or reactionary security. Commoning requires the equality of participants and so where asymmetries of power or capacity exist, as they inevitably will, it requires a commitment to care in order to safeguard the more vulnerable.

Commoning and the more-than-human

Commoning is one way of *doing* care, of translating matters of care into practice. This insight enables us to think about commoning in relation to the more-than-human. Euler (2017:12) defines the contemporary understanding of commons as 'the social form of (tangible/intangible) matter that is determined by commoning. Commoning creates commons'. While this may initially appear to be somewhat circular, it moves our attention away from seeking a definition of commons as an object, a thing. Focus turns instead to the processes by which boundaries and exclusions are broken down. More than a way to mediate conflicts over space, it is a way of 'maintaining relationships between human and non-human communities' (Garcia Lopez et al. 2021: 1201).

Despite this carefully argued demonstration that commoning enables a bridging between the human and the non-human, a majority of work on commoning considers commoning as a purely human practice and action. The question remains as to whether, therefore, the commons is a neatly disguised sidestep back into a reinvigoration of arguments based on the state of nature. In other words, commons might stand in for an unexamined and ultimately critically unexaminable state of nature. Certainly, historical arguments on the commons and enclosure might seem to indicate this.

Historic examples, as Linebaugh shows, have been vital for enabling and revitalizing the commons and commoning. Yet we need to be wary of over-literal connections and recognize that we cannot simply transpose arguments from the past situations to to-day. Nor should the commons be fetishized as a perfect or ideal state in which natural systems are worked without fundamental alteration. After all, the Diggers, seventeenth-century England's most famous opponents of enclosure, proclaimed their task to change the ecology of the heathlands by fertilizing and bringing them into productivity (Winstanley 1989 [1649]).[2] This was understandable as a response to the widespread poverty and exclusion resulting from enclosures and landless unemployment, but not a model that fits comfortably with the assertion that commoning today necessarily and always

---

[2] I would especially like to thank Nye Merrill-Glover for his advice on historical agricultural processes and the ecological implications of commons and wasteland reclamation.

provides a means through which to challenge the logics of productivism and extractivism. To do this we need to proceed from a slightly different argument on the value of commoning.

Ryan (2013) highlights the politically transformative power of commoning as a way to promote self-organization, social inclusion and egalitarian participation. At the heart of these qualities is the insistence that commoning is an expression of the social power of the community that insists on the equality of its participations. This brings us back to a connection with participatory citizenship in the Anthropocene and the role and place of democracy within consideration of the commons. It also provides the argument that translates directly to the idea of the roads as commons (Wells 2012) and of their enclosure by motor traffic (Cox 2023).

Commoning and democracy

Emphasis on participation in commoning movements echoes a tradition of radical imaginations of democracy such as those given by Edward Carpenter (see Chapter 2) and a century later by C. Douglas Lummis (1996). If we address the democracy-scapes described by Santos and Avritzar (see Chapter 1), we can see that the processes of commoning can be read as part of the movement towards a democratizing of democracy. It is a way of extending democracy from its confinement within the field of politics into those multiple different areas of life.

Historic commoning around shared rights to natural resources often linked to very specific membership of local communities could (and can) also be exclusionary. Its contribution to breaking borders is not without tensions and ambiguities. Commoning today requires sensitive consideration of how community management practices are devised and articulated without perpetuating damaging exclusivities. Some historic forms of enclosure of common lands were not simply about restricting access, but by limiting the forms of activity (such as tillage) permitted in a commons space. Use of land and resources could be prescribed to particular uses and users, while proscribing others in ways that were not simply a product of collective agreement among peers to ensure commons maintenance. These discussions are vital as a means to understand and find resolution to conflicts over spaces of travel. A question we need to ask about spaces of travel shared between modes is how different users and uses maintain those spaces as commons, or, through their actions, enclose them, dominating or excluding others.

Commoning and care

Nightingale (2019: 19) neatly summarizes the distinction caused by use and user patterns as a difference between 'the commons as regulated resource use, in contrast to open access which has no property arrangements'. State mechanisms that facilitated exclusive rights and wholesale dismantling and destruction of livelihoods dependent on commoning rights were also those that created new commons in mid-twentieth-century provisions for health and welfare. The dismantling of these regimes under neo-liberal reforms in later decades, especially through their privatization, has led to the reinvigoration of discussions of commoning. The creation of new enclosures in areas of life and social goods means that access to those goods now depends for many on finance. Access to goods, formerly provided as commons in recognition of their status as essentials on which we all depend, has been curtailed through privatization. Provision or quality of provision now depends on access to wealth. Basic goods and services have been enclosed. Once more we return to the fundamental entanglement of moves towards commoning and a relational ethic of care.

Care is a realm of reproduction (Gotby 2023). Care's division from the realm of production (and therefore from value in a capitalist mode of production) is contested. Commodified and wage laboured care does not de-problematize the issue. Rather, it further complicates it. It is worth noting again that it is also deeply gendered, and therefore can be deployed as a tool of further gender differentiation and inequality. The mechanism that commoning provides, and which addresses these problems of care (as a conceptual as much as practical tool), is to integrate production and reproduction (Euler 2018). To do so, commoning necessitates the participation of those who can address each other as equals. Commoning cannot be forged between those who cannot address each other as potential equals. This does not mean they have to be equivalent or exactly similar, but they need to be able to recognize each other as peers. We can use this approach to commoning, with its aim of breaking down boundaries, to think about the limits of identity and to analyse the impacts of different ways of moving. While the 'I' or the 'we' is described by drawing a boundary around who is included and who is excluded, the process is one of enclosure. To think relationally is not to assume that the other is necessarily like the self or even compatible, but to address the quality of relationship between them. As Nightingale (2019: 16) puts it, 'commons is not a resource or place, but rather a set of more-than-human, contingent relations-in-the-making that result in collective practices of production, exchange and living with the world'. Each mode of travel creates realms of inclusion and exclusion in its availability and use, in the material spaces and resources employed and in how it relates onto others unlike itself.

By thinking through commoning, we can also address some shortcomings and limits to an ethic of care identified by Beasley and Bacchi (2012). In parallel to their critique of the a-sociality of writings on the body considered in Chapter 1, they also raise the objection that the language of trust and care offer insufficient attention to embodiment and are not properly capable of offering an alternative to 'the political ethos of neo-liberalism' (Beasley and Bacchi 2012: 104). By linking care to a critique of enclosure and action to restore commons and through a critique of relationships of control that dominate asymmetrical interactions, their principal objections can be overcome. Extending the relationality of care outside of inter-human relations into more-than-human relations further engages Beasley and Bacchi's emphasis on embodied co-existence. To illustrate all of these reflections on the value of commoning, we can turn to the practical example of thinking about mobilities in terms of commoning.

Commoning as critique: Mobilities

High-speed, high-energy travel encloses. It requires the sequestration of resources: spatial, material and energetic, deploying them in ways incompatible with co-existence. For example, high-speed use of roadspace by high mass motorized vehicles threatens and makes vulnerable other road users, human and animal. Provision of separated spaces for the non-car users under these circumstances becomes not a facilitation of wheeled and pedalled travel, but their segregation from formerly common spaces of travel. The historic development of high-energy road travel has been a process of the colonization of lifeworlds and of travelscapes. The financial implications of high-energy travel are unravelled in Urry's (2004) multidimensional analysis of automobility as a system. He identifies how the car is only part of a system of infrastructures, finances, employment processes, spatial reorganization and the general reproduction of capital. Urry gave the name automobility to this system of interdependencies to distinguish as something structurally different to the practices of driving (which we may refer to as automobilism). Automobility shapes the lifeworlds of car users and non-users alike in its consequences, from employment patterns and physical locations of housing, education and amenities. Its impact on the spaces of travel is only one aspect of these broader interconnections.

Examining factors in the destruction of the commons and the imposition of exclusions and privation brings us to analyses that demand proper attention to the processes of colonization. Particularly important here is the degree to which automobility colonizes mobility spaces. Commoning challenges this sequestration. To make common is to take down the fences that partition off the spaces and practices of privilege. Commoning mobilities requires us to consider the impacts of mobility practices on others. How does one set of mobilities curtail others' capacities to be mobile or create demands that to survive they must also be more mobile?

We should not forget that 'enclosure can be understood as a process of spatially orchestrated dispossession, aimed at dismantling autonomous, collectively produced and managed forms of common wealth and value regimes' (Sevilla-Buitrago 2015: 1003). It is not a process that arrives automatically and without mechanisms of implementation. Consequently, Sevilla-Buitrago (2015: 1001) argues that 'we need a more thorough theoretical inquiry into the spatial mechanisms of dispossession: What techniques are involved in the process? How do they operate and change in time? Under what political-economic and regulatory regimes? What are their morphologies?' These questions provide a very useful basis for thinking about the enclosure of the road to be pursued in more depth in the following chapter as we begin to look at the ways in which cycling as a mundane mobility practice confronts and challenges automobility's enclosure of the travelling commons. This confrontation connects concepts of 'slow travel' with self-limitation (Illich 1973; 1974; Popan 2018; Ingold 2021). If travel and travel spaces are both decolonized and commoned, how does this change the possibilities of walking and cycling, and how might it affect the experience of those actions, especially in the opening up of spaces currently made unsafe and exclusive?

Commoning, scarcity and plenitude in mobility

One final resource that arises from the recent rethinking of commoning concerns the issues of scarcity and plenitude (see also how these are a factor in care, above). Thinking through the commons-enclosure binary allows us to move away from degrowth imaginaries centred on scarcity and austerity. Scarcity, argues Esteva (2023: 74), is a 'concrete historical creation that colonizers and developmentalists tried to impose on us'. Scarcity depends on an expectation of ever-expanding needs and dwindling resources. Consequently, scarcity is an inbuilt condition of growth economies coupled with extractive colonization. Challenging both of these premises allows us to step beyond a scarcity model. This is not to deny the possibilities of shortage but allows us control over our responses to those conditions. Collective responses to shortage produce rationing – appropriate allocation of goods – as a response model of shared responsibility.[3] We can contrast it with what are today described as austerity measures, the restriction of goods and services, especially those common provisions that express the state's relation to its subjects. Rationing (as I use the term here) is not to be read as a restriction of individual rights but the institution of allocation based on fair share of limited resources. It is a form of infrastructuring based on equitable distribution (Cox 2020c). Moving away from a language of limits (which is simply the obverse of assumptions of unlimited, cornucopian possibility) points us towards a language of sufficiency, recognizing biophysical realities not as constraints to be overcome but as conditions of our existence. Sufficiency moves the debate into consideration of well-being, rather than consumption, as a measure of social good (Esteva, Babones and Babicky 2013: 90). The question then becomes on addressing whether persons can achieve a level of sufficient provision to meet needs.

Judging by the available data on mobility patterns, the scale of existing mobility inequalities would suggest that vast numbers of people would actually have more and greater possibilities of access to goods and services under a regime of allocated privileges of use. However, that is beside the point. Embedded in these mobility patterns, and in the reasons why mobility rationing might be an interesting thought experiment, is the entangling of mobility with carbon capitalism, that is, carbon consumption as part of a regimen of privatized production, distribution and consumption.

Enclosure creates scarcity by concealing the size of the resources available. Defining exclusionary boundaries prevents transparency and the possibility of collective responsibility for sharing and co-operative long-term management. This works for more than material goods. Braidotti (2022: loc4259) links 'possessive individualism that prioritizes locating the acquisition of commodities as the ultimate object of capitalism and desire', with the constriction of desire to something that emerges as a response to lack and negativity. Desire can only be recognized as a useful value when framed 'as positivity and relationality' (Braidotti 2022: loc 4284). By reframing beyond a model of scarcity created by assumptions of enclosure and exclusion (which a negative form of desire seeks

---

[3] Rations are here thought of in terms of provisions, not of restriction, as in, 'we carried our rations with us'. The framework is one of sufficiency not scarcity.

to overcome), we can see new opportunities for what Kate Soper (2020) has described as alternative hedonism. She explores the creation of joyful desire that seeks to embrace experience not through the acquisitive ego-driven hedonism but in finding exuberance in the everyday. It is notable and not co-incidental that Soper uses riding a bike to illustrate a practical means by which this alternative hedonism can be realized.

The paradox of mobility reductions is that in, for example, the planning of fifteen-minute cities and twenty-minute neighbourhoods (or even thirty-minute environments if we want to move away from the exclusively urban bias of much of the conversation on sustainable mobilities), reduction of journey times to access basic amenities increases accessibility for many of the population. Reducing mobility requirements (and therefore reducing actual volumes of travel) increases the access that travel is the means to achieve. To reach such a conclusion, however, requires a conceptual shift from scarcity and austerity as the framing towards a commoning and sharing of resources conceived as sufficient.

There is one final element in relation to these ideas of social change that needs consideration before moving on to examining mobility and the world around us. In short, it concerns the capacity we have to make and control the very processes of change we wish to initiate. What level of capacity or agency do we have? Reflecting on Marx's observation that we make history but we do not make it as we please, we need to ask what limits there are to our shaping of change, especially in light of the relative failure to address issues of climate change that we have known about for more than a generation and been unable to arrest.

Uncontrollability

Reflecting on the processes that lead to resonance, Rosa (2019) concludes that an important part of their dynamic is that such experiences cannot be 'made' to happen. Resonance is serendipitous. It cannot be engineered. Conditions can be established to make it less or more possible but at its heart there is a degree of what he terms Unverfügbarkeit, translated as uncontrollability, although this doesn't quite capture the meaning of the term (see Box 2.1) (Rosa 2020). Despite the social and cultural yearning that is expressed for resonance (in response to conditions of alienation), Rosa argues, resonance cannot be produced on command. Institutions may be established to nurture its possibility, but, ultimately, resonance remains firmly unpredictable. Nor can the outcomes of the transformations wrought by resonance experiences be foretold or predetermined. From the perspective of mobilities research, uncontrollability echoes the attention given to emergent properties in complex systems, a break from mechanical linear causality.

Following this argument through, Rosa importantly observes that this unpredictability sits uneasily with broader political and socio-cultural emphases on control and predictability woven into the politics and economics of advanced capitalism. A key characteristic of modernity is that relationships of control and mastery replace those of a dialogic relationship to the world. More than a simple observation on the transformative processes of resonance, therefore, uncontrollability taps into a much deeper critique of modernity. Rosa's (2013) analysis of Western modernity begins by noting its primary characteristic of acceleration. Capital reproduction today is based upon an economic and cultural model that relies not simply speeding up as a linear process, but a constantly increasing rapidity in throughput of resources, energy and even social goods. There are few pauses in the constant rush from one thing to another, where the possibility of being able to consider multiple options or interpretations is crowded out by the need for results.

What we lose in the acceleration of modernity are spaces for resonance. Considering resonance seriously as both a worthwhile pursuit and a means to critique and challenge the accelerating society brings Rosa to emphasize the importance of uncontrollability. The corollary of the acceleration of modernity is its fear of losing control. In order to maximize productivity, predictability is essential. Things that cannot be controlled and predicted have little place in modern productivism, whether the product is material goods or education.

The close relationship between control, order and modernity, and the potential negative impact of this trio has long been observed, from Weber onwards. In his classic 1970 book *The Uses of Disorder*, Richard Sennet drew on Erich Fromm to argue that the desire to control embedded in the modern condition reflects societies that operate collectively on a level of adolescent greed. Desire for control is a will to power. As a response, Sennett advocated embracing and celebrating dissonance and the possibilities of surprise, contingency and disorder against a search for purified and 'authentic' identities. Half a century on, in collaboration with planner Pablo Sendra, Sennett reflected on the way this societal condition has become embedded in physical space through the monocultural single use spaces that increasingly define urban planning (Sendra and Sennett 2022). These are, they argue, overdetermined functional spaces where predictability and order are expressed as socially desirable values. These observations concur with geographer Justin Spinney's (2021) analysis of urban mobility spaces, in which he notes how they are also crucial to the definition of urban space as the site of the reproduction of capital. Importantly, in Sennett's original analysis it is precisely those qualities of disorderliness (that are in danger of being erased) that allow development of an 'appreciation of otherness in the world' (Sennett 2021 [1970]: loc 1438). To let go of the desire to control, Sennett argues, is to let go of the myth of omnipotence and recognize the limits of human capacities. Acknowledging disorder and uncertainty, the limit of human capacity to control and predict requires the development of other skills of sensitivity, responsiveness and adaptation: precisely those qualities that are central to the construction of care. Caring-about is the primary mechanism by which we can negotiate uncertainty, an acknowledgement that returns us to earlier discussions in this chapter. Uncontrollability involves risk and vulnerability. Recognizing and negotiating uncertainty requires care. Conversely, it also requires trust as a means to negotiate and become responsive to contingent and every changing processes. Care is a corollary of uncontrollability for a responsive Anthropocene citizenship.

Uncontrollability and uncertainty

Uncontrollability acknowledges the inherent impossibility of the modern project. It accepts that resilience needs flexibility and adaptability (as opposed to monolithic defences and boundary building). For Anthropocene citizenship, its importance should be obvious. Acknowledging that we do not and cannot control our world is an exercise in humility. Accepting uncontrollability warns us against promethean delusions that aspire to control or to the comforting fictions that our technological capacities will somehow magically bring about a world of cornucopian energy abundance at no cost to environment and society. The acceleration of modernity is a key characteristic of the entrance into the Anthropocene (Mauch 2019). Recognizing and collectively owning what we have done and continue to do, and our inability to control the consequences of these actions, is crucial for developing forms of citizenship that can cope with living in the Anthropocene.

In one sense this very much comes back to a series of means-ends debates concerning action and activism that have long been a staple for political, social and environmental activism. Rather than considering if the end justifies the means, acceptance of uncontrollability stresses that the means become all important. We cannot know whether in the long term actions taken in all good faith turn out to have devastating consequences. If nothing else, these are direct political implications of where we find ourselves in the Anthropocene. Destabilization of planetary systems was not an intention or desired outcome of the harnessing of energy powers. The burning of fossil fuels was designed to bring about better life conditions, at least for those with access to and control of them, potentially for a majority of people. A utilitarian justification was possible, in whose calculus the development of high-carbon lifestyles could be approved as an overall good. Yet we find ourselves today the inheritors of the tragedy of these developments, facing the prospect of devastating climate impacts. What at one time seemed like a good idea, and even proved so temporarily (economic expansion through harnessing natural resources), has proven deeply problematic for the majority of humanity when seen in a longer-term time frame.

One further corollary of control is the production of violence. Writers as diverse as Wendell Berry (2020; see also Smith 2003) and Vandana Shiva (1988; 1991) note how trying to control the conditions of our existence and find predictability leads to violence, brutality and cruelty. Indeed, Berry's advocacy that a fully human life requires the cultivation of virtues of moderation, prudence, propriety, and fidelity, and the understanding of (and dependency on) one another, sounds very like the qualities needed for Anthropocene citizenship.

Uncontrollability, instrumentalism and traditions of resistance

To embrace uncontrollability is not to surrender to an idea that nothing can be done, or that since outcomes cannot be guaranteed, it is not worth doing anything. Conversely, it shifts the debate for action and intervention towards much greater emphasis on the qualities of action. It provides us with a criterion by which to challenge instrumental analyses of action and activism that focus only on outcomes and achievements. The illusion of control and predictability has significant implications for action and agency. There is a temptation in the interpretation of action, especially actions of care and commoning, to start with a criterion of efficacy. This imparts a utilitarian value to actions. What is likely to achieve the best outcome and how is it to do so? What reward might arise from any given action? These are the wrong questions if we acknowledge the centrality of uncontrollability in the resonant experience. If outcomes are predictable, expected and produced by intentional action, then no element of transformation is possible, only cause and effect in a linear relationship. There can be alteration and amelioration within a system but no breakout from it.

Yet this demonstrates how deeply and totally an economic valuation of action has penetrated collective thinking. Rosa posits control as a master mechanism of modernity. To recognize and enlist *un*control is to present a radical critique. I suggest that in formulating resistance we may go a step further and draw from intellectual and practice traditions of resistance. Dorothy Sölle, for instance, wrote her last major book, *The Silent Cry: Mysticism and Resistance* (2001), as a reflection on a life embedded in activism for peace, justice and the integrity of creation. She asked what would be required to act consistently in pursuit of such an agenda. A pivotal factor for her was to let go of the calculation of success or achievement and recognize the importance of actions taken *sunder warumbe*, that is, without why or wherefore, for their own sake and sufficient on their own. She adopts the phrase from Meister Eckhart, an important figure in Western mysticism and one whose work has been explored by a number of writers seeking to develop a radical ecological critique. A more familiar phrasing of the same principle might be acting without counting the cost. Calculation of the probability of success and cost-benefit analyses are simply not part of the thinking of this form of resistance. Sölle cites Adorno to illustrate the point:

> As far as possible, we ought to live as we believe we should in a liberated world, in the form of our own existence, with all the unavoidable contradictions and conflicts that result from this … Such endeavour is by necessity condemned to fail and meet opposition, yet there is no, option but to work through to the bitter end. The most important form this will take is resistance. (cited as proem to ch. 11 in Sölle, 2001)

Transformative action

Constituting climate action as a vanquishing of existential threats focuses action as a preservation technique (Colebrook 2020). This leaves us with an unasked question – 'just what is it that we are trying to preserve?' Transformative thinking is not preservationist or defensive. It is not an attempt to stabilize and defend within old orders but to move with the shifting sands of current realities (at least it is when it exists within the context of climate change). There is an express need to problematize interventions designed to preserve, to allow replication or maintain current conditions that are already defined as necrophilic. Action on climate change cannot be framed as a redemption and rehabilitation of all that has previously been if these actions have produced the destructive situation that we find ourselves inhabiting. Again, Dorothy Sölle's (1976: 425) observations are helpful: 'once in the learning process of anti-capitalist analysis, the small hope that reform within capitalism will enable it to take on a human face will die'. It is by taking action that we come to better understand the socio-political context and the processes in which we are bound. Her immediate circumstances were of trying to work out how to move forward in light of recognition of social and economic inequalities within societies structured by capitalism, while being faithful to the social realities of the church through which she had come to recognize these factors. Thinking radically about Anthropocene citizenship requires us profoundly to challenge the social, economic and political frameworks that have produced the Anthropocene dilemma without pretending that we can somehow radically step outside of our own complicity in it as beneficiaries of the inherited privileges of the Global North. Choosing to walk and cycle when driving might be easier and more convenient (because of embedded mobility structures) becomes an act of resistance; choosing a car light or car-free existence, an act of care.

In embracing transformative action, we should not be misled into assuming that complex problems have simple solutions. There is no single blueprint of a unified vision of change. Pluriversal thinking embraces diverse perspectives and multiple solutions. The dangerous project is the one constituted around the certain declaration of the elimination of threat, ignoring the uncertainties of uncontrollability. Political demands for certainty always risk becoming totalitarian. Even amid climate breakdown, there is a need for humility not hubris in our attempts to forge change.

Conclusion: Care and commoning for Anthropocene citizenship

Bringing these factors together allows us to build a less hubristic model of how we act and relate. The assertion of citizenship as a claiming of rights for the self looks out of place when considered against the foregoing discussion. One might still assert the rights of others as part of the process of care and commoning, but it is a long way from an ego-driven possessive claiming of rights over other persons and objects. Anthropocene citizenship challenges the use of rights as a tool of domination.

If we concede that these three factors have positive value in relation to our responsibilities and response-ability as Anthropocene citizens, that is, that they can be considered as 'virtuous' actions, then we need to think about how practices and habits can be remade so as to foster these virtues. Conversely, their recognition enables us to evaluate existing mobility practices for the ways in which they nurture or hinder their development.

Accepting that there is such a thing as a social good, then it surely behoves us to act in accordance with the fostering of these social goods rather than undermining them at every point. This is not to say that we can create a perfect world or that we demand that everyone conform to some deterministic blueprint. The element of uncontrollability requires us to be relatively modest about our power to determine the outcomes of our action, which makes it doubly important to engage in action for change or resistance to dominant ways of being that we are able to recognize as destructive. Even if we cannot be certain about the positive outcomes of our acts, we can identify those actions that have negative consequences and choose to refrain from them. As David Banister (2005) has argued in the context of transport planning, it is easier to identify unsustainability than to define sustainability, but this does not mean we cannot act.

We need to ask whether our actions support and construct institutions that make resonance less or more likely. Rosa reminds us that,

> while it is true that I want to re-introduce the quest for a good life into social theory, … resonance is not a teleological, but a strictly relational conception. For me, the good, or eudaimonia, is not definable in any substantive terms, but only with respect to the quality of relationships. (Rosa 2020: 412)

Consequently, to understand the impact of mobility practices it is vital to examine the quality of relationship that they foster. To institutionalize the 'good' is to take up the classic imperative to build situations where it is easier to be creative rather than destructive.

These are the considerations that we take forward into the next chapter which considers both how we perceive the world and the pedagogies that mobilities provide through their interactions with those capacities for perception.

4

Pedagogies and mobilities: Learning and perception

Introduction

A recent development in educational studies has been the emergence of what are called wild pedagogies (Jickling et al. 2018; Paulsen et al. 2022). Recognizing that dominant ways of learning in education in the Global North are not equipping us with the sensitivities that might be needed for sustainability transformations, proponents of wild pedagogies are developing programmes and exercises to explore our relationship with the world appropriate to the challenges of the Anthropocene. How can we learn ways of being-in-the-world that foster attitudes of care and commoning and open up possibilities of resonance? Wild pedagogies develop themes from outdoor and environmental education. In the words of some of its leading proponents in the field of educational studies, 'Wild pedagogies are about rethinking our relationships within the world and represent a desire to let go of an overabundant sense of control, to invite the places we visit to become an integral part of our work, and to respond to provocations in spontaneous, and at times unforeseen, ways' (Morse, Jickling and Quay 2018). We can already see how this picks up echoes of the analysis of the previous chapter. Care, commoning and caring for the commons connect with and embrace uncontrollability.

A major focus of wild pedagogies is an emphasis on place, coming to know our surroundings to be aware and sensitive to them. The approach follows on from a longer tradition of ecological writings and activist practices, such as David Abram's work, *The Spell of the Sensuous* (1997), cited in Chapter 1 or Joanna Macy's *World as Lover, World as Self* (1991). Of course, walking as a practice to combine both meditation and political activism can be traced for centuries. Joe Sheridan (2002) loosely connects a history of modern political activism between Gandhi's Salt March as an adaptation of the padayatra tradition, Woody Guthrie's 'hard travellin", John Muir's forest walks that grounded his activism and organization, and the activism of Fred Thompson and a myriad of others in the Industrial Workers of the World, all through the pivotal role that walking actively played in the development of a political consciousness. Summarizing the contributions of Sheridan and others to the tradition of environmental education, Jickling et al. provide an image that underpins the argument presented here.

> Walking in a landscape, using mind and feet in concert, he reminded us, is the oldest educational method. Walking is the most fundamental pedagogy known to humans. Humans are physical, sensuous beings; and, we learn through this physicality – though our lived experiences in the world. Through *being in the world* we learn differently, and we learn to be different people. (Jickling et al. 2018: ix, emphasis in original)

Adapting ideas from wild pedagogies in order to read the learning processes of everyday travel is not entirely straightforward. Morse et al. (2018) lay considerable emphasis on locating learning within spaces of wildness and wilderness, defined as *self-willed land.* Spaces of everyday travel are always constructed, built and managed environments, infrastructures of everyday life. Only perhaps weather and atmospheric conditions could be described as fitting their definition of self-willed. The realities of climate destabilization are that even these increasingly bear clear testimony to the effects of anthropogenic action. But within the scope of wild pedagogies, 'wild' has two more important dimensions that are more pertinent for understanding how we learn through travel. The first of these 'reflects the central place and agency "more-than-human" factors have … with spontaneous connections to the more-than-human world as the starting place' (Hempsall 2022: 224). The second useful dimension of the wild in wild pedagogies is the uncontrollability of outcomes, important in education given the increasing demands for controllable and measurable products – learning outcomes. Since this discussion is not strictly concerned with formal educational processes, it is more useful to continue to use Rosa's language of uncontrollability to describe this last use of 'wild'.

Encountering and becoming sensitive to the more-than-human world through which we travel and in which we participate is no automatic guarantee of developing greater sensitivity. What it does offer is a potentiality. We can create situations and practices that offer the capacity for learning values appropriate to responsive Anthropocene citizenship, or we can create situations and practices that stifle opportunity. How we choose to travel builds sensitivities and reinforces values.

Travel is an everyday experience. How we travel dictates how we encounter the world. Each way of moving through the world creates a different story and different memories. Stressing the relational perspective, we can focus on how different ways of travelling shape different ways of being-in-the-world. Questions naturally arise: How does the use and performance of various ways of travelling make us care? What relation does it have to establishing and developing commons? What are the qualities inherent in the physicality of each mode and how do they render resonance more or less possible? Mind and body, affect and emotion, are participants in dialogues with spaces, technologies and histories of travel. Complex interactions of human, environmental and technological factors construct experiences. To start unpacking these complexities, we need to define how we understand ourselves as travellers, and the ways in which as travellers we apprehend the world.

The traveller as assemblage

Previous discussions have already established the primacy of relationality: that relating comes before being, our being-in-the-world not as isolated subjects but always as interacting. Akrich and Latour's (1992) elaboration of human and non-human assemblies in the context of actor network theory and Deleuze's concept of the assemblage (Colebrook 2002) point towards further ways in which our relationality is tangled up in more complex ways involving technologies and place as well as other people. These parallel ideas have proved very fruitful for mobilities scholars to think about how our moving bodies are constituted through sets of connections. Even in something as basic as walking we are rarely naked but clothed and shod. Our interface with the surfaces we walk on is mediated by our footwear, our interaction with the atmosphere by our clothing. Each application of technology to the process of movement introduces a new element and new actor in the sense that these elements have agency: they shape how we as persons interact with each other as well as with the more-than-human. The extent of these interactions is such that as Dant (2004) has suggested we cannot think of driving as just an action undertaken in which the technology and the person remain separate. Instead, the act of driving creates a driver-car assemblage that can be construed as a single entity and subject. It allows action and experience not reducible to car and driver as separate beings. Elsewhere I have made a similar argument to understand the processes of cycling (Cox 2019). Adding another element to the rider and machine assembly, I argue that we also need to take into account the space in which the traveller-technology operates. Different kinds of spaces afford or encourage different sorts of action. During a six-month research project (Leverhulme IAF2024-16) spent filming everyday cycling journeys, it was noticeable how different designs of cycleway infrastructures on a single journey could change not only the speeds that riders travelled but also the style in which they rode and their social and spatial interactions.

The consequence of this entanglement between ourselves and our technologies in travel is that we come to understand how technologies are part of our sensuous selves. Part of the sociality of the social fleshly body remarked on previously is its social relationships with technologies. To think through our experiences of travel is necessarily to think through the ways our mobility experiences are co-created by technologies and spaces. The corollary of these recognitions is that to encourage and support greater participation in active travel, designers and advocates of changing travel spaces, environments and machineries of travel need to pay attention to all these dimensions (Koglin 2020).

Extraordinary and mundane travels

As we focus on acts of travel as ways of learning it is worth making some distinction between the different implications of regular journeying and the special event journeys, irregular and one-off travels. We are probably all familiar with how memory encapsulates and enshrines the journey made for a holiday or as a deliberately chosen outing (the word itself is particularly revealing). We easily understand and recognize how such journeys become part of us as persons, memories that we can return to and that form part of our identity, who we understand ourselves to be is partly constituted by those travels. Over-concentration on extraordinary journeys makes mundane, everyday trips slip out of mind. We rarely remember or notice those ordinary walks to the shops, trips to school or work, journeys made again and again because they are simply mundane. Whatever mode of transport (or combination of modes) we take, driving, walking, cycling, catching the bus or the train, these experiences are far less likely to remain conscious, if only because of the sheer repetition. Yet it is these journeys that are vital to consider when we are thinking about the environmental impacts of journeying.

These everyday, frequently unconsidered, experiences have an important role to play in learning precisely because they largely remain non-conscious.

They are the travels that establish norms. They are the journeys that provide a baseline of what is deemed acceptable. They inform how we react to others, the impacts we make upon them and the relationships we establish, both with other people and with the more-than-human. These ordinary personal journeys are vital to scrutinize if we are to establish new norms, less destructive ways of being-in-the-world. Because they are regular and unconsidered they occlude their role in establishing our values, simply because of that regularity. For this reason, the scope of discussions of journeying has to exclude a range of ways of moving which may be exceedingly instructive of how we are in terms of our fleshy, social interactions with each other and the more-than-human world, both animal and non-animal. Authors as different as social theorist Donna Haraway (2016) and elephant ethnographer Piers Locke (2017) who have studied human-animal interactions closely alert us to the unique complexities that inter-species interactions create. Taking regular walks with companion animals is also excluded because, although vital for social life and being, and being journeys that have to be made every day, they really warrant their own examination because of these specific interactions. Most of the comments made about everyday walking are, however, applicable to such journeys. In focusing on journeys with practical purpose we also largely have to ignore those journeys where animals provide the source of movement. Animal-human interaction requires a very different analytical treatment to that which can be explored within the limitations here. The elements themselves also can provide power for movement. Harnessing wind through sails and rotors, or by gliding, requires specific skills and fosters very different sensitivities to the physical environment. These ways of travel again demand exploration especially as they sensitize us to the more-than-human world but fall outside the scope of movement that can be studied here in a concentration on mundane and everyday mobility.

Wild pedagogies of mobility

The core argument throughout this book is that everyday, mundane walking and cycling journeys provide particularly strong mechanisms through which to nurture forms of experiences that foster values of care, processes of commoning and the humility of adaptability that comes with the recognition of uncontrollability. That's not to say that other means don't, or other ways of travelling are unable to provide resonant experiences. Mobilities have their own pedagogies. We learn through doing; the ways in which we move around nurture different experiences and ways of seeing and knowing (Cresswell 2010). The aim is not to make claims for the moral or practical superiority of walking and cycling but to investigate how they create their own distinctive epistemologies – ways of knowing (Popan 2018) and to distinguish them from other ways of moving. Anthropocene citizenship requires us to nurture ways of knowing and being other than those that have led us to this phase of destructive care-less-ness.

To explore the different pedagogic potentials and functions of various mobilities is not to justify them through the sensations and perceptions they may induce and assuming that these will have specific impacts on world views. This would fail to recognize the principles and comprehension of wild pedagogy. Nor is it to emphasize the measurable positive impacts that activities involving 'exercise' have on health and well-being. These functions can be and are valuable, but the importance of these activities for Anthropocene citizenship lies beyond such utility functions. The emphasis on walking and cycling as a means to greater well-being transforms action into production: the very opposite of the approach I have been advocating here. This is why wild pedagogic perspectives are important. Not just because we citizens of the Global North spend upwards of 95 per cent of our time indoors, and being outdoors would improve our health and fitness. Rather, because I want to explore how those actions that we take for granted are more than functional, they are foundational.

Action theories supply one way to bypass this productivist reading (Adlof 2016). Value exists in creativity, freedom, love and care, spontaneity, a 'doing' without a 'why'. The efficiency of walking or cycling for short journeys or the health gains to be made from regular exercise are justifications within a productivist framing, but entirely secondary if we are thinking about Anthropocene mobilities. How walking and cycling allow us to share the spaces of travel, and to attune to the bigger pictures of environment and the micro-realities of location are not just adjuncts and nice-to-have extras. Rationalities and dialogues need not be dismissed because they fail to function in either utilitarian or normative justifications. Direction sensation and response (fleshly, body-knowledges) are valuable in and of themselves.

A word of caution is necessary to counter the undue optimism that may attach to a hermeneutic of experience (the production of knowledge through doing). It is all too easy to promulgate a progressivist faith based in trust that greater experience will bring us increased enlightenment. Such progressivism ultimately relies on a quasi-religious assertion of an inseparability of rationalism and progress. It assumes that the more we know, the better persons and societies we become. To counter this, we need to highlight the ambivalence of experience – that very element of uncontrollability central to Rosa's understanding of the outcomes of resonance. Here we move into the territory of what Michael Löwy (2018) describes as a revolutionary pessimism, a useful assertion against optimism. A connected observation comes from a collective of the leading analysts of sustainability science (Brand et al. 2021: 273):

> Most mainstream efforts to promote more sustainable modes of living tend to focus on better informing individuals, nudging people to behave better, encouraging green consumerism, or introducing more efficient units of technology, approaches which have been criticized as being too limited in their understanding of social life.

The objective of exploring how everyday travel journey practices shape travellers is less about possession of such information to encourage different actions, but more important comprehending how travel creates us as social beings. Learning from experience and understanding the pedagogies of practice is not just about creating more enlightened travellers. It is a way to explore routes of liberation from dominant systems. The logic of current mobility provision and advocacy is focused primarily on repeating the idea that more is better: more speed, more distance, more expansion. More walking and more cycling equated to more well-being. Simply demanding more cycling, more experience, without critiquing and leaving behind actions destructive or undermining of responsive citizenship is self-defeating. There must be a concomitant embrace of degrowth in mobility. Like economic degrowth within a framework of pluriversal politics, mobility degrowth as call to action is aimed at changing the mobility practices of the already privileged. Better survival conditions for non-motorists in an unchallenged realm of automobility contributes little to Anthropocene citizenship. More walking and cycling without less motoring achieves little in terms of a transitions for the Anthropocene. Arguing for more cycling is only valid for Anthropocene mobility when increased distances covered by cycle travel are a correlation of decreased distances travelled by car. Learning and finding new and different ways of experiencing the world must be integrated into wider processes of change, somewhat beyond the scope of this book.

Bodies in movement

Even though the discussion above argues for the importance of understanding acts of travel as necessarily being assemblages of persons, technologies and spaces or environments of travel, we should not overlook the sensate body itself: the social flesh that is entangled with the technologies of travel. An elaborate description of embodied travel is given by D. R. Koukal, drawing on the phenomenological tradition:

> Phenomenologically, the body is not just experienced as any other spatial thing subject to physical laws [Körper] but rather as something lived [Leib]. The lived body is a synthesized, indivisible, reciprocal, and intentional unity of sensory powers and experiential modalities that is dynamically oriented toward the world. In its various modalities the lived body communicates with this beckoning world through mute gesture, opening itself to new kinds of conduct while at the same time reorganizing and transforming that aspect of its world through a particular manner of taking up that world. The lived body is the bearer of felt sensations and is always co-given in experience as a center of orientation. From this center all else is understood in terms of near or far, in front or behind, within or beyond reach, etc. (Koukal 2020: 718)

The careful distinction between Körper and Leib, the corporeal and the lived, allows an insight into two different dimensions of physicality, two aspects of feeling and sensing that the English language struggles to differentiate even though they are recognizable when we reflect on our experiences.

As we travel, technologies expand the capacity of the corporeal body, and thus the potential to feel to experience. As we think about the intensity of experience provided by different technologies of travel, the capacity of each to provide moments of resonance is clear. We should not think of resonance simply in terms of the volume or intensity of connection. To do so would be to dismiss the complexity of both affection and emotion. Resonance is not simply the product of accumulation of experiences but rather being attuned to the world around, the moments of harmony with the situation, when one feels fully alive in the experience.

Bodies vary in their capacities; our habitual actions develop and change our capabilities to perform those actions. The intention is not to focus here on the capabilities of differing bodies but to think about how modes of travel and everyday habits of journeying afford experience to the traveller.

Each assemblage of traveller and travel technology provides its own characteristics. Dant's (2004) driver-car combination has specific parameters of sensitivity and engagement with the world around. Certain senses are dulled or nullified (e.g. smell) and others, particularly the visual, are intensified. Indeed, in driving, visual information is the most important of all the sensory dimensions and dominates other forms of perception. The degree of engagement with the more-than-human world that any form of travel can provide is clearly linked to the degree of enclosure that the traveling body has from the world. Fundamental distinctions need to be made between walking and cycling, in which one is generally exposed to the elements, and travel by motor vehicles as either a passenger or a driver, in which one is enclosed, separated from the world beyond.

How that lived experience permeates every dimension capable of sensing is vividly described in an account compiled from fieldnotes by Cosmin Popan, recorded in his study *Bicycle Utopias* (2019). In a chapter exploring senses, again proceeding from a phenomenological perspective he writes,

> The visual field expanding ahead of my bicycle is often complemented by a deafening roaring of traffic, the tactile experience of the wind blowing in my face and the sweat trickling on my abdomen, the mild pain in my leg muscles as I accelerate when the green light turns on, the intimate sense of balance that I feel I could lose at any time as a heavy truck passes me by and the nauseating, yet strangely appealing scent of exhaust gas. All these attended at times by a tiresome back pain from and old bike accident. They, all blend into a total sensuous experience where the whole is bigger than the sum of its constituent parts and where the experience of one sense cannot be effectively separated from others. (Popan 2019: 124)

Two elements immediately stand out for further analysis. First, that the senses Popan records extend beyond the familiar five-sense model of perception conventionally used to describe physical sensation, and second that the experiences of cycling he has are not just shaped by the body, road and space but are also profoundly affected by the others in that road space, the motor traffic that surrounds him. Both these dimensions of experience need exploring before we can move on in subsequent chapters to consider some everyday experiences of travel and how they relate to the development of values for mobile Anthropocene citizenship.

Modes of perception: Meeting the world around us

Learning and perception are deeply intertwined. To unpack how they are entangled it is useful to consider how others have thought through the worlds of perception and learning. As Vannini, Waskul and Gottschalk (2012) observe, the usual ways of thinking about human sensation and perception are based on a dualism that separates body and mind, raw sensation and cognitive perception: a problematic position when proceeding from the non-dualist position advanced here. One model that refutes this stance is found in Herbert Read's work, *Education through Art* (1961). Read's stance on education has many affinities with the concerns of wild pedagogies. Though not concerned with human interactions with 'nature' it is deeply concerned with the constructed environment, how we interact with the artefacts of human creativity. It is firmly experiential, emphasizing participation, not simply observation or intellect. It does not depend on targeted outcomes but seeks to find value in all forms of perception and expression.

Read identified six modes of perception associated with learning through art. These have obvious parallels with learning through moving, especially if we comprehend journey as performance (Cox 2019). Table 4.1 takes Read's original categories of aesthetic education and expands them in light of work on kinaesthetic in cycling (Spinney 2006; Clayton and Musselwhite 2013). Read's modes of perception, ways of being and seeing, integrate four of the five senses

Table 4.1 Modes of perception

Mode of aesthetic perception and expression (from Read)	Mode of mobile perception	Comment
Visual	Sight	
Plastic	Physical touch	Mediated through skin
	Temperature sense	
Musical	Sound	
Kinetic/movement	Muscle movement	Bodily sensation
	Movement through space	
	Balance	
	Fatigue	
Verbal/linguistic	Language (expression and communication)	Finding ways to describe
Cognitive	Sensation	Mental processing reflection and reaction include tacit mental perception (intuition)
	Intuition	
	Feeling	
	Thought	
	Smell	
	Spatial	Proximity. Includes proprioception

classically recognized in Western (dualist) thought. But he adds movement and imagination, or mental cognition as modes of perception, allowing us to reintegrate body and mind, not separate them. Thus, he identifies the visual, the plastic, the musical, the kinetic, the verbal and the constructive (i.e. mental or thought as a mode of perception). This last can be further divided into sensation, intuition, feeling and thought. These distinctions are not a sequential series of processes but different dimensions of comprehension.

Perception is multifaceted and multilayered. Read doesn't mention smell as a mode of perception, since he is primarily dealing with the Arts (as defined in Western society in the late 1950s), but this can be usefully added to the list. We can also add in a category of spatial perception. Read himself recognizes this but includes it in his discussion of eurhythmics as the meeting of music or rhythm and dance. Valuably, Popan (2020) also refers to eurhythmia, following Lefebvre, to express that condition of movement when the various rhythms of movement harmonize, the moment when everything 'feels right', a form of resonance. It stands in contrast to the arrhythmic, the disharmony of elements, what musically one might call glitch. What both uses have in common is the sense of the coordination of elements leading to an outcome that demands the eu- prefix to indicate it as a 'good' or positive state of being. Through recognizing the cognitive dimensions of perception, we can see how positive physical sensations of the moving body can align with moral value-judgements: 'this is a good feeling', 'everything feels good'. Another illustration of the constant cross-linkages, indeed the inseparability of the sensory worlds described here is how we recognize tacit, intuitive evaluations and knowledges about locations and processes. We talk of the atmosphere, the feel of a place, of a journey. These are expressions of indefinable combinations of our individual acuities and emotions and the intangible or inexpressible qualities that we sense in the combination of the human and more-than-human contributions to the social and physical life and spaces of travel. Each way of travelling expands or contracts the perceptive horizons, our capacities to become aware of the world beyond ourselves, the world on which we are dependent and with which, through the Anthropocene, we are becoming increasingly aware of our interconnections.

While it may seem both artificial and over-complex to distinguish ways of perceiving, breaking down the multiple ways we encounter the world around us allows a sharper insight into how we can understand them, and how areas of perception and encounter are opened up or closed off to us as travellers. They give us stronger reference points when we come to consider how mobility modes provide sensations and allow or prevent situations that foster resonance.

We participate in a culture in which the visual dominates. Description of the world usually starts by seeing the world around us. The gaze, as a measure of a person's or group's awareness and perception of others, has become a vital tool in critical analysis (Laing and Willson 2020). Connecting the gaze to mobility, John Urry and colleagues (Urry 1990; 1995; Urry and Larsen, 2011) have explored how travel creates new forms of commodification of space and location in which travel is not just relocation and destinations not simply other places to be, but both become and produce objects of consumption. Technologies, not just those for physical travel, feed this objectification of locality.

Digitalization emphasizes the cultural roles of the visual with information and requirements communicated through screens. Touch sensitive the controls may be, but the feedback remains largely visual. Consequently, the visual as a mode of perception gets separated from other sensory experience. We see this formalized in the separation of aesthetics from kineasthetics. Bicycle simulators, such as that developed at the University of Delft (Dialynas 2019) to investigate safety perceptions and decision-making, provide a dramatic contrast to the experiences of, for example, flight simulators. Although one engages in the physical act of riding and control, and lean-cornering and other dynamic elements have been incorporated, airflow over the skin can be mimicked by a fan, the experience remains somehow dissociated. The world around is missing. Travel modes in which the traveller is seated in an air-conditioned capsule, the exterior world mediated by a windscreen, provide a profoundly different experience, simulators being good enough to train those skills required for piloting.

Overemphasis on the visual occludes or hides differences between travel modes. If the visual is almost the only significant factor, then the more visual the stimuli the better. Reducing travel sensations to sights and images has consequences. Since all travel provides visual stimulation, logically, the higher the speed, the more the stimulation. Volume of experience dominates over the opportunity to savour it. The title of Mauch and Zeller's (2008) volume on roads and landscapes is telling: *The World Beyond the Windscreen*. The 'world' is always out there, othered and mediated as the authors show. Fascinatingly, the cover photograph is of a somewhat extreme cross-over 270-degree mountainside turn. It shows one car and eight motorcyclists. Let's consider what these twisting roads afford to these two modes of travel. For the motor traveller on two wheels rather than four, these extreme bends provide more than just continuous sideways forces as one navigates the extended curve. On two wheels, lean is everything, a correlate of speed and tightness of curve. Such terrain offers unmatched experiences. As the novelist Iain Banks (2004: 340) described it: 'Compared to driving a car, riding a [motor] bike feels halfway to flying. There's suddenly a third dimension involved. Cars basically stay flat. ... On a bike, with a little experience and confidence, you find yourself leaning all over the place; angles you'll never see in a car unless you are, technically, crashing.'

Renewing emphasis on the embodied, enfleshed self has become an important task for academic sociology over recent decades. Exploration of the sociology of the body in the 1990s preceded a wider concern with the material, in turn enhanced by explorations of the agency and vitality of matter (Shilling 1993; Bennett 2010). New materialist studies stress the sensory world of touch, taste, smell as important in themselves, essential if we are to understand the interplay of environment and society (Connolly 2010). In dialogic terms this enables us also to consider how we encounter the other, not just through mental perceptions and discourse but also as material beings. Dialogue requires interaction. It is a helpful reminder of basic dimensions of aesthetics and interaction that Read moves from the visual and plastic into the kinetic. His focus was on dance and the dramatic arts as a means of communication and expression, mine here is on the impact of everyday movement on our perception and reception of the world. Walking, wheeling, cycling (including motor-cycling) require coordinated bodily movement, 'feeling' the terrain, maintaining balance.

> You become more sensitive to the road surface. ... when you're on a [motor] bike you suddenly become hypersensitive to the presence of stuff like a little gravel on the road's centre line, a curved sear of mud extending from the entrance to a field, the rainbow hint of colour that indicates a diesel spill, metal manhole covers slicked with rain or a patch of autumnal leaves lying in a shady corner. The point is that a car just sits there. (Banks 2004: 339–40)

In contrast driving is an essentially sedentary process that requires hand and foot coordination responding to processing visual information (Ingold 2021). Sensitivity to road surfaces and conditions is important but far less crucial. In these bodily registers and the interaction with the world beyond the vehicle of travel, passengering becomes almost entirely passive. This is only the case, of course, while in transit. Part of the passenger experience always involves the travel to the points of embarkation and the spaces of waiting. These are not value judgements but observations on the distinctiveness of differences between ways of moving and being moved. Nor should it be ignored that being the passenger in a kinetic mobility in any form of transport does not eliminate one's dialogic interaction with the world, whether of other travellers or the landscapes through which one travels.

Read's emphasis on verbal and constructive thought as modes of perception stresses our enfleshed, embodied existence as perceiving selves, not just data receptors who collect external stimuli that have predetermined meanings. We interpret, we respond, we communicate in and through our interactions. Our varied bodies shape our perceptions and our repeated actions shape our bodies. We inhabit worlds simultaneously constructed by both discourse and materiality. Actions prompt response and our capacities to communicate our own responses to others, even in the wordless sounds we make in response to situations (e.g. of joy, of threat, of bodily overwork or surprise) are part of being human.

Feeling the travelscape

Cognitive perception emphasizes the role of memory and imagination as well as the discursive production of knowledge and experience that accompanies the material. Our experiences of the world around do not just consist of individual and instantaneous reaction to stimuli but continue as journeys of socialization and education, stretching back through time, and projected into the future. We learn to move, we learn to see, feel and hear. We learn to attune or to filter out the world around us. How these different ways of experiencing, learning and knowing interact at different levels can be illustrated by a reflection from Walter Benjamin. In *One Way Street* (1928) he suggested that the difference between observing a road from the air and walking along it was the difference between reading and copying a text. Only through copying or walking does one really come to understand a text or a route. The physical action and time taken change the dynamic of experience.

> The airplane passenger sees only how the road pushes through the landscape, how it unfolds to the same laws as the terrain surrounding it. Only he who walks the road on foot learns the power it commands, and of how, from the very scenery that for the flier is only the unfurled plain it calls forth distances, belvederes, clearings, prospects at each of its turns like a commander deploying soldiers at a front. Only the copied text thus commands the soul of him who is occupied with it, whereas the mere reader never discovers the new aspects of his inner self that are opened by the text, that road cut through the interior jungle forever closing behind it: because the reader follows the movement of his mind

in the free flight of daydreaming, whereas the copier submits it to command.
(Benjamin 1928: loc 668)

The bird's eye view of Benjamin's aeroplane passenger sees the world as a map. Remember that this is the passenger flight experience of the 1920s, not the enclosed, pressurized cabin, air-conditioned, high-speed airline flight of the twenty-first-century airline passenger. There remains a relatively close contact between the ground below and a very visceral feeling of carriage through the air, comparable with early motoring. Benjamin's last sentence is useful because it also reminds us that the difference between walking and being a passenger involves a degree of discipline. For the copyist, the discipline is mental and artistic, required to ensure accuracy; for the traveller, the bodily discipline is to provide motion.

This passage also recalls the difference between control and uncontrol and agency. Benajmin's walker is compelled by the three-dimensional physicality of the road. Only, however, in submitting to the instruction of the text, reading it through the bodily movement of walking, can the walker truly come to know, to be fully open to hear what the landscape is saying. Skimming the text with the eyes is not sufficient. Using this observation to think about the dynamics of comprehension, of interior exploration and of movement we can see how each mode of travel, increasing speed and taking away from the bodily encounter of the roadscape, takes us further from the possibilities of encountering new aspects of ourselves through our interactions with it. If the road is a text and the journey a performance of that text, the more time that is spent with it the more possibilities of encounter are opened up. Slow travel is perhaps not simply a means of thinking through low-energy pathways but also of engaging in an exercise of perception. The human speed traveller sees the route unfurl, sees how the landscape accommodates the traveller, meets the sensory dimensions of scent and sound, responds to the texture of the path or of the landscape, connecting to its history and geology (the logos of the geos or the word of the land itself).

If the route has importance in this manner, then we might consider how routes are created. For what purpose and how did they arise? Are the infrastructures of travel the hardened and asphalted routes tracing paths created by generations of movement from one locale to another, or are they routeways carved out for the specific purposes of facilitating one or other forms of travel (road, canal, rail) accompanied by or rededicated to human-powered travel? The reuse of railway lines is a frequent source of cycling infrastructure in Europe and North America.

Being direct connections, usually into settlement centres, they serve utility purposes very well, but repurposing redundant infrastructures built for other modes raises questions for their ability to engage with terrain. Since cycling is a linear mode of travel and gradients take more work, then the straightened lines and minimal gradients of former rail trackways with their cuttings and embankments ease the cyclist's journey. At the same time, these routes reduce the sensitivity to changing landscape. Jan Gehl's work on human-scale planning allows us to recognize the importance of subtle details of urban architecture for liveability (for an overview, see Gehl 2010). So too, we might extend this into the details of landscaping for human-scale travel, especially in the planning of routes in non-urban areas.

Motor traffic shapes the world

The dominance of motoring in contemporary society has led to a wide critical literature building on Urry's (2004) analysis of automobility as a system that structures social, economic and cultural realities (Featherstone et al. 2005; Wells 2012; Popan 2018; Cass and Manderscheid 2018). Together with the physical and material presence of cars and their dominance of the cultural imaginary, automobility shapes our experiences of non-car travel and the ways that we are able to think about other modes of travel, whether walking, wheeling or cycling, or motorcycling (Sachs 1984; Miller 2001). It also affects the ways we think about being a passenger, whether on road or rail. Even air travel is shaped by automobility as airport hubs demand connectivity with passenger origins and destinations (Cwerner et al. 2008). Discussion of some background to these problems needs to be made before we think about how different ways of moving provide different dimensions of experience and how these allow us to be-in-the-world.

Life for the majority of people in northern Europe today is unimaginable without the car, even if they themselves do not drive. The dominance of driving has been facilitated by numerous factors, state provision of infrastructures being only one. Indeed, the state has played an immense role in the reproduction of automobility as part of what Lefebvre called the society of controlled consumption (Lefebvre 2014 [1961]; Schmid 2022). What appear to be individual 'free' choices are facilitated and made attractive by actions of state intervention (though often obscured or covert), through tax interventions, subsidies or infrastructure provision. These are coupled with actions that can make alternative choices less attractive, for example, lack of investment or infrastructure provision, even the deliberate underfunding of public transport, justified on expectations of and normalization of private motoring. This facilitation has been crucial given automobility's own role as a central form for the reproduction and accumulation of capital.

Since 1945, European cities that existed and functioned for centuries prior to the private car have been rebuilt and reorganized around it, assuming futures of universal and unlimited car travel. Yet significant numbers of people do not, will not or cannot drive, for a variety of reasons (of which youth or old age is the largest factor). Their mobility may be compromised when set against the mobility privilege of the car driver, and dependencies can be produced by this exclusion from dominant practices of driving, but these are not necessary or foregone outcomes. Transport inequalities are produced by political decisions on mobility provision and space use. We also know that current patterns of personal transport are deeply unsustainable both in environmental and social terms. A range of effects from air pollution to congestion (let alone CO_2 emissions) make current levels of motoring untenable for future sustainable mobility scenarios (Sperling and Gordon 2009).

International political commitments to low(er) carbon transport policies in response to awareness of the realities of climate breakdown place us, theoretically at least, on the edge of a significant travel transformation. Yet I venture to argue that we will not *see* any dramatic shift. Transport technologies can and do change with surprising rapidity, but these changes are often invisible, below the threshold of conscious attention. A simple reason is that overall patterns of mobility are enmeshed and inseparably entangled in the social and physical structures of society. Spatial distribution of opportunities for work, housing, education and leisure determines the needs and possibilities for everyday journeying. Access to these opportunities is further determined and constrained by personal and familial wealth, or lack thereof. This is often inherited. Another constraining factor is the legacy of public investment in and provision of infrastructures from public transport to roadways, cycleways and footpaths, specific to any given locale. Put simply, who we are and where we are determine our mobility actions and possibilities. Who we are shapes how we travel; how we travel tells us who we are. Prior expectations of mobility inform where we can choose to live; if unable to drive, we necessarily have to seek out locations close to workplaces or with reliable public transport connections.

This is not to argue that there can be no change. Low-carbon and low-emission options from vehicle electrification and the widespread marketing of alternatives to the car as the ubiquitous vehicle option will inevitably change the overall makeup of the transport fleet. Alternatives here particularly include small, light electric vehicles designed for lower speeds. Reducing maximum design speed lowers the power requirements and simultaneously lessens the scale of safety features required (because of inertial vehicle mass), allowing for increased energy efficiency (through not having to move redundant mass).

These factors also demonstrate why the spatial thinking of the fifteen- or twenty-minute neighbourhood is so important. Such plans propose that one should have access to most everyday amenities available within a fifteen- to twenty-minute travel time. Of course, one can choose to go further and make any distance journey one wants, but localization of goods and services is designed to ensure that one no longer depends on making longer distance journeys to access everyday necessities. The implications of such strategic thinking are obvious for both social equality and for transport-produced pollution. However, we can also consider how reduction of need for longer distance journeys for quotidian requirements can have a major impact on vehicular requirements for the individual or family traveller.

Automobility, the systematic structuring and dominance of the private car, has achieved a level of hegemonic dominance such that those who have lived their entire lives under its shadow find it hard to imagine what life could be like without the private motor vehicle. One consequence of this level of domination is that the imagination of what might be an "otherwise" possibility of mobility regimes is very difficult. A second implication is that current experiences of other mobility modes have to be read through their existence as subordinate – even subaltern – practices. That is, their form and the experiences they offer as modes of interaction are not self-determined but created in light of their relation to the dominant system of motoring. Walking, wheeling, cycling and passengering all remain secondary experiences while the domination of driving remains the norm in both expectation and policy provision.

One of these consequences is the normalization of risk and fear created by the inherent violence that motor traffic creates for all road users, not just, but especially, for walkers and cyclists (Braun and Randell 2021). Any observations of the potential forms of interaction and their capacity for resonance offered by walking and cycling therefore have to be taken from observations made in segregated/separated facilities made in a context of car dominance in a system of automobility.

The average car is an immensely wasteful machine for the majority of journeys it makes. Even in the 1920s, Charles Mochet, a pioneer of velomobile and microcar manufacture, noted the ridiculousness of the amount of power (energy) and resources used in everyday motor journeys (Cox 2023, see also www.Mochet. org). He also noted what might be called the overkill capacity of much driving and how superfluous mobility capacity was closely tied to proclamation of social status. Driving or being driven was conspicuous consumption. In an article for the motoring press of the time he described the absurdity of watching a one-tonne, eighty-horse-power (chauffeur-driven) limousine for a simple shopping journey to convey an eighty kilogram traveller with a couple of luggage boxes. Today's everyday driving practices are almost incomprehensible in their relative squandering of resources.

Conspicuous consumption has always played an inordinate role in transport choice. In Mochet's interwar era, low overall vehicle numbers allowed it to remain an amusing observation. We may have dispensed with the expectation of a chauffeur, yet the basic perversity of everyday urban motor mobilities remains. Not only vehicle numbers are unrecognizable. Comparing the average weight and power of today's mass-marketed cars with those from the 1930s, one is immediately struck by the huge differences in scale. Even in the last fifty years the size differential is significant – a 1960s Mini was 3 m long compared with up to 4.3 m for today's Mini and widths are similarly increased (Deutsches Museum Verkehrscentrum 2023). Gains in engine efficiency have been nullified by increases in vehicle mass (and hence higher degradation of brakes and tyres) and in vehicle use (total kilometre travelled). Powerplant substitution from internal combustion of on-board petroleum to electrical motors drawing power from battery storage or hydrogen fuel cells does little to address the overkill status of automotive design, and of the regulatory requirements for vehicle safety that determine many of the necessary features. A vicious spiral is entered into, where increasing vehicle mass necessitates greater onboard safety measures which then increase vehicle mass further (Cebrat, Cox and Gustavssson 2009).

Mochet's means to address the problem was one that centred on sufficiency. He started from first principles. What were the requirements (volume-wise) for a typical ordinary family journey and how might these be best provided so as to be available to the most persons (i.e. democratic)? The minimalist vehicle he designed could be entirely pedal powered or augment its human power source with a lightweight, low-power motor. Capable of carrying two persons and luggage (or children) the microcar was redefined. Other manufacturers, including DKW and Citroën, also pursued this line of minimal motoring to make driving more affordable (Thirlby 2002).

Yet ultimately, mass motoring and a safety discourse that externalized the risks of driving produced vehicle styles that increasingly isolated those within the car from the world outside. Externalizing risk ensured increased safety for the drivers and passengers while unsafety from the higher speeds secured was transferred to other road users (Adams 1985; 1995). It is not necessary to provide a history of motoring and how its dominant position was achieved but to note how the growth of mass motoring was accompanied by significant changes in auto design. Democratization of motoring was also predicated on making the driving experience increasingly more mundane and predictable, making the world inside the car increasingly separated from the world outside.

In today's mobility transition, innovative lightweight electric vehicles (LEVs) that blur the line between cycles and motor vehicles abound. Legal definitions and vehicle category requirements attached to them are currently the primary barrier to e-bike and LEV innovation. Thus, when we think about cycling, we should not limit our imagination to the classic image of a diamond-framed solo bicycle that has, with minimal variation, dominated cycle production since the 1890s. Cycling includes a range of designs of bicycles, tricycles and quadricycles, pedal powered and handcycles, for one or more persons, for cargo carrying, for different uses and with different capabilities, all potentially with or without power augmentation or assistance. There are also many other forms of human-propelled wheeled travel from scooters to wheelchairs. Some provide essential mobility aids, others, consumer choices. Between them, these devices for personal travel provide a range of options any of which can be used given the provision of appropriate infrastructure. What I am interested in here is not what moves us to make particular choices but what these do to us when we use them. How do they shape the ways we can see and experience the world and how do they affect our interactions with each other?

Conclusions

We learn from our everyday travels, and one of the most profound lessons that appears to come from the past century of dominance by internal combustion-powered motor traffic is that profligacy of energy use has become unremarkable. Those who have argued for sufficiency and supported ideas of minimal motoring (Thirlby 2002) have generally been overrun by the designers and providers of ever larger, ever more powerful motor vehicles, encouraged and supported by government investment in the facilities that make higher speed motoring feasible and safe – at least for the motorist. That these changes have come at immense expense for people and planet is slowly becoming inescapable, as we shall see in more detail in Chapter 6. The reality of climate breakdown makes it imperative that personal travel habits need to challenge this energy profligacy.

By turning attention to ways of learning and producing a model of perception we have a set of criteria that allow us to understand the ways in which different forms of action, in this case, travel action, might be interrogated to work out their specific relationships with the values for responsible Anthropocene citizenship highlighted in Chapter 3.

To make an analysis of the experiential dimensions of personal travel, the following chapters will make a distinction between machines and forms of travel powered by the human body, even when augmented by some form of extra power, and those that are fully powered vehicles and which require no power input from the traveller. For the driver of a powered vehicle, the primary task is to control the engine and the consequent movement of the vehicle. This is the same requirement whether the power source is animal, steam, internal combustion engine or electric motor. Some modes of travel are much more visceral than others, exposing the traveller to the elements or not and involving different levels of driver control (e.g. in the differences between powered wheelchairs, motor cycling and driving). Likewise, there are differences between two-wheelers and multitrack vehicles, powered or non-powered. Motor cycling and driving are very different experientially as noted above. Dynamically stable, two wheelers require skills and kinetic balance that make them immensely different from the statically stable multitrack machines.

Moving away from the straightjacket of assessing movement by vehicle type, there is a third category of travel that is important – that of passengering. Neither controlling movement nor providing tractive power, from rickshaw passenger to railway passenger, from taxi and bus to passenger air travel, even just travelling as an everyday car passenger, there are deeply connected similarities. Interpersonal trust is at the centre of the journey trust in the driver, or pilot and in the machine. One's relationship to those in whom one's trust is invested may vary wildly from an intimate loved one to an impersonal organization. Passengering in the Global North is almost always the result of motor-powered travel and so, as Chapter 5 deals with walking and wheeling and cycling, Chapter 6 will connect passengering and driving.

Returning to our categories of care, commoning and uncontrollability, we see how different modes engender specific relations with the material world, our bodies and each other: the social fleshly and the material relations of travel.

We can return to the questions raised earlier: How does each form of travel make the possibilities of resonance more or less likely? With what dimensions of resonance (with ideas, people and things) can it occur? No action is perfectly contained or innocent, so when considering potentially resonant experiences within one form of action, we need also to consider how those actions impinge on others who are not participants. Recognizing that our answers may overlap and contain both advantages and disadvantages simultaneously, we might, for example, ask whether any chosen mode allows for peaceful coexistence or results in enclosure and exclusion? Having explored how motoring shapes the world especially through its current dominance, one might also speculate, as the examples are developed, whether dominance in other forms of travel might alleviate existing inequalities or perpetuate them. Is the problem of exclusion grounded in the very factor of dominance, rather than the particular way of travelling? My own reflections on this will be explored in the final chapter but I will not claim that these are definitive. With these questions in mind, we can now turn to thinking about ways of moving.

5

Human scale movement: Walking, wheeling, cycling

Introduction

This chapter clusters together a range of ways of everyday movement distinguished by what can be called human scale movement. That is, they provide movement within a speed range or ability to cover distance as experienced by humans for most of our history. This includes histories of animal co-mobilities. The majority of these also rely, in part at least, on the human body as a primary source of power.

For survey and data collection purposes, travel is commonly categorized by type of vehicle, by trip purpose and by trip length. As resources for thinking about the relationship between everyday travel experiences and the relationships they engender, these categorizations reveal little. To provide a useful way of relating travel experience to the pedagogies of travel, and to assess these for their appropriateness for nurturing the qualities necessary for Anthropocene citizenship, a different approach is needed. Discussion of actual mobility practices will therefore focus on journeys and travel experiences for their relationality: the ways in which they develop interaction. There are three areas of relationality of concern. First, those within the travellers themselves; physical experiences of bodily perception and exertion; and how it is interpreted and understood. Second, there are the interactions between travellers and other persons. While these may be obvious when we travel together, or in the visible interactions with other travellers, there are also invisible interactions, impacts upon others that are not seen by the journey maker. The third category of interaction is that between travellers and environments. These may be the direct physical encounters provided by spaces and infrastructures of travel, or they may be more distant effects. Effects occur from the construction of those infrastructures or from the construction and use of vehicles or products necessary for travel. Material assemblages of travel link travellers to supply chains of goods and services, to infrastructures and to forms of exchange.

When we apply these considerations to everyday journeys, these three forms of relationality are shaped by the speed of travel, the scale and intensity of exposure to other persons and to the more-than-human, and to the scales of infrastructure required for that travel. There are two further correlates of these variables, the energy input required for travel and the specific design of vehicles and infrastructures. Higher speeds and increased acceleration rates require proportionately greater energy. Infrastructure design can encourage or actively prevent different speeds and accelerations. It can also be deliberately used to favour or disfavour modes of travel or vehicle types. Vehicle designs also affect the ways we move, whether exposed to the elements or enclosed, for example.

Taking all these factors into account we can make a basic distinction between what I am calling human-scale travel, and travel that is enabled by high-density energy systems, primarily powered by fossil fuels and notably from oil-derived products. Historically, we can see a general distinction between mobility practices that were possible prior to the mid-nineteenth century, and those made possible by oil-fired internal combustion at the end of the nineteenth century. Steam power provides an interesting transition. Coal and coke are fossil fuels but not as energy dense as oil, high-pressure steam was needed for successful rail and road travel. This is not to endorse a periodized analysis in which one technology replaces another. As David Edgerton (2006) has shown, technological innovation generally adds, not replaces. Other factors than power plant alone are also important. The relatively late arrival of the bicycle as a viable transport technology (in comparison with rail travel, for example) reflects its dependence on materials that are part of global resource supply chains and technologies for their processing, most notably of rubber for pneumatic tyres.

Human scale speeds and travel

Human scale travel is easily imagined as operating within the parameters set by pre-fossil fuel travels: in other words, the bodily capacities of humans or animals used for traction and riding, and its augmentation by simple machines, from oars and sail to skates and skis and carts and carriages. These technologies allowed international trade as far back as the Bronze Age. The mechanical advantage of the bicycle raises human capacity towards that of horse riding, but both are still subject to the self-limitations of muscle fatigue. If this needs quantification in speed terms, this is roughly a normal maximum of about 35 km/h on level ground – the speed of the fastest sprinters. This is not an absolute or a necessarily clear-cut boundary, but using this measure provides a way to restore physical body movement and capacity to the centre of the discussion. Mechanical devices such as bicycles are force multipliers, transforming human effort not only into forward motion but also providing mechanical advantage (multiplying the effort put in). As such they are easily capable of speeds higher than 35 km/h (especially when assisted by gravity, for example!) but for the majority of everyday journeys this is not really an issue.

Adding electric motor power to cycles and scooters or introducing other new micromobilities is often seen as a problem for legislation, defining vehicle types and the necessary power restrictions and permissions for use. I suggest that framing the problem in terms of vehicle types is problematic. The issue is not one easily defined by absolute power or whether the machine relies on human power input or not, but whether the motorization takes the machine and rider beyond the parameters of human scale movement. The EU decision to limit e-bike assistance to 25 km/h is conceptually grounded in this way of thinking, but underestimates the capacity of effectively designed bicycles. Heavy laden cargo bikes and trikes may need relatively large amounts of power to cope with loads but still travel at human scale speeds. The legal status of micromobilities and their management within traffic systems of course need to be addressed (O'Hern and Estgfaeller 2020; McQueen et al. 2021). Taking an historical perspective, it is worth noting how legislative definition and restrictions have been used to eliminate previous attempts to encourage low-power-assisted cycling, with cyclemotors, for example. One important function of low-power-assistance is to provide parity between people's different bodily capacities, reflecting diverse levels of health and fitness (from whatever cause). Designing for higher speed travel requires additional external power and a transformation of thinking about safety, for travellers and others. Fully powered travel modes shift users from active contributors to movement, in the sense of being the power source (or part of it), to being drivers or passengers.

The idea of human scale speeds of travel used here corresponds to Jan Gehl's work on human scale in thinking about city planning. Gehl (2010) considers speed of travel to be all important to the human capacity to interact with our surroundings. But his prime focus is on how urban design interacts with our perception. Design can induce feelings of discomfort or engagement. Similarly, speed of travel through environments, built or grown, affects the degree of engagement possible. Although the bicycle multiplies the capacity for movement by about a factor of four, most normal cycling speeds still fall below the speeds that can be sprinted on foot: they rarely exceed the capacities of the unassisted human body. Professional racers may come to exceed speeds double that of 35 km/h in a sprint, but normal riders, even those with aerodynamically efficient cycle designs such as velomobiles, rarely sustain more than 35 km/h for practical purposes. Hence cycling falls into what might be considered as a 'natural' pattern and action of human movement.

It is almost too obvious to state, but most journeys are short distance (under 10 km). Therefore, human scale journeying is entirely possible and appropriate and human-powered (or augmented) modes of travel, coupled with public transport provisions, provide practical possibilities for almost all of these journeys. Distance being a product of time and speed, these limited distance journey, even extended to 20 km and beyond, could be relatively easily accomplished under these means, given adequate provision of facilities and access to the technologies of movement. What is lacking is not the technology but the political will to enable change to happen.

As an aside, the more-than-human world may have much to teach us about sufficient and sustainable mobilities and human scale travel. The speeds of fast cycling correspond to the speed of birds in flight, which typically fall between 30 and 35 km/h for smaller birds and 40–55 km/h for larger birds (Hedenström and Åkesson 2016). There are other lessons on energy use: birds automatically select the most efficient flight speeds and patterns, for example, sheltering in a vee formation to minimize energy expenditure. Walkers will seek straight lines between points and cyclists will duck down into the wind or take advantage of each other's 'wind shadow' when riding in company. Self-powered travel is not an asocial behaviour. Mapping speeds of animal travel sheds light on the different speeds and intensities of travel. Birds in flight seem to have two distinct speed modes, one roughly twice the other (Schiffner and Srinivasan 2016). My own research observations of urban cyclists and pedestrians (using GPS-linked digital video recording to correlate speed of travel with spatial location and qualities of travel space) reveal similar patterns. One mode which we would recognize as ambling, which proceeds at about half the speed of the other, is purposeful travel towards a clear destination.

Studying historical documentary film using the same analytical tools developed in that research project (Cox 2020b) shows that when urban motor traffic speeds remained at human scale, the interactions of motorists, walkers, cyclists and wheeled traffic (including handcarts) remained largely conflict-free. There were speed differentiations, but the scale is such that there is time for negotiation. No vehicle aimed to reach higher speed beyond human scale. Designs for urban shared space operate under similar assumptions about human scale movement. As long as the spaces of travel are not overcrowded or restricted in area, this remains a feasible goal for redevelopment. It is not easily achieved when the street has become understood as a space primarily for flow of traffic (Karndacharuk et al. 2014).

To explore human scale travel and its interactions, the rest of this chapter will examine walking, wheeling and cycling more or less in turn, paying attention to the variables of speed, scale and intensity of interaction and to infrastructures. Of course there are many commonalities, as will be observed, but there are also factors that make the experiences distinct. Each way of travel is a way of being-in-the-world. Each heightens specific sensitivities and, in its interactions, raises issues of power relations and ultimately of vulnerability. How those relations are managed provides an insight into their connections with and potential for care and commoning. Human scale travel provides a baseline against which we can also consider other modes of travel which will form the basis of the next chapter.

Walking as a way of being-in-the-world

> Imagine you are out walking in the street. To go for a walk is to create, through the endless flow of interaction, bodily and spatially. With each step – and within each step – perceptual, sensorial and social possibilities are opened up, assemblages of forces gathered, altered and reconnected, complexities multiplied, memories activated. The moment is saturated with affectual relations and intensities ... With the fall of the same step, previous possibilities perish, simultaneously propelling the endless opening of fresh possibilities of connection. (Goodman 2018: 11)

Reduced to the language of travel planning, 'pedestrian' imposes a uniformity and mundanity on this most basic of mobility functions. It even becomes pejorative; pedestrian is used as a synonym for dull. So ordinary that it becomes unconsidered, invisible.

> Try to map all the relations that go to make up one instant, one occasion: within your body, between body and world, mind and body, object and object – all the various 'machinic' combinations producing experience. You will have to consider subatomic, atomic and molecular forces with their general disregard for what we view as discreet bodies. You will want to account for the way the texture

and gradient of the terrain shapes movement, rhythm and posture; how sensory perception, vision, hearing and touch and so on begin to ready the body for the next step; how the force of physical habits and body memory shape patterns of movement in the moment. Also present will be all the events of relation that have gone into making each tree, stone, person and sound you are interacting with, affecting your body more or less forcefully. Then there are the mental forces – 'inextricably intertwined' with the physical (Whitehead 1978; 325) – memories, anticipations, evaluations, random associations made and forgotten, affects that will subtly or bluntly alter you, the myriad mental processes that sit behind conscious perception, yet nevertheless shape and reshape your body. (Goodman 2018: 11–12)

Goodman's beautiful and poetic dive into the possibilities that the very simple, basic act of walking opens up invites us to imagine walking as a set of connections that fundamentally place us in the universe as bodies: as moving bodies for whom the earth itself is not a terrain to be trodden but an integral part of our moving interactions.

To walk is to be-in-the-world. Perhaps everything starts with crawling, and for some, mobility impairments mean that a wheelchair is a necessary means to this primary activity. For the majority of most people's lives, walking is the first and last act of every day's mobility. The second of the two quotations cited above makes it clear that what is covered in the generic 'walking' is all movement, whatever assistance, aids or prostheses are required or engaged, that enables us to move forward at an ordinary, walking pace. This is way I want to use the term, as an inclusive not an exclusive marker of activity. Within our own living spaces, we walk around between functions necessary to maintain life: from beds to bathrooms to cooking spaces. Journeying begins when and if we step outside. Immediately on crossing the threshold we sense the world beyond. Our capacities to perceive, and to give interpretation and meaning to those perceptions, are engaged. How light or dark it is, the temperature, weather, humidity, all those environmental cues that confront us, however invisibly or unconsciously, with a set of indicators that there is a word beyond us, not in our control. We sense, we interpret, we perceive. We may choose to ignore, we may not know how to react appropriately, but the capacity is there even if only latent.

These observations become mundane, to the extent that they rarely come into conscious reckoning except when we are surprised by unexpected extremes or sudden shifts. The passing of seasons may make an impression but often only at moments of transition when the colour of the landscape changes in spring and autumn, a process more marked the further from the equator one is. In urban landscapes, trees are an essential marker of this annual cycle. Every location has its subtle signs, recognizable and interpretable only through regular exposure.

If our walk is minimal, for example, only to get into the car, then to a certain extent we can ignore having made clothing choices that might not bear sustained contact with outdoors. Depending on the degree of sophistication (and reliability) car interiors are relatively controllable environments. Public transport less so, and one also has to be suitably dressed for the walk to the station or halt and to wait for the service. Outdoor bus and tram halts, with minimal or no shelters, confront us with the sensory world, but not one that entails moving through it for the moment. So let us get back to walking.

How long is the walk going to be? Journeys to work, to education, to public transport services, to shops and to social engagements are regular, repeated occurrences. These are our everyday journeys. Our selection of mode depends on a series of evaluations. Distance, time and energy requirements compete with an assessment of our desired exposure to the elements and available modes. Everyday walking and cycling speeds are relatively constant.[1] At my walking pace, a kilometre will take somewhere between ten and eleven minutes. Cycling, I take a little over three minutes for the same distance, less on the journey home which has a lot more downhill. For the 4 km journey from my apartment to the university where I am writing this, for example, that's about half an hour difference if I walk or cycle. That's also about 5,000 steps each way. The bus is part way between the two. Being in walking distance for primary everyday journeys is perceived by some as a privilege. Yet those who for whatever reason cannot drive are always forced to seek proximity or efficient public transport routes between housing and employment. A dependence on not-driving obligates certain wider life choices that produce what others call mobility privilege.

Everyday travel, although it can be instrumentalized to provide specific benefits as 'exercise' or as a means to ensure well-being, cannot be reduced to function. As Frederic Gros reminds us in his philosophical meditation on walking:

Walking is not a sport. Sport is a matter of techniques and rules, scores and competition, necessitating lengthy training: knowing the postures, learning the right movements. ...

---

[1] Extra exertion can produce higher speeds, running or riding fast, and these may be occasionally required to meet deadline or transport connections, but for general purposes I am considering as fundamental the basic movements that do not unduly stress the body.

> Walking is not a sport. Putting one foot in front of the other is child's play. (Gros 2023: 1–2)

Walking, skipping, dancing, running: to watch the remarkably non-linear movement of children alerts us to the potential richness of simple, short journeys as ways of encountering the world around us (Kahn et al. 2021). Adult leisure activities similarly point to the potential of different ways of being attuned to the spaces around. Parkour, the creative and athletic traverse of urban environments in a manner that is half athleticism, half dance, hardly constitutes an everyday way of moving through the city, but it vividly demonstrates the potential of the built environment to be seen and interpreted differently (Loo and Bunnell 2018). It graphically illustrates how important it is to understand how we assess and react to the spaces around us as spaces of movement, potential movement and constriction (Kidder 2012). Hill walking and climbing require constant conscious assessment of the potential of the terrain faced, and a balancing of possibility with a knowledge of one's own physical capabilities, skills and endurance. Far less extreme, any walk through the city or anywhere else requires a parallel assessment of the capacities of that space, the presence of other objects moving in it (persons, vehicles, animals) and of the obstructions (pavement edges, trees, street furniture, uneven surfaces) that require negotiation. As physical capacities are limited by age and infirmity, greater caution is required to cope with diminished agility and lowered endurance: a short walk may be all that is reasonable. Surfaces and textures underfoot become more crucial. Unevenness that may once have been a visual and textural delight can become a barrier to movement. The materialities embedded in infrastructures become crucial in small details (Cox and Koglin 2020). With a wheeled walking frame or trolley, even kerbs can become problematic barriers that confine one's progress or desired route.

Repetition

Travel becomes a discipline of learning not through intense study but through repetition; familiarity permits recognition of nuance. Repeated journeying, even if only over a relatively short period of time, brings familiarity with a route. On the same daily journey, I often see the same people who I come to recognize. For example, in a commute that I undertook daily for over a decade, I was always intrigued by the slowly changing roster of people, who I would see both morning and afternoon as we crossed paths, always going in the opposite direction. We smile and acknowledge each other's presence, though remaining strangers. Nevertheless, they become part of this journey, their presence a reassurance, their occasional absence a concern.

Becoming aware of the world around, learning to care for one's surroundings, requires more than occasional observation. The boring mundanity of journeys made regularly, to work, to the shops, to education, to town from the suburbs, over the same route, through the same spaces, is what allows us to recognize how the world changes. It sensitizes us to the seasons, to year-on-year changes to weather patterns. Without regular exposure the pleasure of an occasional event remains just that, an isolated experience. Perhaps memorable, but as easily forgotten. Repetitive activity forms a narrative, produces a sense of expected and unexpected. The more familiar I become, the easier it is to spot sudden changes. But some changes are harder to spot than others. On one route I have used for years, I become so familiar with some features that I stop noticing. Only when being away for a month and then returning do alterations become visible.

Consequences of climate destabilization now become part of the experience of everyday walking and cycling. One notices longer periods of heavier rainfall, more intense periods of heat. The effects of climate change on rainfall patterns are measurable in increased volume and intensity of rainfall. More intense rain requires surface drainage. Systems established decades ago are no longer sufficiently resilient, incapable of dealing with run-off. Standing water and puddles increase, a hazard and difficulty for both walker and rider. Because of the increased regularity of flooding on my route into town, I have to take the bus more often than I did fifteen years ago. Now there are days when even the bus can't get through.

The sensory journey: Perception and care

Walking and cycling demand exposure to the elements. This involves our plastic sense of aesthetics, one of the modes of mobile perception (see Box 4.1). While we are sensing beings, the environments we encounter are not fixed, 'natural' phenomena. We constantly travel through environments created by human intervention. Contours, buildings, reflected heat, the shade of trees, the winds created by tall buildings all contribute to the multi-sensory walking journey. We use clothing to mediate temperature. Skills have to be learned to assess what the appropriate layers might be from what is available. Temperature control, responding to sunlight, breezes and the physical work required by the travelscape, becomes important. Steps and slopes require effort to conquer gravity. We sweat, we get chilled and take action to avoid extremes. We walk, but in everyday travel we rarely walk constantly for the hours that we might spend commuting by train or by car. Breaks, interruptions and changes are used to reduce fatigue.

As we build spaces for everyday walking, malls and shopping centres incorporate mechanical devices, escalators and elevators (lifts), to nullify the effect of slopes and stairs over multi-levels. Both are required to provide access for wheelchair users. Travellators speed up walking in airports. All are valuable mobility devices but all offshore the energy demand of the cityscape on the pedestrian. They take the energy cost from the traveller and place it on the electricity grid that powers the city functions.

For walkers, devices and elements as basic as paving and street furniture ease access or corral pedestrians into particular patterns of action. All transport infrastructures, from trails and pavements to rails to motorways, are an investment of materials, energy and finance: capital costs for construction and running costs for maintenance. The quality and quantity of these investments demonstrate the valuation of travel modes by the state or private authorities tasked with their provisions. Citizen demands, financial and ideological factors in governing authorities and, increasingly, recognition of the impact of travel on climate change all shape what is provided and for whom. Travel infrastructures, their physical spaces, design and routing, determine both what is encountered and what is not seen and felt in a journey. Different surface materials can differentiate spaces and uses. Not all routes are designed for maximum ease of use. Heritage and distinctiveness can also dictate choices (e.g. the use of cobbles or other textured surfaces in city centres). Care needs to be taken that the surface finishes do not discriminate against users with impaired walking, but this need not result in uniformity.

We all too easily think of walking as a uniform practice, but again, reflecting on the different purposes of everyday journeys we should also note the differences of velocity according to needs. These are most profound in spaces of intersection with public transport. Simon Cook's fascinating study *Rushing, Dashing Scrambling* (2017) examines how the railway station itself creates what he calls 'emergency' or 'reluctant' runners as people scramble not to miss services in the midst of spaces designed primarily for waiting, for non-movement. These contrasts and contradictions though forcefully highlighted in this specific context are to a lesser extent constant in all spaces of mobility interaction. The very human negotiation of space, the need to take care not only of oneself and one's own movement but also of others are constant themes of pedestrian spaces. Paths of movement weave in and out of more static elements, both people and street furniture.

Each journey is also a soundscape, affected by its routing. What does any environment of travel sound like? The sounds of walking are not just ambient, those produced by and reflected off the buildings or the landscape around us but those produced by footsteps themselves, engagement between shoe and surface. Different shoes, different surfaces, different sounds and feel. Other walkers around us create a range of walking sounds and other noises. In addition to conversation, the sounds of headphones and all the ambient sounds of human social life create a general hum. Even in low human population density areas, where the sounds of birdlife and weather might predominate, one is rarely beyond a further background tinnitus of motor vehicle noise.

The advantage of walking is that it is so much easier to stop and pay attention to an unfamiliar sound. My outdoor listening is fascinated by birdcalls, especially birdsong. With the help of an app, I can identify these, even in the middle of town. Similarly, I can learn to distinguish different trees and plants, deliberately training my curiosity to engage with the world. Walking doesn't take every element of attention, so I, like many others, often walk phone in hand, checking things as I go, whether they be objects of my immediate surrounding, my social networks or the web of political power plays making decisions that will ultimately affect this world around me.

We also mediate our journeying with personal soundscapes. Earbuds and headphones serve multiple purposes. They may mask noise we do not want to hear. They may allow a journey to be an occasion to continue conversations, whether for work or social life, catching up with friends and family. Sound can be creatively used to recreate and reinterpret spaces (Bull 2000; Jungnickel and Aldred 2014). Listening to voice and music need not be a way of separating us from the experience of the other, but a means to augment that encounter. I may choose music to suit my own mood, but sometimes, to deal with the monotony of the same journey taken every day, I play games with sound, selecting a style of music to see how the journey feels different when given a different soundtrack. Folksong or psytrance? I notice from the records of journeys made for this book how higher music tempos subtly speed up my walking: the march gained its name for a reason. These ways of dealing with sound in movement are not necessarily confined to walking, and in thinking about the sensory scapes of other modes of travel we can make similar reflections.

As we walk, what do we smell? Animal and human odours pervade our senses as we move close to them. Breath and sweat are a reminder that each of us is a microbacterial system. Our 'leaky' bodies are porous, not solidly bounded and contained (Goodley and Runswick-Cole 2013). Perfumes and deodorants are used to disguise and to mask our own bodily odours, and in turn contribute their own layers to an olfactory journey of encounters in every space we walk. The smells of asphalt and cement, heightened by the effects of warming sunlight. The smells of smoke and combustion, of manufacture and industry, fresh cut and seasoned timber for construction, of old wood and rot from tree felling. A range of odours associated with the constant presence of food preparation, domestic and commercial: citrus fruit and coffee, spices and herbs, roasting meats and frying doughnuts. Some scents are tied specifically to the rhythms of the day and the seasons, some ubiquitous. Organic smells of flowers and foliage that change even within the times of day. The specific yeasts of baking and brewing rhythmically pervading townscapes. The acrid smells of rot and waste, urine and faeces that change with weather and temperature. As we move, wherever our location, we often subliminally recognize the smells of our location. We remember how particular locations can be dominated by specific smells, shaped by the weather, heightened in the warmth and dulled in the cold. Our subjective reactions connect with our own histories and past encounters. We do more than receive this information as data, we interpret and give value to them.

Walking engages all these senses, these modes of perception. None dominates, none is supressed. Perhaps this is not surprising as we have been honing our senses on the basis of being ambulatory as long as we have been humans. One thing to note is that walking rarely overwhelms our senses, our mental processing capacity is easily able to cope and allows plenty of time for contemplation and reflection, the mental processing of cognitive aesthetics (Table 4.1). One aspect of this processing capacity and space for reflection is precisely that it allows for a heightened aesthetic sense. Nothing disappears instantly. Sights, sounds and smells that we find unpleasant are not fleetingly passed by. We can choose to turn our attention away but passing by takes time. Walking presents us with a heightened capacity to be disturbed. To be affected, to be upset is itself a reflection of our ordinary propensity to care for our surroundings. To not-care about the condition of the spaces we walk through is something that has to be learned, we have to learn to be unaffected, not to care.

We touch the landscape, and the landscape touches us. 'Walkers envelop the landscape and are enveloped by it, an overlapping of folds', as Gros (2023: 95) expresses it. Stressing the repeated nature of walking he continues seeking an appropriate metaphor for this interaction.

> The right image for conveying this repetition is the caress. Caressing lies something between two extremes: gripping it and brushing lightly against it. The latter almost amounts to disdain: one does nothing more than signal one's presence, or else one's departure. It is a form of detachment. Gripping something is always about power, domination, dominion and possession. Both approaches are of a fleeting nature. (Gros 2023: 95–6)

The caress is also a physical expression of care.

Exclusive space and the commons

Processes of enclosure that destroy the commons of walking spaces can be subtle and invisible. Leslie Kern's *Feminist City* (2019) sharply depicts the gendered impacts of urban infrastructures; even when accommodating foot traffic, they are frequently unsuitable for pushchairs and pushed wheelchairs, for prams, buggies, walkers, trolleys and hand carts. All these devices make it possible to walk with children or those with impairments, to shift loads associated with shopping and other functions of the reproduction of everyday life. Using any of these devices opens possibilities of interaction. All increase the possibilities of walking. But their use is frequently overlooked in the detail of urban construction. Off camber surfaces that make balance difficult, kerbs and steps that limit access, uneven surfaces that make progress difficult – all are far from uncommon. Worse still is the elimination of walking spaces, destroying any possibility of meaningful pedestrian traffic. The relative funding and investment of authorities tasked with mobility provision can tell us much about how human scale travellers are constructed as citizens: whether they are valued, and their movement facilitated, or rendered second class to motorized traffic. Unmaintained areas and frequently disrupted areas for walking often contrast with the regularity of smoothly asphalted roads.

Spatial elements are most noticeable when we consider how non-motorists travel the city. The first historic innovation was the segregation of walkers through the introduction of pavements/sidewalks. The North American terminology is more descriptive here, the walker is moved to the side. Road space that once was a commons, shared among a multitude of users and uses, was separated into zones of segregation, walkers here, moving traffic down the centre (Longhurst 2015).

The road was redefined as a space of traffic flow. Canalizing rivers controls and speeds the flow. Water management concepts were transferred directly to the language of traffic planning using liquid metaphors to conceptualize traffic flow and identify impediments to smooth progress (Verkade and te Brömmelstroet, 2022). In these ideals, none should stop nor deviate from onward movement, only separating from this primary flow at the last minute as destination is achieved. No space for play, for pausing distracted by something or someone seen or heard. Perhaps a friend, birdsong or an interesting view; perhaps the shape and texture of a tree that you pass by. These are all null in the insistence on unimpeded traffic flow. Travel ceases to be a means of encounter with the world but part of the urban machinery, delivering persons to destinations as efficiently as possible. In societies already shaped by distinctions of class, race and gender, restrictions on use and access are inevitably read through those same lenses of privilege and distinction on the one hand and of subordinate status and lower worth on the other.

Separate spaces make sense when carved out by the marginalized for their own self-determination. When defined by those rendered subordinate in regimes of dominance, inequality and oppression, they can provide opportunities safe and secluded from otherwise dominating forces. Separate spaces allow the possibility of imagining conditions without the presence of the oppressor. Conversely, when separate spaces are allocated by the dominant party, such locations are spaces of segregation, constantly at risk of ghettoization. These considerations of place give us an insight into the issues facing spaces for walking, wheeling and cycling for transport. Whose power, whose priority do they reflect? What relative space is given to different modes and numbers of travellers?

As we identify constriction of pedestrian activity to the margins of prioritized motor vehicle traffic, for example, permitting crossing from one side of street to another only at specified locations, the difficulties put in place of a variety of wheeled pedestrian traffic become more visible. Into this category fall a range of types, from wheelchairs to scooters, sketes and skateboards, all of which offer ways to move around, but all of which are constricted by the design of streets focussed on roadways and separate pavements. The tragedy of all this is that walking is fundamental, it is the source of maximum sociality, it engages us with the world around, built and unbuilt environments. Walking and engagement with the physical world is widely recognized as key for well-being, physical and mental. In the midst of pandemic lockdowns, it was preserved as absolutely necessary. Yet even under these measures it was still primarily construed as a leisure activity, not as a basic means of personal travel. Necessary perhaps for the maintenance of social reproduction, preserving the mental health and well-being needs of workers otherwise confined to home but distinct from the 'real' mobility needs attached to work and economic accumulation.

Walking, wheeling and cycling in a motoring world

Motoring creates the worlds of human scale travel as we experience them today. From the 1950s, European urban areas were replanned and rebuilt to facilitate the growth of mass motoring. Only twenty years later, disillusion with this model was to set in (Gunn 2018). For many cities, the transformations were much harder to undo than they had been to put in place; historic buildings and spaces once removed cannot just simply be put back (Feddes and De Lange 2019). Reaction, particularly in European cities from the 1970s, was to pedestrianize surviving historic town centres and to create new car-free developments. These measures can be interpreted in contrasting ways.

Positively, pedestrianization can be understood as recognition and reaffirmation of the centrality of walking in spaces that had become saturated with motor traffic, both in motion and parked. Historic urban development (prior to the twentieth century) had taken place without cars and so restricting cars from spaces they are ill-fitted for makes logical sense. However, another reading of recent move to pedestrianization is possible. Preservationist tactics can actually be a way to promote more car travel and car dependence. Pedestrian enclaves become stranded in masses of ring roads and access routes, inaccessible without motor travel. This intention was clearly signalled, for example, in the Buchanan report in the UK in the 1960s in which two options were outlined, either complete rebuilding of cities around the car or preserved pedestrian areas with increased traffic flow around (Gunn 2011). Pedestrian activity was conceived only as ambling, as leisure to take in the historic past and engage in casual engagement with shopping. It is an attitude that, although it had largely lost credibility by the late 1970s, still echoes today.

Organic interrelations of different parts of the city, all accessible to the non-motoring citizen, were brushed aside in favour of zoned activity (whether formally recognized or not) and greater dependence on car travel between the various zones of activity. Or, for the visibly progressive administration, the construction of mass transit systems along these identified corridors offered an alternative. Concentrating functions necessary for survival in one area and hosing in another with work and education in a third creates longer distance travel dependent citizens, idealized as car travellers. The preservation of historic enclaves makes the reconstruction of spaces beyond the urban centre easier and more justifiable. Transit beyond the pedestrian zone without a car becomes increasingly difficult. As routes to the city centre areas are redesigned for higher motor traffic flows, to walk or cycle into town becomes more difficult and more unpleasant among the traffic.

Cars are space hungry. Within the walking spaces of most cities more than a century old, adaptation to their requirements impacts heavily on pedestrian spaces and pedestrian experiences. Cars necessitate the allocation of significant amounts of land space to their storage, since they are static most of the time. Geology and finance may permit construction of underground parking which puts cars out of site but not out of central importance in city planning. The cheaper option is the multi-storey carpark. Inserted into city centres, both options equally still require access and egress routes, bringing motor traffic into the heart of the town. Routes between towns and their surroundings become increasingly dominated by motor vehicles.

Cars are intimidating companions for pedestrians in shared space; even more so today when average weights and sizes of the car are rapidly increasing. Even when stationary, the effects are felt. Car parks are rarely pleasant areas in which to stroll. However, expectation of driving allows towns and cities to sprawl, occupying more and more physical territory, and as distances increase, these spaces become less and less accessible to the pedestrian (Kern 2019).

In motion, cars pose an ever-present threat. The moving mass becomes more lethal the faster it moves. The aim of traffic planning for years has been to ensure the increased flow of traffic and maintenance of speeds, usually by the removal of obstacles such as pedestrians. Consequently, all the complexities of mixed-use spaces that make them desirable sites to walk and to encounter in a multisensory world are suppressed.

Cars also dominate the sounds and smells of the city experienced by the walker. Drivers and passengers are increasingly isolated by air-conditioning and acoustic suppression, coupled with in-car sound systems (Bull 2004). The internal and external acoustics of vehicle travel are remarkably different, the soundscape of traffic engine noise, mitigated only by exhaust silencing and the noise of tyres on asphalt or concrete provides a constant background soundtrack to most city life. Combustion effluents and tyre and brake degradation are not just accidental or incidental side effect. They are a fundamental and necessary aspect of vehicle design. Only the first cluster of these products are removed in changing from internal combustion to electric battery power. Tyres abrade in contact with surfaces, and brake pads wear on discs, all creating an invisible miasma of micro-particulates, toxic and carcinogenic (Cox 2010). In shared travel spaces, the air breathed by pedestrians is formed by motor traffic.

Perhaps the most profound effect of the ubiquity of car traffic for walkers, wheelers and cyclists is on our political imagination. Motor travel's omnipresence occupies social, mental and physical spaces, all three axes of resonance (see Chapter 3). To redefine and redevelop more sustainable urban life, car-free spaces have long been one of the major focusses of high-profile advocacy (Topp and Pharoah 1994; Nieuwenhuijsen and Khreis 2016). Yet without examples to see and experience, it is hard to imagine a city without cars. Even those cities that are internationally lauded for cycling and walking, such as Copenhagen and Amsterdam, are still dominated by motor vehicular traffic. Even when in a minority of journeys, they claim and are given the majority of travel space.

Wheeling

Free-rolling wheeling devices aid everyday movement. Wheelchairs may be the most obvious, but all sorts of scooting devices (from blades to skateboards) also serve the same function, allowing travellers to move by gliding. Others, from pushchairs to handcarts, pushed or pulled, allow travellers to propel those unable to propel themselves, or to carry goods. Travel on wheels changes the relation of the traveller to gravity. Movement is no longer one step at a time, it no longer requires the constant activity of walking. Movement initiated continues, only slowed or impeded by gravity and forces of resistance. Efforts made to move along are retarded only by the rolling resistance of wheels on whatever paving surface is available and by the resistance of air. Continued progress may require continued input, each impulse from hands or feet followed by a rolling forward. Given suitable conditions, wheels may increase the speed over that of unassisted walking, permitting greater distances to be travelled. They intensify the feeling of movement. Though not necessarily currently common for everyday travel use, all could potentially be.

Scooting and wheeling can be remarkably efficient. But topography and travel surface become all important. Walkers know the extra work that going uphill requires. Wheels change one's relation to gravity. Uphill, extra energy is required to propel both the traveller and vehicle, gravity retards progress. Without propulsion, no movement occurs. Any form of indirectly powered travel (wheeled vehicles that roll rather than are propelled by drive systems) risks surrender to gravity and even backwards movement if not adequately braked. The payoff for all uphill wheeling comes in the other direction. Downhill acceleration is free speed. Energy banked in the ascents becomes available to roll downwards. All, however, rely on infrastructures. Without smooth surfaces, wheeled travel becomes difficult. Kerbs and drops can prove problem barriers, especially to wheelchairs. As long as there is an uninterrupted surface, the glide can continue. Gravity-assisted, speed picks up until it becomes uncomfortable or difficult to negotiate with other travellers. Wheels allow faster movement and the sensation of gliding, those moments between propulsive efforts, a new sensation unavailable on foot. All the encounters of walking are there, but in the greater volume of perception, the more rapid consumption of distance, finer-grained interactions are lost. There can be no instantaneous pause or redirection as there can be for the pedestrian. Speed increases intensity, decreases sensitivity.

Wheeled travel is especially vulnerable to processes of enclosure. Physical barriers easily impede or make journeys entirely impossible. Non-continuous routes shut out users who cannot just dismount and carry their wheelchairs over even small barriers. Gravelled surfaces that may suffice for walking are rarely usable by those dependent on wheeled travel in ways that are often only recognizable when one tries to navigate. While the human scale of speed is maintained, wheeled travel does not generally preclude shared space with walking; however, the speed differential between a pedestrian amble at 5 km/h and the 25 km/h plus of a brisk cycle journey is considerable and may feel intimidating if there is insufficient space or if the purpose of a travel space is unclear (Delaney et al. 2017).

Being-in-the-world as a cyclist

Cycling is simply a specific form of self-propelled wheeling. Propulsion is independent of body contact with the ground and, hand or foot cranked, can be constant. The modes of perception engaged in cycling are similar to those of walking with notable exceptions in terms of kinetics and cognition. Muscle movement is more constrained and regulated, movement through space is speeded up and therefore sensations intensified, and more concentration is required. Balance, on two wheels at least, is a function of movement.

The cycling body is held in space by contact points with the machine it is riding. With fixed points of contact, saddle, pedal, handlebars, the body's actual movements are fairly limited – which means that if the fitting and posture are badly set up one can never get comfortable. The movement of legs is rotational so there is no impact from the fall of the foot onto the ground, only the transmission of surface unevenness. It is a little less easy to read fatigue cycling than walking, easier to overdo the effort and put more work in than when I walk. This can make journeying faster, in ways not possible when walking, but it has its price. There is also a thrill in moving fast, which uncertainty moves across into fear. There is no need to put in more effort cycling than walking, but the temptation is always there, partly because of the lack of impact. Cycling in close proximity to faster moving motor traffic, the temptation to speed up (if one can) is heightened, so as to decrease the speed differential and thus increase the sense of security. The speed of the faster and more powerful determines the feel of the situation.

The encounter with nature, the visceral and physical meeting of the body with the atmospheres, and materials through which we travel cannot be fully socially mediated. Its meanings and import are socially constructed, our encounters defined through culture, knowledge and experience, but the physical process of encounter is a thing of the body. We may use digital media of a variety of forms to locate ourselves, find routes and points in space, communicate our images and impressions, and have our visions and comprehensions formed by the communicated information, but the physical movement, the body memory of muscle, stretch and compression, tension and relaxation, breath inhaled and exhaled, and heartbeats raised and slowed, remains matters of bodily concern and reality. The sensory experiences of everyday cycling are close to those of walking, with the difference that the heightened kinetic perceptions demand more concentration and focus of the cognitive senses. The plastic senses of physical touch are no longer direct with the ground but mediated by tyres and the different absorbencies of bike design and materials.

Gros insisted that walking is not a sport, nor is cycling for everyday travel a sport. It is not about times, speeds or performance. It is not a matter of bodily power and the triumph of the athletic. Plenty of forms of gamification try to commodify or justify cycle travel as performance enhancers and training programmes, just as step counters do for the everyday pedestrian.[2] But this is to miss the point. In thinking about riding for everyday journeying, weakness matters, vulnerabilities matter. These activities are not described in dialogues

---

[2] In preparing to write this book journeys were mapped and recorded. The commercially available devices used continually notified me of ways to 'improve my fitness', 'create a training plan'. Hard to resist, they attest both to the increasing commodification of normal bodily function and to make the everyday journey remarkable, not just a normal mundane function.

that describe the conquest of distance, or of the attainment of speed or body-power through record journey times. Those are the measurements of athletics, of training and fitness regimes. Regimes, the word emphasizes the imperial control and domination, the power of rule over one's body as a separate object. They may have their place in body discipline. Outside the fitness concerns of a small self-selected and self-identified few, they do not relate to mundane life. Sport cycling exists through its delineation from the commons. Sport cycling is that which, despite the advocates of 'sport for all', remains meaningful only if undertaken through the application of levels of disciplines not present in everyday non-sporting life. One may run or jog for pleasure without identifying as an elite athlete with competitive inspiration. One may break into dance in response to music without it being a performance to observe correct movement. Even the organized activities of amateur cycling or athletic clubs or networks and their social runs are far from the world of elite and professional competition. Nor, despite the claims of cycle sport bodies who might claim it to be so, is competitive sport a logical outcome or progression from everyday travel (Cox 2007). Cardiovascular health developed through regular walking and cycling in a sedentary society is important, but there is a significant gap between everyday healthiness and well-being (and the activity required for it) and athletic competition (and the training required for it). This is not to decry the value and possibilities inherent in trained, honed and disciplined bodies. The point to be made here is that the encounter I am interested in is not constrained to the experiential horizons of an elite few. It is about our everyday mundane activities, the choices we take or fail to take, and the uses we make of those activities.

There is an undeniable thrill arising from the ability to move faster than one can unaided, of coasting down a hill and feeling the air against one's skin in a way that is only otherwise possible standing outside on a very windy day. There is the satisfaction of reaching the top of an upslope, whether having pushed the bike or ridden up: the promise of a downhill reward on the return journey. Unless the terrain is absolutely flat, these are experiences regularly encountered in everyday riding.

For cycle journeys, only in actual riding do the qualities of the ridden journey become apparent, hence the importance of the repeated trip. This allows reflection on the process of the journey, not its novelty. The body remains physical: sweat, tiredness, exhilaration or just air on the face. Light, dark, twilight, rain, winds: elemental forces engaged with, whether journeying through built-up streets or ex-urban areas of agriculture or forestry. Restressing this visceral encounter, emphasis on bodily action neither decries nor seeks retreat from the digital world. It is to note that one common attribute of digitalization and of gamification is to restrict awareness of the modes of perception described in Chapter 4. The kineasthetic and sensory experiences of the more-than-human world cannot be grasped without some grounding in the physical. They require acceptance that not all physical sensation can be captured as data. Perception is more than numbers. In digital and electronically mediated communication the visual and auditory modes of perception become all important, touch is reduced to a fingertip sensation. Of course, we can be moved and emotionally affected by this limited exposure: for almost all of us our appreciation of the arts is not through performance but as spectators. However, the experience of a body moving through space is akin to the complexity of synaesthesia. Multiple sensory engagements are simultaneously linked and thus the emotional response to stimuli is not limited to a mental cognition but felt through other modes of perception including, therefore, the creative response. As those who walk, wheel and cycle through the world, we are performers and creators, the artists of travel. As such we need to recognize the creative potential not only of the 'good' or 'successful' travel experience, but to accept discomfort and in vulnerability as meaningful modes through which to nurture and develop responsibility and care-fulness (Sliwinska 2019).

The cyclist, as any wheeled traveller under their own power, is vulnerable to the elements, to tiredness and fatigue. Rain and wind can delay or enforce extra preparation. One is never immune from the environment. To return to the central themes of Chapter 3, cycling undermines the apparent control of air-conditioned, alienated travel. It challenges the timetabled predictability of public transport services. It allows for autonomy but highlights the dependencies we have as humans on the world around. Mark Augé (2014) makes the point that the plot of a novel or of a film is already set. The journey, he suggests, while it may have a destination, retains the unpredictable, the unfinished. Though the endpoint is already set, if we imagine the journey as a story, a text, its reading remains unpredictable, even if apparently tediously familiar through repetition and overuse. There is always the possibility of intrusion by forces beyond the control of the individual. Good things and bad. Weather, punctures, wind, people, animals and birds. Combinations of light and shade, and qualities of light changing through the year. Each ride reshapes the unfolding of the travelscape through which it passes. Each distancing from these forces by the technologies of travel makes us further removed from their impact. Development of powered, enclosed travel has increasingly focussed on the predictability of the journey experience, non-engagement with forces of chance, the invulnerability to disruption or disturbance. While we walk and ride we can plot and trace our courses on a map but never entirely control the process.

Technologies of cycle travel

The kineasthetics of everyday cycle travel are further complicated by the intimacy of the body's interaction with the machineries of cycling. Different styles of bike, different gearing ratios and ranges provide different possibilities of travel experience, even if in only short rides. The regularity of repetition provides familiarity, with the idiosyncrasies of any particular riding characteristics soon being forgotten. But how do we relate in a wider sense with the technologies of everyday travel?

Augé (2014 Kindle Locations 771–3) argues that our contemporary situation may be characterized as one in which 'we are no longer capable of addressing our relation to space and time – the basis of the symbolic activity that defines the essence of man and humanity – except by means of artefacts elaborated by industry and available of the market'. Such a deeply pessimistic view is problematic. While there is considerable verity in his observation, it also implicitly assumes that there could be some artefacts or technologies that exist outside production and commerce. All material goods including the necessary elements for human scale travel – shoes, clothing, bikes – are artefacts 'elaborated by industry' but it is their use, not their artefactual existence that allows us to explore and address our relation to space and time. If the central point of his argument is that we lost our ability to locate ourselves in space and time as soon as these basics were commercially produced, bought and sold, there can be no way back from alienation; this alienation is inherent in humans as creative beings, people that invent things, make them available through organized production and exchange them. Are we to return to an exclusively handmade and nonmarket economy or is it possible that we could order relations of production to overcome alienation? The part of me that aspires to create conditions sympathetic to resonance, the overcoming of alienation, certainly hopes so.

Machineries of travel are sold as products with different designations of styles but their potential and possibility are only discovered in use. Subtle and small changes in design do provide very different experiences. Users adapt machines to suit their own needs, to make the most of the specificities of regular journeys. Histories of cycling developments are dominated by user innovation. Racks and baskets enable goods to be carried in various ways. States of maintenance and repair also make a difference (Abord de Chatillon 2022). For example, relatively small changes in tyre pressure can effect a considerable difference to how a cycle rolls and how it feels as you turn a corner or cross uneven terrain. How a cycle rides can be as much to do to its state of repair as to any intrinsic properties of the design. How it is elaborated by industry may be far from the way it ends up in use as an everyday object.

Even if bicycles are produced as commodities, cycling as an activity remains difficult to commodify. Perhaps a more useful approach is to consider Augé's statement as a critique of capital accumulation. A more fruitful line of discussion would then be to distinguish between two contrasting types of travel technology. First are those that conform us to processes and demands outside of our autonomous action and require us to engage in and maintain processes of accumulation. Second, there are those that assist our liberation from dependence. Here we are returned to a reflection on critiques of technology that recalls Illich (1973; 1974). Illich was a major advocate of the bicycle as a convivial tool, one that remains in the service and control of its user, rather than as a technology that impels its users into a particular way of action in its own service. If it should be that the second group of (convivial) technologies of movement also allows us greater possibility of resonance, then they have a double value. Reading Augé this way provides another means to challenge the myth of freedom attributed to motoring.

Travel technologies and alienated labour

All technologies are made and produced. The bicycle is a good example. Its history is bound up with the expansion of global markets under imperial regimes. Cycles in their modern form (the safety bicycle) owe their existence to a global web of connections. Karl Drais's running machine of 1817 used only wood iron and leather – material resources locally available, as did the steam engines that were being experimentally harnessed in the same period to provide motive power. Michaux's bicycle of the 1860s was innovative in its use of a leg-driven crank drive to turn the front wheel, but it was still forged from locally available metals. The big shift to widely usable cycles depended on access to rubber to make cushion tyres, first solid and then pneumatic, indispensable for absorbing the shock of any less than perfectly smooth surface. By the time that we get to the pneumatic tyred safety bicycle, we have a machine that only exists as a product of the globalized empires and their grasp of resources. The bicycle is a material product of imperial trade. This is not to make anyone feel or appear guilty but to illustrate our inescapably entangled realities. We are where we are. What we have power over is how we respond to that past, to those entanglements. We cannot, as Bruno Latour made vividly clear in his writings, escape from those entanglements (Krarup and Blok 2011). Denialism is appealing but reality will eventually catch up.

The bicycle is a machine born of modernity yet tied to the archaic. Reliant on the body it appears as the last mechanical mobility, obsolete almost as soon as it merged according to the logic of a linear evolutionary narrative of motorization (Cox and Van De Walle 2007). This narrative of motorized mobility follows a logical sequence of harnessing the power of others for mobility. Harnessing horses demonstrated the domination of human over animal, the sedan chair demonstrated the domination of one class over another. Carbon exploitation is morally valuable in this calculus. It is more humane than the harness of animal energies, or of other humans. Ironically, however, what the harnessing of carbon power does is ultimately not to end dependence on human and animal exploitation, but simply to offshore and obscure continued reliance upon human bodies and labour. Automobility requires the construction of an entire class of labourers bound into a vortex of commodity production and exchange. The perceptual boundaries of human scale mobilities are a way of reconnecting with the realities of space and time as parameters of our existence.

Elsewhere, Augé (loc501) notes the distinction between the 'sociological reality' of a place, for example, in its markets, roads, farms, towns, dialects, and 'the force of its landscapes, its sounds and smells'. What I have here called human scale travel, and which often coincides with that labelled slow travel (Popan 2019), provides a way to reconcile these divided realities. Being open to the elements and open to the multi-fold perceptions of quiet movement under one's own motive power allows a far greater degree of integration of these two perspectives than the aggressive transit provided by bus, let alone car movement. The latter reduces the forces of landscape to a visual spectacle. Velomobiles (cycles usually three or four wheeled, with a full streamlined body shell) present an interesting intermediary. Despite the body shell, the rider is still fully responsible for power (with or without e-assistance) and the fairing is partially open. One may be able to don a rain hood for protection, just as one might put on a raincoat, thus the fundamental connection with the elements is not broken. Conversely, the desirability of convertible (soft top) cars follows the logic of desire for encounter with elemental forces while driving.

Human-powered travel contains its own limitations and sufficiencies. In a final observation we can therefore consider technologies and practices of travel, not in their relation to production and marketing, but instead in the degree that their augmentation of movement increases the divide between the sociological realities and the force of landscapes. The importance of cycling as a means of everyday travel is that whatever its technological form, whatever the shape and capacity of the machinery involved, it still places us in direct contact with others (human and more-than-human), unshielded and at a pace where we can still recognize, acknowledge and respond to those others.

Encounters care and commoning

On the bicycle – or more properly, with-the-bicycle … we encounter not only new spatial horizons and places but also other lived bodies, with which we co-constitute place through bodily gestures that generate what could be called a kind of 'social attention.' This attention begins in the simple recognition of others when there is a mutual recognition of another in such an encounter … through friendly nods or the ring of a bell. In these encounters there is a degree of intimacy that opens up the possibility of further engagement. (Koukal 2020: 722)

The social interactions of cycling, like walking, are personal and shared. It is easy and necessary to acknowledge the sharing of travel space as the cyclists, like the walker meets other participants of journeys face to face, as one human to another. To ride successfully together as one may do in any well-frequented location requires the development of trust and the nurturing of an ability to be trusted, to take care not only of one's own self and progress but also to ensure that one is not the cause of another's misfortune.

Shared spaces for cycling and walking are frequently assumed as unproblematic in infrastructural planning. However, outside of specific, low-speed areas of shared space, these can often be difficult sources of conflict. Cycles are vehicles that have certain physical characteristics, they need space and time to accelerate and to slow down. They travel in paths that trace lines and curves without abrupt changes in direction. The distinction made between walking to get somewhere and ambling (made earlier) is more acute given the higher speed capabilities of cycling as everyday travel. It is not that pedestrians and cyclists don't or can't mix successfully, more that play and travel may have different demands on space use. What then of the commons?

Pedestrian and cyclist conflicts are largely products of the scarcity of space. When travel spaces are taken up by cars that threaten non-motorized traffic, all other activity involving movement is confined to narrow corridors. It is the bigger picture of democratic Anthropocene citizenship that needs recall. To pit two forms of mobility, both marginalized by a dominant regime of automobility, against each other is to concede power to that regime. We fall back into the assertion of the competing rights of cyclists and pedestrians at our peril.

Human scale limits as virtues

Walking and cycling are often underrated or felt as a burden. It takes bodily effort to do either. In spaces and infrastructures that construct human scale mobility as the province of the second-class citizen, it is often difficult to imagine the organization of services and socialities in ways that do not depend on long-distance and high-energy travel. In light of the need to address the current overshoot of high energy mobility beyond the boundaries that indicate the safe limits of human action, the difficulties and limitations posed by an emphasis on human-scale mobilities as primary may appear differently. The central importance of reimagining walking, wheeling and cycling as primary mobilities for the Anthropocene lies in what are often perceived as their limitations. Human scale speeds, and therefore, distances that can be travelled without taking an excessive and exclusive amount of time, highlight the necessity for decentralization and for local provisions of goods and services. It may be obvious but is often overlooked that if necessary services are beyond walking range, then they are unavailable to anyone without access to other means of travel. This increases dependencies, another case of the compulsion to move being structured into society. Conversely, planning provisions around human scale speeds decreases social exclusion based on lack of access to goods and services – particularly important in age-based discriminations currently felt by those dependent on public transport.

One of the more obvious objections to walking, wheeling and cycling in everyday mobility is that they are reliant on the unpleasant and objectionable use of one's bodily labour in order to move. Surely, the history of the civilizing process is synonymous with harnessing other forms of energy to overcome the necessity of physical work? In any conversation on active mobility, it is necessary to distinguish and to consider the relation between bodily labour and mobility labour. By bodily labour, I mean the general, physical work that we have to do in order to achieve any task. Mobility labour concerns the efforts made to accomplish specific acts of journeying. Both are complicated when read through the lens of social class.

Work can only be done if the means to do it are provided to the do-er. Marx's analysis of class defined the difference between classes through their relationship to the ownership of that means of production. The proletariat are defined through their lack of resources, they have only their bodily labour to sell for a wage. Consequently, it is easy to see how those involved in human-powered travel can be construed in class terms as lesser: reliant on bodily labour for their movement they constitute a travel proletariat.

Yet mobility labours are not quite the same. The ownership of the means of mobility are not necessarily easily quantifiable or identifiable. Those who rely on their own bodily capacities for movement are perversely liberated from control, either to timetable or to reliance on external power sources. One might even contrast the driver's dependence on petroleum as a form of captivity, while those who rely on their own motive power are liberated to go as they please. Wolfgang Sachs described this in his classic work, *For the Love of the Automobile*. 'Whereas the purchase of an automobile is a gesture of submission to the transportation machine, the purchase of a bicycle becomes a demonstration of trust in one's powers' (Sachs 1984: 200). Class is a useful lens to use in thinking about mobility futures but one might need to distinguish the very different effects of economic class (in a Marxist sense) and mobility class, defined in relation to the ownership and control over the means of mobility, including dependency on external energy sources. One might also consider the relation between paid work and the purchase costs of mobility forms, as Illich (1974) did in his oft-cited calculations of social speed. Speed of travel is calculated as distance divided by time. However, Illich sought to calculate that time factor not simply as that elapsed in journeying, but including the hours worked in wage labour to earn the money required for purchase (and maintenance, etc. if required) of the specific mode of travel used. Consequently, if one allows for all the hours one needs to work in order to meet the purchase and running price of a motor vehicle, then its social speed compares unfavourably with the social speeds of non-motorized, human scale travel.

A second area of analysis opens up by using the perspective of social class analysis to think about the distinctions between different travel purposes. Returning to the relation between bodily labour and mobility labour we see a distinction between two separate histories of travel. First there is leisure travel: travel undertaken for its own sake, not for any purpose in terms of economic or social production. While travel experiences may be deemed educational or have other measurable outcomes (e.g. in health or fitness), the initiation of leisure journeys is without a specifically utilitarian justification. This is travel as bourgeois leisure. A second category of travel might be that of (proletarian) utility: journeys that have to be made for the purposes of some other action. Commuting is perhaps the classic form of utilitarian travel. Always calculated as a time-cost, preferably minimized unless 'work' can be carried out, whether related to employment or one's own 'work' on the body as an active traveller. Time spent on travel is lost time, unproductive in a context of time scarcity, productive only if an extension of other tasks as in the much vaunted ability to work on train journeys. Yet these separated histories of leisure and utility and their respective modes of analysis of travel also profoundly overlap. They are not mutually exclusive. Though histories of social class and mobility are important, the twentieth century saw consistent challenges to the separation of the two. The histories of walking and cycling clubs explicitly founded as self-expressions of the intersection of working class and leisure mobilities demonstrate the constant desire to reappropriate travel and deny its constriction as a mode of bourgeois privilege.

We might even further complicate this intersection by thinking about the role of sensual gratification and bodily work in this equation. Can pleasure only be assigned a bourgeois value? Returning to the context of the Anthropocene can we afford to identify sensitivity to the conditions of planetary deterioration as something as a matter of bourgeois privilege? To do so would be to repeat the mistakes of separating these histories of concern and denying their mutual entanglement.

Perhaps one way to move beyond the binary options presented in this framing of the problem is to relate this more closely once again to the problem of time. Is it a commodity to be spent, understood as something surplus, or a scarce resource to be managed in a framework of scarcity? Quite clearly, the answers to this are bound up with socio-economic class, and it would then be easy to fall back, even reinforce the dichotomous framing that the previous discussion has highlighted as a problem.

The availability of time cannot be disconnected from wages and incomes and the time required for making a sufficient living. One important response is to comprehend how therefore Anthropocene mobility practices are inseparable from the arguments for basic incomes within an economic narrative of degrowth. Only the removal of time as scarcity allows for equitable active mobilities. Freed from necessitarian and ultimately proletarianized travel we can look towards the valuation of the sensory, not as a divisive bourgeois privilege but as a common birthright of human and more-than-human interaction.

Mobility, leisure, aesthetics and knowledge production

Even though the focus here is on mundane, everyday journeying the enjoyments gained through mobility remain important. They connect us to desire and motivation. To develop this discussion further, we can think about the relation between travel and leisure. Does leisure belong to the category of surplus or is it a mode of knowledge in its own right invaluable and indispensable? In a critical essay on Herbert Read, whose framework of aesthetics and perception was outlined in Chapter 4, Raymond Williams (2022) noted that Read dismissed H. G. Wells for explaining art as an aspect of leisure. Art, suggested Wells, was nothing more than 'an outlet for … surplus energy', one of a number of 'useless but quite delightful occupations'. Read (1937), in contrast, insisted on the primacy of art, a vital way of knowing and comprehending the world. Art is a mode of knowledge, its production is therefore not a matter of leisure that can be dismissed (even if only implicitly) as an exclusively bourgeois privilege. Escape from the dilemma of mobility as work versus mobility as leisure is found by refuting the assignation of leisure either to the category of an unnecessary luxury activity, nor reducing its value to the performance of utility functions. Highlighting travel as an aesthetic mode of knowledge production allows us to reassess the value of travel experiences and their basis as a way of learning.

We make a parallel analysis to Read's assessment of art in considering the role of cycling and walking as active travel. Shifting our comprehension of them away from arguments based on utility and luxury as an antithetical dyad enables us to understand the ways in which active and human speed travel functions as a mode of knowing. It has pedagogic functions, but these are not in themselves justifications. To do so would be to fall into the trap of assuming that resonance can be manufactured. To think in terms of the utility function of learning is to work within a mindset still dominated by a productivist logic in which actions and persons are justified through their commodification as means of reproduction and accumulation. Indeed, so many forms of education today are governed by this problematic productivism and accumulation-ist logic. Although I am concerned to highlight the pedagogic functions of active mobilities and to stress their value for developing the qualities necessary for Anthropocene citizenship, these are not ultimate justifications. A degrowth approach insists on the break from utilitarian approaches in its stress on the quality and fulness of life rather than the pursuit of accumulation (hence its status as a critique of capitalism).

To clarify further, we can return to Williams to employ his distinction between art as object (product) and art as practice (production). The object is very quickly commodified, exchanged and acquires its own peculiar value. The production process involved in its creation is much harder to commodify, its value remains within the ownership of the creator or performer. If we think about performance art in the same manner, then there is also an audience to consider. Performances that take place in public space and in forms that are replicable are difficult to commodify (or to re-present). Extending the performance metaphor to think about social actions and the ride or the walk as performance, we might then see the way that the craft of its production works on the producer, while the outcome of the action works on further observers. If walking and cycling produce different ways of perceiving and comprehending the world, then others in the presence of those so transformed will also have new possibilities of perceiving the world differently. Walking, wheeling and cycling do not only change the worlds of their participants but for a wider public.

A final observation using the parallel of walks and rides as performances is that they also exist in notational forms, as routes and guides that allow repeat performances by new participants and new interpretations and re-creations of prior performances. Notation extends the relationship of the performance and the performer across time. This may be thought to push a single idea beyond the obvious, but it provides an access point to help us to think about the experiential world not just as the privilege of the experiencer themselves, but in what the practices communicate to others. Applied to mobility practices, these become more obvious. What does any mode of movement say about the relationship between the mover and those in attendance? These external interactions become more and more pronounced as the power differentials between travellers and their 'others' increase, as we see in the impact of automobility.

Conclusions

Human scale mobilities, primarily those dependent on human power, but also including fully electrified travel aids that allow users parity of movement share many features in common. Walking and different forms of wheeling and cycling have distinctions and divergences. They are not always easy to combine in limited spaces, but they share much of importance. As ways of moving through the world and ways of being in it they force us into encounter with the more-than-human in ways impossible in the enclosed spaces of vehicular travel. Moreover, the encounter with other humans differs from that created by the spaces of public transport and other forms of passengering as we will see in the next chapter.

6

Passengers and drivers

Introduction

Human scale travel explored in the previous chapter was characterized primarily by its non-reliance on external power, or if added, serving as an augmentation of human input. This chapter explores forms of travel made possible only through harnessing external power sources, what for simplicity's sake can be called high-energy systems of travel. Throughout the twentieth century these have been dominated by internal combustion engines, but animal traction, steam and electric power vehicles have their own histories, and in the search for rapid decarbonization of mobility systems, electric drive using stored energy battery systems or direct transmission for rail and trolleybus public transport is becoming increasingly important. What should be noted before proceeding, however, is that the amount of energy required of any vehicle is independent of the type of powerplant. Energy use per kilometre travelled is a function of vehicle mass, acceleration, speed and induced resistance from air and ground contact. It is independent of the energy source. The energy demand is not changed by powerplant type.

High-energy travel systems place a considerable burden on the global commons. The transition to decarbonized transport requires significant increases in the mining of a range of rare earth metals and other minerals vital for low-carbon technologies, usually referred to as 'transition minerals' (UNEP 2024). Before we even think about the experiences of personal travel, either as passengers or drivers, we have to factor in the impact of the extractive industries required to power vehicles. Adjusted for current occupancy rates, car travel requires about 2.2 times the energy of bus travel, and about 7.3 times the energy of rail. Increasing rail and bus occupancy rates, further increasing their efficiency, makes these differences even greater. Domestic air travel for longer distance journeying is more than double the energy intensity of car travel, fifteen times that of rail. Approximately 94 per cent of the total transport energy use in the EU (277 megatonnes oil equivalent) is accounted for by road transport (all data from odyssee-mure.eu (2024)). Tackling car use and dependence therefore requires the highest priority in planning transitions to sustainable mobilities for the Anthropocene. To the burden of energy use we also have to add the breakdown products of each mode of travel. All vehicles (even shoes and bicycles) require energy and resources for manufacture, roughly proportional to their mass and lifespan. All these impacts are offshored, experienced far from the locations of those who benefit from the mobilities provided.

Battery electric vehicles that remain fundamentally similar to internal combustion powered vehicles, differing only in their power source, may contribute to lower carbon emission scenarios, but don't herald a lower energy transport future. The energy they require still needs to be generated and stored. And battery systems are usually heavier, thus requiring even greater levels of power for the same performance.[1] Consequently, longer term imaginaries for Anthropocene transport indicate the need for much greater stress on passenger transport modes and major reductions in car use. These discussions are beginning to take place, but for the present, and in keeping with the discussion so far, I want to return to thinking about how powered travel shapes the ways in which we as travellers experience the world and the pedagogies associated with different ways of travelling.

The first distinction to be made is that arising from the difference between being a passenger and being in charge of motor vehicle transport. In the worlds of motorized travel, one is either a passenger or a driver: in charge of the vehicle or being carried. Both rely on power external to the traveller. There is an element of being a passenger in every form of motoring, even as a driver or motorcyclist where, though the driver is in control of all aspects of the vehicle, it is only through the control of that external power source that movement is achieved. One is a passenger of the engine, in charge but also as part of an assemblage, a car-driver system (Dant 2004). A specific set of relations between traveller and travel provider is established: we have to trust the vehicle and, as transported passengers, we also have to trust the driver or pilot. We might even think of these two positions as being passive passengers and active passengers of motor transport.

---

[1] Lightweight electric vehicles make much more sense but this would demand considerable reimagination of performance and safety expectations in private vehicle use.

This chapter will explore the relationships and values that motorized travel, whether as passenger or driver, makes possible. As before, rather than working through individual modes of travel and contrasting bus journeys with trains, taxis and air travel, motorcycling and driving, the approach is to ask how the common elements of travel create different relationships and (inter-) dependencies and how we might learn from them. There are also social inter-relations between travellers both within their vehicles and in waiting spaces necessary for passenger service. There are further interactions between vehicles and their environments of travel, both as they move and in the time spent static. Even regularly used cars often spend more than 90 per cent of the time parked. Cycles similarly spend most of the time parked but take up considerably less space. However, in locations of large-scale use, cycle parking is a considerable problem and cannot be ignored but must be properly provided and organized.

Returning to experiences of travel, we must ask what attitudes we bring to and take from interaction with others in travel spaces? How, we can ask, do these foster a sense of care of other humans and the commons? How does using different vehicle types affect non-travellers, both human and more-than-human?

Passenger sensations

Common to the human scale travel that has been examined previously, one unspoken characteristic is that discussion so far has almost entirely been about solo travel. As we move to thinking about passenger experiences, we move into an area dominated by collective transport. Nevertheless, even in mass transport in close proximity to others one may also be travelling solo, alone in a group of people, bound up with one's own thoughts and reflections. Being passive, even belted-in to one's seat, kinaesthetic perceptions are relatively limited. Forces of acceleration and vibration from engines and vehicle and surface interactions (including air turbulence) provide sensate feedback on the spaces travelled through and the way those spaces are travelled. But as passenger rather than driver, this information requires no response. Walking, (motor)cycling and driving, these sensations are essential elements of cognition, requiring action to maintain balance and control.

Being a passenger is not always a status derived from a desire to travel. Much travel is forced upon us, both as passengers and drivers. In the context of the Anthropocene this needs interrogation. Just as the previous chapter noted the creation of dependency and liberation with respect to motorized and non-motorized travel, so too the issues of freedom, agency and possibility need examination in light of inclusive citizenship.

Most vehicular travel takes place in closed vehicles where ambient conditions can be (at least minimally) controlled or determined by the traveller, even if that only amounts to an opening window. Consequently, the design of interior spaces is important, enclosed within the vehicle, oriented towards a world beyond it, or towards its interior either engaging fellow passengers or not. So too the spaces, interior and exterior, where we wait for transport services to arrive. We have to think about how the organization of waiting spaces encourages and discourages interactions and the narratives they create about our citizenship. These will be explored in turn. The most important interactions arising in motorized travel are therefore interhuman, person to person.

Categories of passenger

Families, strangers and degrees of trust

Being-in-the-world as a passenger is less about the precise vehicle of travel and more about the relations of trust that are required for travel. The essence of being a passenger (by choice) is a partial surrender of one's agency. You may choose to travel but you travel on the terms of the travel provider. Whether travelling by car, bus, train, tram or air, all of these journeys require, to a greater or lesser extent, conformity to a service provided by another. The chauffeured car journey, where the driver is under the full command of the passenger, might appear to break this but (paid) chauffeurs are hardly part of ordinary daily travel for adults of working age. Much more common is the chauffeuring and transport of children and family members, especially those who cannot drive. Trips are dependent on the availability of the vehicle, the driver and their willingness to undertake a journey. The relationships engendered in this shared travel can be generous or mean-spirited. They test the capacity and willingness to provide care, simultaneously exploring negotiated assessments of what is reasonable either as demand or offer. Paid taxi services require faith in the professionalism of the service provider. The taxi driver is a stranger requiring trust that is fundamentally different from that within family and close friendship circles, though even these cannot be taken as a given.

This surrender of agency is not presented here as a negative factor. It illustrates that we always work within limits. Freedom is not and cannot be an absolute, especially in the case of mobilities. Every choice of travel imposes on others, through its requirement of infrastructure, its use of space and the residues it leaves behind. Collectively, we make decisions about how much travel is acceptable for ourselves and for each other. Maldistribution of travel privileges produces 'enforced passengerization', the dependency on transport services and provisions that prove undependable or inadequately designed for inclusions of those with mobility impairments. It highlights how far we have to go to be able to structure and recognize appropriate mechanisms and organization for Anthropocene mobilities. Service providers shape the experiences of travel for their passengers, and for those with mobility impairments, experiences of public humiliation during travel remain worryingly frequent.

Public transport services require faith in a timetable and in the reliability and safety of services. From a social practice perspective, without these qualities a service cannot attract users. Provision may exist and may give access to desired destinations, but if trust in that service is not available, the relationship between traveller and means of travel is incomplete. This raises an interesting point with respect to the interaction of trust, agency and uncontrollability in mobility practices. Journeying that has a utility function – in other words, making a journey to get somewhere – is the exercise of desire (to reach one's destination), and of the agency of travel and capacity to fulfil that desire within the resources available (including economic resources). Pricing regimes, subsidies and the regulation of public transport (services and vehicles) combine to provide radically different experiences. Comparing different states and cities across Europe, for example, attests to a variety of different attitudes to public transport provision and to those who travel on public transport.

The attractiveness of private vehicle ownership and use (including cycles) is the degree of control linked to agency. One is not tied to the existence of a service or not, or to its timetabling. But there are negative dimensions to this apparent freedom. Should a breakdown or mishap occur in private travel then the traveller has only recourse to their own resources. Inadequate as these may be, it can be comforting to sense that even though things are going wrong, the sense of agency remains. Breakdown services have existed alongside private motoring almost from its inception to cope with these situations, augmenting the lack of specialist skills of the driver (and in car-sharing arrangements the support these give can be collectedly owned and shared). In the case of similar occurrences on public transport, the feelings created in the traveller depend entirely on the degree of trust and the flow of information available from providers. It becomes easy to feel the lack of agency as a deficit. Yet in both situations, the delay is the same, the capacity for remedy varies. It can be even greater in the case of public transport. But these considerations illustrate how the desire for control is built into the development of mobility systems through the differentiation of moving and being moved.

Dependent and compulsory passengers

Many who travel as passengers are not passengers by choice. They travel as passengers either because there is no possibility of travel under their own agency, or spatial ordering is structured to demand more travel for everyday life than would be undertaken of their own volition. This is especially the case in relation to the separation of housing and work or education opportunities. Whether as a passenger or not, this latter, being impelled to travel by one's spatial and social relations, is described by Cass and Manderscheid (2018) as the compulsion to travel. Again, a key aim of fifteen-minute city planning (Moreno 2024) is to tackle the necessity of travel dependence. A consequent effect of that is also to tackle the exclusionary impact of travel compulsion on those whose capacity to travel is impaired. Mobility impairment, whether through age or physical conditions that prevent one from using normalized expectations of motor travel, especially when public transport services are far from inclusive, creates what we have elsewhere called 'enforced passengerisation' (Ogden and Cox 2009). Where people are forced to travel, whether in displacement or by lack of options as to how they can travel, it has to be a serious concern for mobility justice (Sheller 2021). Enforced passengerization remains a reality for many.

Age and impairment are the obvious categories that may preclude power over one's ability to travel. It is worth noting that a number of medical conditions, including visual impairment, may preclude driving while the slower speeds of cycling are not a problem. A literature has developed around the concept of care mobilities: those mobility practices that accrue around the exercise of care relationships (Sánchez de Madariaga 2013a; Rubin and Parker 2023). According to Inés Sánchez de Madariaga (2013b: 58),

> The mobility of care includes all travel resulting from home and caring responsibilities: escorting others; shopping for daily living, with the exclusion of leisure shopping; household maintenance, organization, and administrative errands, as opposed to personal walks for recreation; visits to take care of sick or elderly relatives that are, again, seen as different from leisure visits; and the like.

Sánchez de Madariaga makes the point that mobilities of care are fundamentally gendered. To observe the imbalances of care mobilities is not to approve their perpetuation.

The need to travel arises from everyday practices of care, and gendered social roles generated by the burden of care need to be taken into account in the provision of mobility services and opportunities. Providing mobility is a means to express care, but if mode of travel and its consequent impacts are not part of the discussion, then providing mobility has little intrinsically to teach about care as a value. It is possible to express care for specific persons while disregarding others.[2]

Beyond journeys necessitated by the tasks of social reproduction we can also note the care mobilities that come from family members, friends and neighbours who provide travel for those who cannot travel themselves. Such journeys are particularly important over longer distances and in circumstances where even accompanied travel is not possible. Young, old and mobility impaired persons are carried as passengers every day, and not always by car. Journey providers express care and value through provision of travel, those travelling are enabled through the provision of travel by those who accompany them.

We can consider public service transport this way, as a means of providing care. Doing so highlights the importance of mobility service provisioning as part of the infrastructuring process that defines the relation between state and citizen (Cox 2020c). We can understand it as a potentially key relationship in Anthropocene citizenship. In this framing, the state (or other provisioning authority) provides mobility services and infrastructures for human scale travel not as a matter of obligation or duty, nor for the more efficient production of capital, but as an expression of the obligation of care that it needs to have towards its citizens if they are to be encouraged to care and value each other and the planet. Conversely, the denial or degrading of services has the opposite effect. States fail their citizens by failing to ensure adequate and inclusive public transport.

As noted in the broader discussion of care relationships (Chapter 3), there is a potentially darker side to this case of care that requires us to consider the relations of dependence that can result from unequal distribution of mobility

---

[2] Discussing travel patterns and rostering with workers in care provision in the UK reveals them to be high-mileage drivers as they move from client to client. Because many employers do not pay directly for the costs incurred, journey patterns forced on workers are often profoundly inefficient when compared with the planning approaches utilized by logistics providers for whom induced travel is a direct cost.

opportunities and means. Inadequate provision, that allows some but not others to travel, is an especially common experience for wheelchair users, where provision of possibility and accessibility is not made on an equal basis. Other functional impairments such as those to hearing, to sight or to general infirmity create other barriers to travel.

Independent travellers who use wheelchairs (and/or other mobility devices) on public transport often become recipients of 'special passenger' status, expected to feel grateful for the provision, while simultaneously remaining in a constant state of uncertainty whether the provision will actually be fit for purpose and allow their travel (Ogden and Cox 2009). Poor design and delivery are only part of the problem. Another, sometimes more insidious issue can be the social relationships of inequality engendered by approaching the wheelchair-using traveller as a special, 'needy' case, a status often reinforced by the language used to describe the necessary provisions in a mobility context (see also Chapter 3 on the limits to care). At best, however, the services we provide to others, not necessarily to those classified as 'needy', can be an everyday expression of care. Sharing mobility resources in the context of the Anthropocene is a way of expressing care and affirming mobility as a commons, not as an exclusive private domain.

Passenger transport as public space

A shared characteristic of higher speed powered travel is the need to isolate the traveller from the elements. Usually this is within a vehicle.[3] Contact with the more-than-human world from inside the body of a car, bus or train is almost exclusively visual. Consequently, the primary form of sensory interaction other than visual in passenger travel is social interaction with other travellers. Immediately, the social safety of interaction with one's fellow passengers has to be taken into consideration. When travelling in a private vehicle with family or friends we know what to expect. How do we react to being confined within a vehicle with strangers?

Travel takes place in public space and so the individual perception is contextualized and framed by broader social expectations and fears around

---

[3] The 'prophylactic suite of helmet, armoured leathers and Serious Boots' (Banks 2004: 339, capitals in original) adopted by motorcyclists (even though only the helmet may be compulsory) reflects concern to avoid the inevitable consequences of speed and bodily contact with road surfaces that comprise the space of travel. Balance and control for powered two wheelers does involve a lot more bodily sensation, precisely why it is attractive to those who use it.

Table 6.1 Closed and Open Views of the Other

Distinctions	Closed views of the other	Open views of the other
Monolithic/diverse	The other seen as a single bloc, static and unresponsive to new realities	The other seen as diverse and changing, with internal differences, debates and developments
Separate/interacting	The other seen as separate: (a) not having any aims or values in common with the self; (b) not affected by it; (c) not influencing it	The other seen as interdependent with the self: (a) having certain shared values and aims; (b) affected by it; (c) enriching it
Inferior/different	The other seen as inferior: e.g. irrational	The other seen as different but of equal worth
Enemy/partner	The other seen as violent. Aggressive threatening to be defeated and perhaps dominated	The other seen as an actual or potential partner in joint co-operative enterprises and in the solution of shared problems
Manipulative/sincere	The other seen as manipulative and deceitful, bent only on material or strategic advantage	The other seen as sincere, not hypocritical
Criticisms of the self rejected/considered	Criticisms made by the other of the self are rejected out of hand	Criticism of the self are considered and debated
Discrimination defended/criticised	Hostility towards the other used to justify discriminatory practices and exclusion of the Other from mainstream society	Debates and disagreements with the other do not diminish efforts to combat exclusion
Hostility towards the other seen as natural/problematic	Fear and hostility towards the other accepted as natural and normal	Critical views of the other themselves subjected to critique, lest they be inaccurate and unfair

Source: Adapted from Runnymede Trust (2000).

safety and public space. Are other people just other humans feeling and struggling as we are or are they a potential threat? In 2000, the report on *The Future of Multi-Ethnic Britain* (Runnymede Trust 2000) contrasted two ways of comprehending social interaction with those who can be classified as 'strangers' inasmuch as they are not part of one's immediate circle of recognized peers. Table 6.1, adapted from the original report, shows how it identified two extremes of approaching social encounters. In the literature on public space and public transport, social interactions have broadly been assessed as operating between two poles of understanding of the spaces of public transport, being either arenas of conviviality or anxiety-inducing spaces (Neal 2010; Bissel 2018). Using a broader framework of social interaction allows us to expand our ways of thinking about the spaces of public transport, indeed in travel spaces more generally, in a multidimensional manner. We can open up our thinking about social interaction in the spaces of travel through reflection on how those 'closed' and 'open' views of the other in the table correspond to ways of thinking about reactions to others in the spaces of travel. Open views stem from an ethic of care: closed views deny such relationships. These categorizations are not limited to considering reaction to fellow travellers in public transport. They can also be used to understand better the conflicts between different modes of travel in shared spaces.

The growing literature on public transport encounters stresses the role of public transport as public space (Tuvikene 2023). As public space, it is where citizenship is enacted. Public space is a democratic necessity. Without public space there can be no recognition or negotiation between fellow citizens. To be effective, those public spaces need to be structured so that participants can meet with relative degrees of equality; they need to serve as commons. Public transport providers are enabled by the state, even if only through the provision of basic infrastructures. Degrees of regulation and direct or indirect service provision in public transport systems vary widely, yet whatever the format, public transport for everyday travel creates its own particular publics. Regular service users become familiar with their fellow travellers, much more so than in walking and cycling. Expressions and explorations of citizenship in the context of the public spaces of public transport are not confined to interpersonal action. The actions of provision and providers also define the status of user as citizen, or at least express the relation of state to citizen. For Anthropocene citizenship, we need to consider therefore how public transport scenarios express or allow care and commoning, and how the adoption of attitudes to the other at the heart of interpersonal encounters is linked to this. The attitude towards otherness is at the heart of care: 'The fact that every being is formed differently from me also lays an ethical obligation on me. Only human beings can bless this otherness, live freely with it, or wickedly destroy it. This is what grounds our ethical responsibility' (Boff 1995: 87).

Read through the lens of resonance, the closed and open views of the other (Table 6.1) can be contrasted in their openness and closure to the possibility of change. Relational encounter always carries a risk because of the possibility that one will emerge transformed by the experience. We can also think of these as a way to reflect upon our responses to perception, to the possibility of alteration and destabilization.

A second way of using these distinctions between closed and open views of the other to foster values for Anthropocene citizenship (and therefore for Anthropocene mobilities) can be seen in how categories of traveller or vehicle users are constructed through the lenses of othering. Researching a previous book on cycle activism (Cox 2023) required reading through almost a hundred years' worth of what appeared to be an endless stream of reflection on cyclist–motorist conflicts in the UK, from newspaper and magazine comments in the 1920s right through to below-the-line commentary on contemporary media sites. The hostility towards cyclists was remarkably consistent. Looked down upon as a separate social class, homogenized as a single identity, in the written comments of motorists, cyclists were consistently 'othered' in the terms described in Table 6.1 (compare Caimiotto 2020; Egan and Caulfield 2024). Where attempts to work together were enacted, towards common resolutions of problems, solutions appeared only temporarily before prior relations of suspicion and alienation resumed (Cox 2023b). For their part, cyclists' comments frequently resorted to othering motorists, but as the weaker group (both politically and physically), sustaining a constant toll of deaths and injuries in road traffic accidents caused by motoring offences, there was a profound asymmetry of consequences. The response of fear had a grounding in physical threat.

In mobility terms perhaps the deterioration or decline in social trust and the growth of othering can be seen in the decline of hitch-hiking. What was once a ubiquitous action for many, its virtual disappearance is not only a function of social fears but also the expectations around driving (Chesters and Smith 2001). As car ownership becomes more normative, those not driving become abnormal and objects of suspicion. A quiet resurgence of hitch-hiking is noted by O'Regan (2012) and Treibl (2018) in the context of the developing exploration of slow mobilities, which holds out promise for a rediscovery of the potential and possibilities inherent in more informal modes of car-sharing.

Waiting spaces

Travel on-demand services, such as taxis, can take the traveller from their immediate location to the required destination. Of course, this happens with all private vehicle ownership where the vehicle, whatever form it takes, is immediately accessible. The theoretical instant access of private vehicles is a major form of their attractiveness. Actually, the practicalities of door-to-door travel depend on the proximity of parking places both at start and destination. To have parking space close to where we want to begin or end journeys depends on not everyone driving.

Most journeys require some form of waiting, even if only for other family members to be ready. Scheduled services with timetable require coordination and submission to the strictures of timing. Sharing journeys with family members also requires degrees of negotiation over time availability. Where and under what conditions is waiting done? Once we shift from private transport to public modes, the waiting spaces of public transport services make statements about the status and the value of the traveller.

Scheduled services have always required waiting spaces, from coaching inns to the most elegant of nineteenth-century railway stations and to the architectural statement designs of international airports. Through the histories of their creation and development we can chart how each has distinguished and elevated the status of passengers or, conversely, disvalued them. Stations of all these types, catering for the stationary passenger, at once provide opportunities for anticipation and afford the provider a management system to process passengers. At one end of the scale of contemporary provision we have the barely utilitarian functionality of a simple bus shelter or railway halt, providing basic protection for passengers with no alternative but to wait for the service with common access to all and making no distinction between passengers. At the other end, the grand stations and airports serve a double function, to create a demand for new forms of travel, associating mobility with luxury and status, and to make a statement about the provider. Again, these are spaces of citizenship, but more frequently distinguished by the semi-privatization of space, only open to those with tickets. Within railway stations and airports, further and sharper distinctions are visible. Waiting rooms, particularly for long-distance travel by rail and air, remain places of segregation by class, or at least by cost. Desegregation of mobility spaces, travel and waiting formed a symbolically and practically central theme in struggles for equality in the United States. The days of formally racially segregated spaces may have been overcome, but differentiation enabled by ability to pay (or to put on the expense account of 'business') remains, and racial profiling of passengers continues. Such distinctions begin in waiting spaces and continue through the provisions of different classes of travel (in air and rail travel at least, though these distinctions once applied to omnibus travel as well). The continuation of fundamentally classed, gendered and racialized passenger spaces reflects social divisions and categorization and the failure to address these social divisions.

Interior spaces

Subsequent to the arrival of our transport, we enter the interior spaces of the vehicles of travel. Each affords its own particularities. Different degrees of sociality and comfort are forced upon us. There is no need (nor would it be remotely possible) to examine every possible form of interior passenger space but some observations may be made, reflecting on how different layouts create contrasting social spaces, and noting how combinations of spaces are used to provide different opportunities for sociality even on the same journey.

The interior spaces of public transport are shaped by design. Maximizing scarce space for seated passengers, rows of seats all facing the same direction provide little chance for interaction, save with those immediately adjacent. No eye contact. A view dominated by the back of the seat or person in front. An encouragement to remain solitary. Layouts that maximize the number of passengers within a restricted area allow minimal provision for those requiring other forms of mobility or unable to be conveyed in standardized seating: airlines are particularly notorious for their inability to provide any semblance of equality of travel opportunity for wheelchair users.

Open spaces allow for wheeling, for all those utilitarian trolleys, prams and buggies necessary for the walked travel of significant numbers of people, as discussed in the previous chapter. Public transport is inevitably intermodal (combined with other forms of movement), and at least one end of the journey will necessarily almost always be walked. Seats that face each other, sometimes with a table, allow for travellers already in groups to remain clustered and continue their togetherness. They may even be explicitly designated as family seating areas. Compartments are the logical extension of these spaces of togetherness but have often disappeared in favour of a move to open flow carriages to maximize security and flexible use. Each design decision has its compromises.

Each of these sets of spaces not only creates different ambiences of passenger interaction but also different relation to the gaze at the world beyond the window. Direct facing or oblique, confined to a narrow window or large open view, being able to see ahead or only sideways all makes a difference to how we see the world. Tim Ingold (2021) speculates on the effect of different ways of sitting on the production of a gaze or of interaction, arguing that the fully seated position of the car traveller forces a much more directed and narrowed forward perspective on the world than is afforded by the standing or upright riding stance of the walker or rider. Each layout both permits and encourages different forms of interaction, encourages us to recognize our commonalities or permits social distancing.

Looking at the world beyond the window does not necessarily separate us from it, we still see, we still perceive even if the image is only through one of our senses, sight is still the most dominant of our ways of interacting. Moreover, the image has the power to be transformative. Writing about this power, Dorothee Sölle quotes an interview conducted with Swiss writer and political activist Otto F. Walter:

> Let me tell you of an experience I had. I was nineteen years old at the time, I guess. I was travelling by train to Lucerne; it was afternoon, the light and moving shadows were signaling a thunderstorm, sun and shadow played on the fields. I was alone in the car, I opened the window and just stared in amazement at this landscape. I was completely overcome and could have shouted for joy. I wept and had the feeling: This is God. That is what lives and what ought to be. It was an image of peace and of harmony of everything thing with everything. I had the feeling that I was part of it; I felt the rhythmic movements of recurrence in their infinite multiformity within in me. It was a mystical, a kind of pantheistic experience, that is, the experience of God in nature. (Sölle 2001: Loc. 1346–1351)

Whatever the naming given to that experience and the language it is expressed in, Walter gives voice to a moment of revelation, of resonance, all the more powerful for its fleeting unpredictability. Recalling how he opened the window emphasizes the multi-sensory encounter, triggered by the visual, as he sought a more unmediated experience of the view before him.

Passenger journeys provide opportunities just to sit and gaze in ways that are rarely possible at other times of day. Yet travelling in the dark can produce the inverse of such connections. In the dark, we travel as passengers through unknown spaces, unable to recognize landmarks. Without the trigger of clear 'next stop' signboards even familiar journeys can feel uncomfortable. We are entirely thrown back onto our fellow passengers.

Understanding encounters

The centrality of the social encounter to experiences of public transport has become a major theme in academic studies, especially following David Bissell's work (2010), in which he stressed the need to explore how the public spaces of public transport necessitate 'being with' others. Whatever form the negotiations of space and encounter take, one cannot control or choose company in public transport spaces. Degrees of control are imposed by transport operators, through ticketing and pricing mechanisms, to provide levels of mediation.

This negotiated sense of being-with is also being-with-in-the-world. We are people together in physical locations. Encounter is mediated not just by interpersonal relations but also with the qualities of the specific spaces provided by different modes of transport (and their spaces of waiting), and of the world beyond the transport. While passengers use journeys as opportunities for screen time or reading, others continue to watch the world go by. To illustrate these interior spaces of interaction we can think about how subway systems create very particular forms of interaction. Their peculiarity is that they have no vista on an outside world: the cliché of commentary on tube travel is that it is characterized by 'studied inattention' – the non-verbal negotiation of space that allows participants to engage with each other without direct contact (Kokkola et al. 2023: 1697). Such actions are not unique to underground systems and can be observed as practices in the negotiation of interaction of most social travel spaces of walking and cycling. However, the lack of a visible external world intensifies the needs to work out ways of negotiating this peculiar public space. As will be noted a little farther on, the interior design of different modes of public transport also contributes.

These observations on interaction also alert us to the degree to which spaces of public spaces of travel are often spaces of 'affect': spaces that generate emotional response not through any specific mechanisms but through tacit perceptions formed from the sum of human and more-than-human elements, the latter including both constructed and designed spaces and the broader elements of 'natural' elements including weather.

What sort of spaces are provided by public transport and whether they support the building of positive social connections or are places of disconnect and alienation remain a matter of ambiguity and debate (Sträuli 2023). In light of the earlier discussions of uncontrollability, it is important to stress rather that encounters open worlds of possibility. There is always a risk that uncontrolled and unplanned experiences may alter one's knowledge or perception, and there is no way of knowing which direction this may go in; will it be a good or bad thing. As Tuvikene et al. (2023: 12) put it, 'The very experience of PT [public transport] journeys does not simply reflect and expose pre-existing identities and differences but can turn them into transformative experiences with positive and negative effects.' Passengers share experiences and this can allow the development of shared outlooks, but outcomes are neither predetermined nor entirely predictable. Kokkole et al.'s (2023) study of public transport experiences during the period of restrictions triggered by the Covid-19 pandemic pointed to both an increased sense of 'strangeness' and alienation, while simultaneously allowing and revealing greater acts and sense of care. Passengers, they found, largely developed greater sensitivities to fellow travellers. Acts of hostility were observed but these attracted social opprobrium. External pressures from the pandemic threat can be interpreted as prompting open view of the other as fellow humans challenged by a threat that remained invisible and hard to comprehend.

Beyond these general observations of interaction on transport services we can turn to some of the specific conditions arising from the peculiarities of different forms of transport provision to consider how diverse experiences are created, and to observe some of the inheritances of history in which deliberate effort has been made to make statements about travellers using differing modes.

Aeromobilities

Perhaps the extreme end of passenger mobility is formed by air travel. Even though it is hard to consider it within the bounds of everyday travel, flying has become 'routine, matter-of-fact, effectively banal' (Cwerner 2008: 6) for many addressed by the 'we' of this book. Its combination of speed of travel and distances covered, together with the almost hermetically sealed environments of travel that flying today provides, makes it almost the acme of powered passenger travel, an almost cartoonish extreme version of the traits that we see in other forms of passenger travel. Greater levels of unequal distribution exist between frequent flyers and those not travelling at all or very infrequently. Strictly classed systems of segregation between passenger groups have major impacts on the non-traveller and the more-than-human world through the environmental and noise impacts of airports and the aircraft themselves. Finally, there is the devastating impact of the contributions of air travel to GHG emissions. All of these combine to make it very difficult indeed to align air travel with the values of Anthropocene mobilities. Yet the externalities have to confront the dependence of a globalized world upon air travel. It cannot just be willed away.

Like the desire to drive, the will to fly had to be constructed. A series of essays edited by Bjørkdahl and Franco Duharte (2022) expose how a single profession, that of academia, became dependent upon and almost synonymous with regular air travel. Mimi Sheller's contribution, a brutally honest assessment of her own complicity in the role of an international research academic, demonstrates the ecological unsustainability of the role and observes that its existence is only made possible through the immobilities of others (Sheller 2022). For some to travel, others cannot. The observations made of driving by Gorz back in the 1970s are writ large in relation to contemporary air travel.

The professional dilemma, that certain careers, even those within institutions externally committed to carbon reductions, depend on high levels of international travel, is not easy to resolve. Sheller's own conclusions especially in light of the enforced cessation of flying during the Covid-19 pandemic are to endorse strong travel reduction, recognizing the degree to which what has become normal in recent past decades is in fact hyper-travel: 'We need to introduce what I call a mobility justice perspective into planning academic travel' (Sheller 2022:72). Although the primary advantage of physical air travel is the face-to-face communication it affords, its sensorial limitations obscure the effects it has on the world around. As Karen Armstrong observes in her wide-ranging reflections on reforging relationships with the world, Anthropocene living will require sacrifice and change, and in travel terms, she argues, we can no longer drive or board aeroplanes 'with our former insouciance' (Armstrong 2023: 99).

Driving in a system of automobility

As we have already seen in the unfolding discussions so far, everyday, regular car travel is the most problematic of transport solutions. It is the one form of mobility that is hard to reconcile with the twin demands of ecojustice; it cannot be distributed equably to all and it cannot exist without dramatic environmental costs. Driving has a history and physical reality that makes care difficult. Moreover, the distribution of the disbenefits of mass motoring is even more broadly inequitable. Those who drive can benefit from the mobility provided but the majority of costs are borne by those who do not drive (Conley and McClaren 2009). Recognition of both social and environmental impacts of mass motoring has a long history, as have campaigns to confront the worst excesses and to advocate for solutions, especially in the pivotal years of the 1970s, when household access to cars in the Global North reached over 50 per cent. An entire literature chronicles these actions in different locations and here I want only to note some particular analyses as they contribute to thinking about how we might address the problems of private motoring in terms of Anthropocene mobility.

Patrick Rivers (1972) was part of the 1970s wave of cultural critics alongside, for example, André Gorz (1980 [1975]) or Ivan Illich (1973; 1974) who all developed analyses of the negative impacts of mass motoring, each extending their gaze beyond the car itself. Rather, the problem could be better described, Rivers argued, in comprehending how mobility had become the new god and the car acted as the saviour, the technology which would provide redemption and access to the desired goal of infinite ability to travel. The car was no longer a tool of travel, but had become a totem, a sacred sign pointing beyond itself. River's fears are echoed by Galeano's discussion of 'The Sacred Car' in which he explains how the objects that promised freedom have come to 'act like travelling cages' (Galeano 2000: 234).

> Cars are like gods, born to serve people like good luck charms against fear and solitude, they end up making people serve them. The church of the sacred car with its US-based Vatican has the entire world on its knees. The spread of the car gospel has proven catastrophic, each new version deliriously multiplying the defects of the original'. (Galeano 2000: 236)

We do not travel just in a world of objects, but of signs. The sign value of motoring, as success, as economic indicator of prosperity, is reflected in the space we reserve for its use and the priority we give it in planning. Leblanc (1999) contrasted the very different ways the world is experienced when viewed from the saddle of a bicycle and the inside of a motor vehicle. In his study of gendered roles in Japanese society, he goes as far as to describe these producing two different forms of citizenship, the 'taxi citizenship' of Japanese businessmen and the 'bicycle citizenship' that comprises the political world of the Japanese housewife. Our perspectives form our political identities.

As an object unseen by those looking out from inside, it is hard to grasp the effect it has on those outside. As design stresses safety, the objects become more massive, more intimidating, more threatening as generations of commentators have observed. The physical isolation of contemporary driving experiences further reduces the sensitivity to those beyond the vehicle (Nixon 2014). This makes it difficult to exercise or experience care for others. Having described the interpersonal communication arising from interactions common to walkers and cyclists by virtue of the face-to-face encounters, Koukal (2020) explains how motoring denies this possibility.

> In encountering an automobile we are only encountering an other by inference through (often ambiguous) signs like brake lights, turn signals, different rates

of speed, or the sounding of a horn. The technology of the automobile veils the lived body within, not only for cyclists but for other drivers as well. We might be able to sometimes catch a glimpse of a driver's head and shoulders if the distance, light, and the reflections off the windshield are just right, but more often than not our attention is drawn to the relative mass of the automobile itself, and the manner in which it is moving. (Koukal 2020: 723)

The only direct contact possible in driving is that between driver and passengers.

Yet for all the negative impacts of motoring, it is not only its practical dimensions and a system that creates driving as an uncomplicated and mostly financially affordable option that give it its appeal. There is also a visceral enjoyment that comes from being in control of a motor vehicle, whether on two wheels or four. Beyond the macho posturing and opinionated absurdities, part of the international appeal of motoring programmes like Top Gear is watching the sheer delight that comes from presenters' test driving. How a car or bike 'feels', its balance, its ability to respond to driver input are valued commodities. Yet these are qualities that ultimately can only be experienced fully in the separate and private space of the test track or closed road. In everyday conditions, they can only be glimpsed. Hence, we also note the importance of the editing of footage, as in car advertising, that emphasizes the driver alone, with rarely any other vehicle in sight. The ideal driving experience is one where no one else is driving.

Motoring as citizenship

Packer's (2008) detailed study of motoring safety discourses reveals how ideas of citizenship have become entangled with motoring. Where early motorists were briefly considered a nuisance to existing road users, discussion soon reversed the gaze to talk more broadly about the dangers and threat that might be posed to motorists by others on the road. Particular motorists of course could be themselves deviant and undesirable, especially in the racialized United States and so, Packer notes, arose a link between an idealized citizenship and motoring. A whole range of groups of road users were identified at different times as posing a threat to the 'proper' 'desirable' motorist. The models of 'car citizenship' Packer highlights are far from the idea of an open Anthropocene citizenship discussed here. Indeed, they might even be construed as its polar opposite; an exclusive club of privileges opens only to those who conform to certain stereotypes of behaviour, race and class.

The idea that roadspaces should be understood as places for an exclusive group of persons is the main theme of Longhurst's (2015) study of road-use conflicts. Starting with the historic recognition of the road as a commons, a resource for all to share and provided by the community he shows how policy has been used to construct increasingly exclusive rights of use and access. Community resources are used to protect the privileges of specific groups. Though he doesn't use the language of the commons, Peter Norton (2011) similarly analyses how the various historical patterns of enclosure imposed on the road as commons have implicitly and occasionally explicitly raised the questions not only of 'whose streets' but of 'what are streets for'. Reconstructions of roadspace were not so much physical as social. Different interests for their own rights to roadspace campaigned on grounds drew on different registers: pedestrians on moral grounds of justice, urban authorities and commercial interests on the basis of efficiency, and automobile interests framing their cause as one of freedom. Of course, the problem in reconciling these various ways of constructing the issue is that each is impervious to the other. One of the potentials of using an idea of citizenship to address the problems is that it may provide a way to connect and to bring into dialogue these very different registers as all form constituent parts of a broader social reality. Clearly, each of these analyses provides us with images that are of vital import if we are to be able to construct an idea of motoring that might be compatible with Anthropocene citizenship.

If Packer noted the construction of the car citizen in the United States, in the very different context of India an important analysis was made in 1996 by a team from the Centre for Science and Environment in Delhi (Agarwal et al. 1996). This reverses the gaze to consider the relationship between a state and its peoples. Despite legislative and policy frameworks to protect citizens from the widely recognized, growing problem of vehicular pollution, minimal action had been taken to enforce standards or to prevent exploitation of loopholes by powerful economic interests. Agarwal (1996: 7) condemns this pattern of inattention and the favouring of specific economic interests and already privileged middle classes as 'a case of state supervised slow murder'. Conventional citizenship, he reminds us, is not simply a declaration of rights but involves the reciprocal obligations of states towards those who legitimize their existence, the basis of my discussion of citizenship in Chapter 2. In the context of the Anthropocene and a deterritorialized citizenship, these obligations doubly accrue to the social relations between groups of peoples. As Agarwal argues, it is not simply that the state has reneged on its responsibilities, but sectional interests within society are pursuing their own interests at the cost of the lives of their fellows. The driver is complicit in this problematic web of relations. Coton Seiler is another author whose analysis examines the web of interaction between motoring, citizenship and the state, clearly brought out in the title of his book *Republic of Drivers* (Seiler 2008). In it, he shows how driving continues to mobilize fantasies of individual autonomy while binding users into specific forms of subjectivity and dependence. The life lived with an automobile cannot be lived without it, and yet we collectively know that this prospect needs to be addressed, since a simple greening of the car is not a credible possibility (Paterson 2007).

Yet for all this knowledge of the devastating implications and impact of mass motoring, we also need to recognize that both the car and motoring permeate deep into the cultural psyche because of the promises and benefits they confer on their beneficiaries. Being-in-the-world as a driver is to attain a status of mobility privilege. Daniel Miller (2001) shows how motoring is embedded in everyday life for a majority in the Global North, drivers and non-drivers alike, not simply as a force of alienation but as something much more complex. He argues that the car has become integral to how we see ourselves as human and therefore despite the negative dimensions it cannot be rejected out of hand. To critique the dominance of driving in mobility provision one must also recognize that many users fully understand its destructiveness and that the unfreedoms caused by being locked into a system of automobility are part of the contradictions of everyday life. Few fully live according to the values they might espouse as ideal. Acknowledgement that 'I cannot live without my car' is not necessarily just an assertion of rights and a rejection of any need to engage in change. It also can be a recognition that the structures of contemporary life make it impossible to live without this addiction. As Sullivan (2021: 142) states in a creatively and tellingly titled article *I'm Sian, and I'm a Fossil Fuel Addict: On Paradox, Disavowal and (Im)Possibility in Changing Climate Change*: 'Under current structural circumstances, I am completely unable to unhook myself from fossil fuel production and consumption. Even consciously "low-impact" and low-carbon lifestyles are bound with the fossil fuel industry and the apparent necessity of economic growth this supports.' Writers who step in to practically address this complex set of contradictions necessarily have to engage with not only the role of the car in everyday life but also the realities of decades of the restructuring of society around car dependence (Alvord 2000). Our personal mobility habits are far from personal choices but responses to social, economic and spatial forces, organized according to political and economic priorities (Soron 2009). Such arguments are bolstered by individual case studies that reflect on how these processes have unfolded in specific regions (Knoflacher 2009) or cities (Wickham 2006).

From the perspective of an academic historian, Wells (2012) demonstrates how built environments have been shaped by auto policies, that the necessity that driving seems to present to us is neither natural nor inevitable – a theme similarly taken up in Bohm and colleagues' (2006) call to rethink what is possible. To undo it, however, requires more than just a simple rejection of the act of driving or the 'greening' of current practices through increased efficiency or changing powerplants (Paterson 2007).

What I want to highlight here is the significant difference between the experiential qualities of car travel and those potential unleashed in walking and cycling. Wolfgangs Sachs put it very well.

> Behind the steering wheel one sees nothing, hears nothing, smells nothing; the perspective through the windshield kills space, makes it into a mere transit route. For the bicyclist, however, the nearby details gain a sharper focus. It is not the gaze into the distance but the attention to the immediate vicinity that keeps pace with the bicycle. (Sachs 1984: 202–3)

Conversely, the potential for interaction between motorists and other users is depersonalized.

The evidence for the unsustainability of mass motoring, its incompatibility with living less destructively in the Anthropocene and thus the need to change everyday driving habits are overwhelmingly clear. The argument made here is not that motoring should be banned but to break with the compulsion to drive: to advance possibilities for minimal driving lifestyles, and to ensure that the positive values arising from not driving are clear.

Cass and Manderscheid (2018) describe this systemic challenge to the dominant patterns of car mobility as one of autono-mobility. Beyond all the rational critiques of motoring mobilities mentioned above they argue that challenges need to be made not just to the ways in which travel is conducted but of the 'socio-economic compulsions to travel' (Manderscheid and Cass 2023: 187). It is clear from their work that Anthropocene mobilities require not simply sustainable alternatives to the ways in which travel is currently conducted but, as was sharply highlighted by the experiences of pandemic immobilities, require also a critique of the need to travel. The emphasis in this work has been on the potentials of more sustainable and lower carbon travels compatible with responsible Anthropocene citizenship, and the emphasis on human scale and speed travel allows us to celebrate movement outside of the socio-economic compulsions that these authors identify.

Anthropocenic motoring?

If the familiar patterns of motoring as a default form of mobility fail to address the criteria for Anthropocene mobilities, then what role is there for motor-mobilities? Wright (1992) suggested that a better way of thinking about the transformation of mobility might be by moving attention away from an obsession with the vehicles themselves. Most responses to challenge automobility are framed in terms of how to replace the car or how to make driving more eco- and people friendly. Wright outlines four axioms that enable the problem of transformation to be reframed.

First, that people appreciate transport for what it can do, rather than for the vehicle itself. As discussed above, they are largely willing to discount the problems caused by particular travel choices as necessary costs and contradictions of everyday life. The second proposition, partly developing the previous, is that the characteristics of travel can usually be obtained by more than one mode, and modes are multiple and can be bundled together. In other words, the advantages credited to car travel are not necessarily, nor even predominantly, the exclusive characteristics of car travel. The same benefits could be obtained by other modes, especially in combination. This latter point is exemplified in Wright's third statement, that combining modes produces different characteristics than are seen in any mode individually. Finally, Wright noted that people value the characteristics of travel differently depending on their social and geographical locations and other variables, unlike those who measure and plan for mobility provisions. As a consequence, Wright argues, modern transport systems and the investments made in them are immensely wasteful of resources.

Although the car as a 'one size fits all' remedy for mobility issues has been discredited (Banister and Hickman 2014), the temptation in recent mobility planning has been to instate the electric car as a suitable zero carbon substitute. To address the scale of the problems a more comprehensive approach is needed such as that explored by Cass and Manderscheid (2018) in their advocacy of autono-mobility as a means to break the compulsion to travel. Attempts to increase efficiencies and to provide technical fixes to the problems of automobility from the perspective of Anthropocene mobilities and citizenship simply prolong the dominance of what Brand and Wissen (20121) call an 'imperial mode of living': one that exists only through the exploitation, suffering and destruction of others, human and non-human. To break from this cycle, based on mobility as an unquestioned good that can be advanced only through ever greater provision, requires us, they argue, to orient thinking around ideas of sufficiency.

Conclusions

Motorized travel, by its very nature, obscures the energetic and the environmental cost of movement. Properly provided passenger services coupled with carefully thought out (and dramatically scaled back) private motoring can provide the needs of much travel. In terms of care, commoning and caring for the commons in relation to the more-than-human world, the contributions of higher speed motor travel are necessarily limited. More importantly are the contributions they make in terms of social interaction. The scale of 'othering' currently embedded in motoring discourses and in the everyday interactions between motor and non-motor traffic on the roads is a problem that must be confronted as part of the building of citizenship. From the earlier discussions we can see the qualities that are necessary, but the question is how we can embed these in everyday practice. Thinking in terms of building responsive citizenship alerts us to the role of state authorities. As provisioners of mobility infrastructures they have an important task and their contribution can potentially do much to shift focus from individual travel behaviours to see how travel demand is produced through institutions. Cars are valuable tools and an essential part of future Anthropocene mobilities but while still considered in their current form as a default mode of travel, as primarily something for individual ownership and as an affirmation of a right to drive, they are very hard to reconcile with visions of Anthropocene mobility.

7

Coda: Towards Anthropocene mobilities

Introduction

The focus throughout the book has been on the experiences of travel and how those perceptions shape the ways that we interact with the world around. Ultimately, these effects are only felt at an individual level: only I can know what my experience is like, only you can know what your experience is like. The stress has been on inter-relationality as we interact with each other and the world around. The I-thou, I-It distinction emphasizes the quality of the relationship. Do we approach interaction as open or closed, instrumentally, for what I can deliver, or as gratuitous, open to whatever responses it invites. In our everyday travel do we seek to cut ourselves off from the elements and from other persons that might demand reaction from us? Each of us can reflect on how these perspectives engage with our own travel habits. Which of our travel processes are unconsidered or deliberately unnoticed? When we have the agency to act, how deeply do we engage?

The stress of recent research in sustainable transport has been undeniably and necessarily focused on systems of mobility and on the precise interventions to provide for or facilitate different vehicular actions. It defines infrastructures that will enable the passage of particular forms of traffic, whether that be through investment in new vehicular infrastructure for cycling, for trams or bus systems. Research understandably seeks mechanisms for practical transition to lower carbon and less polluting traffic. Yet large sums still go into smoothing and enabling the flows of road traffic, not its reduction. The aim of this last section is neither to summarize this research nor to produce a textbook for post-car futures. It is to draw out and revisit a number of elements touched upon in the discussions of this book that when connected might form lines of enquiry and possible courses of action.

Concentrating on vehicular traffic loses sight of the traveller. Counter to easy assumptions that we are able to make free choices from a range of equal possibilities, there are powerful structures and social forces that shape these decisions. We inherit path dependencies in transport planning and actions. The last century of decision-making has been grounded in assumptions of cheap energy, derived from burning fossil fuels. The myth has been an assumption that internal combustion engine-powered travel can be provided for all. The reality is that the ecological cost of high-energy travel on demand is greater than can be sustained and the social cost is the maintenance of privilege for drivers whose continued mobility depends on others not driving.

Transforming movement patterns from the current regime of automobility will not be easy. Nor will it come simply. Indeed, as I have stressed throughout, if all that happens in the current mobility transformation is a transition from one high-energy system to another, with high-speed, high-power electric vehicles taking the place of those with internal combustion engines, the problems of inequality, of space dominance, of poor air quality from particulates will remain. Given the current trend for ever-larger and heavier vehicles, this may even get worse.

Anthropocene mobility systems require abandoning the assumption that high-energy travel is an automatic right. The spatial relationships of work and housing, family life and the reproduction of society can no longer build in unquestioned assumptions of individual motorized commutes, whether for work, education or family life, including shopping, leisure and social life. It requires interrogation of the claimed need to drive: are the circumstances of dependence on private car travel ultimately of our own making? If we recognize individualized motor travel for the privilege it is, we may be better able to begin to comprehend the nature of the mobility transformation ahead.

Sufficiency

> To furnish a barren room is one thing. To continue to crowd in furniture until the foundation buckles is quite another. To have failed to solve the problem of producing goods would have been to continue man in his oldest and grievous misfortune. But to fail to see that we have solved it and fail to proceed thence to the next task would be fully as tragic. (Galbraith 1958: 285)

Running throughout the discussion here as a constant undercurrent to learning and understanding values for Anthropocene citizenship have been the themes of degrowth and its corollary, sufficiency. They have been deliberately underplayed and mentioned less than they might have been in order to focus on the experiential dimensions of travel.

What constitutes sufficient mobility? When is enough enough? What levels of mobility, of energy use, of material resource use, of particulate pollution and of carbon emissions are compatible with a credible politics of equality? What levels are desirable? These are hard questions, but these are questions that must be tackled if we are to think seriously about Anthropocene mobility scenarios. In the *Lancet Planetary Health Commission Report* (Gupta et al. 2024), the authors calculate that on the basis of earth-system justice, ensuring fair shares and equal access while remaining within earth-system boundaries, an appropriate global allocation of surface travel might be as little as 4,500 km per annum calculated on the basis of individual car driving. Beyond that we contribute to transgressing earth-system boundaries, or, alternatively, become dependent on the immobilities of others, those who travel less than their equal share. Although there can be questions about the methodology for this calculation, it provides a stark illustration of how far we might have to go in terms of thinking about fair shares of mobility in the Anthropocene.

The positive element one can take from this is that other modes of travel are much more energy efficient than motoring (see Chapter 6) and so act as multipliers of this base figure. Perhaps even more importantly, human-scale travel is minimal in its pressure on planetary biophysical systems. In these calculations, it is effectively, almost free mobility.

Mobility choices are moral choices. We can choose to be complicit in forms of energy use and waste generation (arising from our mobility practices) that imperil the well-being of those who we condemn to live through the consequences of our current choices. Climate destabilization is already upon us. Reading through the factors outlined in the IPCC sixth report is a sobering experience. Or we can consider what might be a sufficient level of travel for our own use and how that compares with a globally equal distribution of mobility privilege.

We can take a stand. Change will not be easy. Expectations of mobility will have to change. Personal and family sacrifices may be required. What we need to bear in mind, however, is that such changes are the renunciation of privileges that still only accrue to a very small percentage of the global population. The instantaneous accessibility of private motorized car travel only exists because others are denied it, or choose to relinquish their possibilities to drive. Modern European towns and cities function only because not everyone drives. Another area for structural change concerns housing. Cheap and affordable driving has made it easy to live apart from employment. Those with mobility impairments or limitations have never had that privilege. Yet they continue to survive and prosper in the midst of normalized assumptions of driving. We have to look towards the techniques and processes that enable their lives.

Abandoning motoring as an everyday, unconsidered action requires abandoning privilege. Reducing the amount driven is a goal in itself as part of a necessity to reduce the overall amount of travel. If we are to live responsibly in the Anthropocene, considerations of ecojustice (economic and ecological) demand change. The changes required are not those brought about by simple switches of power source or mode while retaining high-energy lifestyles, particularly in respect of mobility. Caring for the commons is simply incompatible with those activities that enclose commons. It is incompatible with unfettered demand for mobility, with more accumulation, with greater sequestration of energy sources, especially those translated into travel.

Anthropocene mobility as an abolitionist project

One way to usefully think about mobility transformations for the Anthropocene is through the lens of abolitionism, through which they can be simultaneously engaged as a process of liberation (Gilmore 2022). As Kathi Weeks (2023) explains, abolitionism as method approaches problems from a systemic analysis, not targeting individual examples. An abolitionist approach to automobility would therefore target it as a social and economic institution, not as the specific practices of driving or individual drivers. An abolitionist approach to the problem of high energy mobility would secondly focus on the transformation of the society that needs it, exploring ways to restructure planning and institutions such that they no longer depend on the mobilities of a previous century. Contrary to some expectations, abolitionist approaches are not hostile to reform. While sustainable transport activists may recognize the undesirability of private motoring's dominance of everyday mobility, it would, in the words of one early prison abolitionist, 'be unsafe to presume on the immediate prevalence of such wisdom in the community' (St. John 1912: 538). Consequently, we can share his desire 'for the present to inquire whether certain modifications are feasible in our ... regime and system' (St. John 1912: 538).

Solutions to current travel inequalities and its unsustainable patterns do not lie in banning or prohibiting any particular form of travel or transport. But there are places to start making decisions, especially in relation to personal travel, starting with those journeys that we have immediate power over. Reducing car use and flying is not just good for the planet but crucial to begin to develop the sensitivities to make us more caring Anthropocene citizens. Every decision we make will require some degree of sacrifice, some discipline. The appeal of mass motoring and its promise have been to make travel apparently available and accessible to all, while simultaneously obscuring the exclusionary effect it has on those not able or not willing to join its ranks.

There is little room for hypocrisy. The excuse that someone else has a more problematic lifestyle, so I don't need to do anything is not credible. The emphasis on the 'we' in the introductory chapter identified that high carbon travel is a privilege shared by all in the Global North, however internally ill-distributed. In Chapter 3 we saw that care is not simply an attitude but a complex ethic and a political action, expressing value. Care applied to everyday travel practices cannot be exclusive if it is to be meaningful; if care for the passenger means exclusion, creating spaces of privilege where the individual can be cosseted at the cost of others' (human and more-than-human) discomfort and disprivilege, then it is not care within the context of an ethic of care.

Non-car natives

'Digital natives are people who have grown up under the ubiquitous influence of the internet and other modern information technologies. Digital natives think, learn, and understand the world around them differently from people who have not been as subjected to modern technology' (AI-generated query response). If we are to consider post-car futures, then one of the pointers to the shapes of those futures, the skills, knowledge and experiences that can contribute to their construction come from those we might call non-car natives. They are not distinguished by a generational divide but as those who 'think learn and understand the world around them differently' by virtue of lives lived without dependence on car travel.

All through this work the emphasis has been on the need to take seriously the experiences of those not travelling. Little planning for vehicular traffic engages with the perceptual world of either travellers or non-travellers. Key to understanding how to build future car-light, flight-light mobility systems is to take seriously not only the mobility practices and strategies of those who already live car-light, flight-light lives but also those whose annual travel budgets, if we can call them that, already conform to the fair shares of mobility indicated by the *Lancet Planetary Health Commission Report*.

There are studies to be made and questions to be asked not only concerning how they navigate and travel but also how they experience and perceive the world. What factors make life pleasant and unpleasant? Travel and mobility researchers need to pay attention to the lives of the mobility impaired and those who electively choose low-carbon mobilities. They need to understand what the world looks like though other eyes, like those of children who are less than 1.5 m above the pavement. How do the designs of a new generation of electric SUV's shape their worlds?

The ambiguity of vulnerability

Campaigns for improvement in walking and cycling, both in terms of status and practical interventions, have long opposed the categorization of 'vulnerable road users'. In policy terms it reduced the non-motorized traveller to a secondary status and is frequently the source of a failure to question what actually is making the non-motorist vulnerable. Vulnerability becomes understood as an intrinsic quality of walking and cycling, an understanding that quickly shifts onto depicting them as inherently dangerous modes of everyday mobility.

Without wishing to revert to classifying all walking and cycling as vulnerable, from the perspective of Anthropocene mobilities, however, there is also something about the language of vulnerability that captures something important. From a care perspective, vulnerability is not a negative quality. In the transformation of limits into virtues and in the context of creating and encouraging a care ethic, it is entirely appropriate to highlight the vulnerability of travellers who are unprotected from the incursions of other, from dogs to drivers. Vulnerability to weather, the need to delay journeys, the unpredictability is a virtue rather than a curse. Relinquishing the control built in to enclosed, power-driven travel requires acknowledgement that such travel is an exercise of privilege, not a right.

Without the shield of the vehicle, one is vulnerable to the elements. This is precisely what created the enhanced possibilities of resonance. Walking and cycling as everyday travel habits help participants foster sensitivity to the environments in which they take place. They connect the human with the more-than-human: technologies, built environments, natural forces. Their limitations challenge the sequestration of resources and occasion a redistribution of privilege. They require that we are flexible, to adapt to changes in the seasons and the weather, to the quality of spaces and the socialities of encounter and interaction. They are self-limiting. They force us to acknowledge that we have to travel differently: not just substitute one power mode for another.

The ability to care needs recognition of our common frailty. Linked to this is the necessary embrace of open view of the other (see Chapter 6). To recognize other as fellow participants in processes of change is not to deny or to elide considerable differences between our travelling necessities and practices but recognizing that the diversity of travellers is part of the necessary plurality of mobilities proper to the Anthropocene. What cannot be embraced is the treatment by those already in positions of power of others as lesser.

To make a common adaption of the famous lines from Mary T. Lathrop's *judge softly*, 'Before you judge a man, walk a mile in his shoes.' Responsibility (responsiveness) requires just this, a degree of empathy. For mobilities, it is an almost literal injunction. It means everyday recognition that the slower, weaker movement is not an impediment to passage, but a part of our common reality. Steam gives way to sail is recognized shipping lore, and it continues to work where the spaces of travel are open water. But these are far from the confined spaces of roadways which operate more like canalized channels with restricted possibility. Two aspects are worth drawing attention to. First, that travel space is a scarce resource, and is made scarcer by the vehicle size. There is often little room for avoidance and so patience must be exercised. Mutual respect is necessary, even when there are disparities of speed and mass. Second, infrastructures are provisioned by state authorities. Authorities responsible for transport provision must also learn to exercise and express care. To deliberately create conflicts through the design of infrastructure to minimum standards (or even below) is to build conflict into encounter and should be read as an action of irresponsibility by provisioners.

Infrastructures

A watchword for any changes to infrastructure, for the actions taken to encourage and support change, must be that senses matter. But not just the senses and sensitivities of white able-bodied males. How do infrastructural interventions enable greater care for the commons? How do they encourage interaction? How do they avoid zones of exclusion?

On a practical level, lower used roads are degraded slower, require lower levels of maintenance. Transferring journeys to bus, to rail and tram will require investment shifts from the current focus on roads provision. Sufficient space for safe and pleasant cycle traffic in all its diversity requires removing space from motor traffic and reducing speeds in mixed traffic zones. To reiterate, this is not a call for an outright ban on driving but to centralize the idea of travel sufficiency: does a journey really warrant motoring? Lower motor traffic levels make it possible to appropriate space currently required for high-speed travel, increasing the travel space for other forms of wheeled travel without having to fundamentally redesign road systems. Infrastructural prioritization is a means by which political authorities can signal their commitment to Anthropocene mobility and to an understanding of sustainability that goes further than just wanting to maintain exploitative social and ecological relations.

There are no magic solutions that will fix the difficulties for every situation. Each location will have to work out what systems might be needed for lower energy travel. In any given situation: historical factors, density, topography, current degrees of auto dependency all have impacts.

One major element is common, however: transforming the need to travel as part of this process. The tragedy of Covid pandemics and the almost complete shutdown of travel options indicated that transformation of travel spaces and practices was possible, but also that changing patterns need support and encouragement. Many meetings, conferences and business activities that previously involved long travel distances shifted online.

These issues of infrastructure highlight the issue of provisioning. Providing infrastructures to include particular groups affirms the relationship between citizen and state. Seventy-five years of focus on maximizing the possibility for motoring and facilitating higher speeds of travel has created the motoring citizen. To an extent, the degree of unquestioned connection has elided the differences. To be a citizen has become de facto an assumption of the right to drive. The expectation of being the holder of a driver's licence allows the driving license to become a legitimate form of identification. Hence any measure by state authorities (local or national) is interpreted as an assault on their rights.

Reversing the narrative to ensure that driving is a privilege is an important first move in creating an Anthropocene citizenship rather than automotive citizenship. Part of the alteration involves the affirmation of other mobilities through not just monetary investment but the symbolic and discursive mechanisms that mediate the relations between state and its interventions. How and where delivery agencies exist, what they are named and where their impact is visible are part of this process.

Conclusions: Frugal abundance

What I've tried to show in these discussions is that reducing travel and travel expectations need not be a 'hairshirt' policy of asceticism. They are rather what Latouche (2018: 22) has described as strategies of 'frugal abundance'. Our current emphasis on quantity obscures the value of quality. Travel less, travel better. The Anthropocene as an understanding of our situation places us in a condition where the effects on ecosystems that we collectively create and maintain through our actions, especially our everyday, repeated actions, can no longer be ignored. Searches for new patterns of mobility can't simply disregard the effects that those everyday behaviours have on others, human and more-than-human. This is an unashamedly moral argument, but one that addresses not just individual choices but the elective actions of all involved in planning and provisioning mobility, and in the institutions that create demand for (more) travel through the structuring of their activities.

Valuing others requires recognizing their integrity. Relationality interrogates our simplest and most overlooked actions to ask what effect they might have on others. If we are currently citizens whose lives are constructed on the often invisible privilege of global hypermobility, whose possibilities of flourishing are constrained by our own exercises of privilege?

A compulsion to travel is not just made possible by high-energy systems, but becomes an apparently necessary part of a linked system of growth. Dwelling allows us to reconsider our relation to place and travel. Belonging and identification with place, together with meaning forged through interaction are positively developed through the direct contact of walking, wheeling and cycling journeys. These are connections with place not based in nationalism but in empathy with the more-than-human, the geos that is beyond the boundaries of political borders and named territory. This form of respect for place, while localized, is difficult to frame in exclusionary terms because it is no longer an abstract identification forged through symbols and concepts but through direct interaction. A citizenship of place can be rooted by these encounters. Through walking and cycling, we come to know where we live. Processes of responsible Anthropocene travel allow us to connect with the world, through the sensing and feeling process that creates a sense of belonging.

At the outset, the discussion posed the problem of how to live together as less-destructive planet-dwellers. The various explorations have sought to explore some of the ramifications of different ways of moving and travelling that can give pointers towards ways of imagining these futures. Framing the debate on reduced mobility as one of good citizenship is important because it alerts us to see this is more than an issue of rationing or austerity mobilities, but of finding ways to share better worlds. Other Worlds Are Possible was the slogan that emerged from the World Social Forum. From the shared investigations from which this study is drawn emerges the conclusion that Other Worlds of Mobility Are Possible.

References

Abord de Chatillon, M. (2022), 'Appropriating the Bicycle: Repair and Maintenance Skills and the Bicycle–Cyclist Relationship', in M. Adam and N. Orthar (eds), *Becoming Urban Cyclists: From Socialization to Skills*, 215–43, Chester: University of Chester Press.

Abram, D. (1997), *The Spell of the Sensuous: Perception and Language in a More-Than-Human World*, London: Vintage.

Adams, J. (1985), *Risk and Freedom: The Record of Road Safety Regulation*, London: Transport Publishing Projects.

Adams, J. (1995), *Risk*, London: Routledge.

Adlof, F. (2016), *Gifts of Cooperation, Mauss and Pragmatism*, Abingdon: Routledge.

Agarwal, A., and Narain, S. (1991), *Global Warming in an Unequal World*, New Delhi: Centre for Science and Environment (CSE).

Agarwal, A., Sharma, A. and RoyChowdhury, A. (1996), *Slow Murder: The Deadly Story of Vehicular Pollution in India*, New Delhi: Centre for Science and Environment (CSE).

Akrich, M., and Latour, B. (1992), 'A Summary of a Convenient Vocabulary for the Semiotics of Human and Nonhuman Assemblies', in W. Bijker and J. Law (eds), *Shaping Technology/Building Society: Studies in Sociotechnical Change*, 259–64, Cambridge, MA: MIT Press.

Alvord, S. (2000), *Divorce Your Car!: Ending the Love Affair with the Automobile*, Vancouver: New Society.

Arias-Maldonado, M. (2020), 'Bedrock or Social Construction? What Anthropocene Science Means for Political Theory', *The Anthropocene Review*, 7(2): 97–112.

Armstrong, K. (2023), *Sacred Nature: How We Can Recover Our Bond with the Natural World*, London: Bodley Head.

Atkinson, M. (2018), 'Hashtag #Affect', *Capacious: Journal for Emerging Affect Enquiry*, 1(2): ii–vi.

Augé, M. (2014). *The Future*, trans. J. Howe. [Originally *Futuro*, 2012], London: Verso.

Bakhtin, M. M. (1993 [1919–21]), *Toward a Philosophy of the Act*, trans. Vadim Liapunov, Austin: University of Texas Press.

Baldwin, A., Fröhlich, C. and Rothe, D. (2019), 'From Climate Migration to Anthropocene Mobilities: Shifting the Debate', *Mobilities*, 14(3): 289–97. https://doi.org/10.1080/17450101.2019.1620510.

Banister, D. (2005), *Unsustainable Transport: City Transport in the New Century*, Abingdon: Routledge.

Banister, D., and Hickman, K. (2014), *Transport, Climate Change and the City*, Abingdon: Routledge.

Banks, I. (2004), *Raw Spirit*, London: Arrow Books.

Bauman, Z. (2013), 'Europe Is Trapped between Power and Politics', *Social Europe*, 14 May. https://www.socialeurope.eu/2013/05/europe-is-trapped-between-power-and-politics/.

Beasley, C., and Bacchi, C. (2012), 'Making Politics Fleshly: The Ethic of Social Flesh', in A. Bletsas and C. Beasley (eds), *Engaging with Carol Bacchi: Strategic Interventions and Exchanges*, 99–120, University of Adelaide Press.

Beck, U. (2016), 'Varieties of Second Modernity and the Cosmopolitan Vision', *Theory, Culture & Society*, 33(7): 257–70.

Beck, U., and Grande, E. (2010), 'Varieties of second Modernity: The Cosmopolitan Turn in Social and Political Theory', *British Journal of Sociology*, 61(3): 409–43.

Benjamin, W. (1997 [1928]), 'One Way Street', in W. Benjamin, *One Way Street and Other Writings*, trans. E. F. N. Jephcott and K. Shorter, 45–104, London: Verso.

Bennett, J. (2010), *Vibrant Matter: A Political Ecology of Things*, Durham, NC: Duke University Press.

Berry, W. (2020), *What I Stand On: The Collected Essays of Wendell Berry 1969–2017*, Washington, DC: Library of America.

Bhambra, G., and Holmwood, J. (2021), *Colonialism and Modern Social Theory*, Cambridge: Polity.

Bińczyk, E. (2019), 'The Most Unique Discussion of the 21st Century? The Debate on the Anthropocene Pictured in Seven Points', *The Anthropocene Review*, 6(1–2): 3–18.

Bissell, D. (2010), 'Pasenger Mobilities: Affective Atmospheres and the Sociality of Publuc Transport', *Environment and Planning D: Society and Space*, 28(2): 270–89.

Bissell, D. (2018), *Transit Life: How Commuting Is Transforming Our Cities*, Cambridge, MA: MIT Press.

Bjørkdahl, K., and Franco Duharte, A. S. eds. (2022), *Academic Flying and the Means of Communication*, Singapore: Palgrave Macmillan.

Böhm, S., Jones, C., Land, C. and Paterson, M. eds (2006), *Against Automobility*, Oxford: Blackwell.

Boehm, S. L., Jeffery, J., Hecke, C., Schumer, J., Jaeger, C., Fyson, K., Levin, A., Nilsson, S., Naimoli, E., Daly, J., Thwaites, K., Lebling, R., Waite, J., Collis, M., Sims, N., Singh, E., Grier, W., Lamb, S., Castellanos, A., Lee, M., Geffray, R., Santo, M., Balehegn, M., Petroni and Masterson, M. (2023), *State of Climate Action 2023*. Berlin and Cologne, Germany, San Francisco, CA, and Washington, DC: Bezos Earth Fund, Climate Action Tracker, Climate Analytics, ClimateWorks Foundation, NewClimate Institute, the United Nations Climate Change High-Level Champions, and World Resources Institute. https://doi.org/10.46830/wrirpt.23.00010

Bohlin, A. (2020), 'The Liveliness of Ordinary Objects: Living with Stuff in the Anthropocene', in R. Harrison and C. Sterling (eds), *Deterritorializing the*

Future Heritage in, of and after the Anthropocene, 96–119, Ann Arbor, MI: Open Humanities Press.

Boff, L. (1995), *Ecology and Liberation: a new paradigm*, Maryknoll, NY: Orbis.

Bonham, J., and Bacchi, C. (2013), 'Cycling Subjectivities in on-Going Formation: Interviews as Political Interventions', *Paper presented to Foucault and Mobilities symposium*, University of Lucerne, Switzerland, 6–7 January.

Bookchin, M. (1973), 'Environmentalists versus Ecologists: An Interview with Murray Bookchin', *Undercurrents*, 4: 13–16.

Bookchin, M. (1980), *Toward an Ecological Society*, Montreal: Black Rose Books.

Braidotti, R. (2017), 'Four Theses on Posthuman Feminism', in R. Grusin (ed.), *Anthropocene Feminism*, 21–48, Minneapolis: University of Minneapolis Press.

Braidotti, R. (2022), *Posthuman Feminism*, Cambridge: Polity.

Brand, U., and Wissen, M. (2021), *The Imperial Mode of Living: Everyday Life and the Ecological Crisis of Capitalism*, trans. Z. Murphy King, London: Verso.

Brand, U., Muraca, B., Pineault, E., Sahakian, M., Schaffartzik, A., Novy, A., Streissler, C., Haberl, H., Asara, V., Dietz, K., Lang, M., Kothari, A., Smith, T., Spash, C., Brad, A., Pichler, M., Plank, C., Velegrakis, G., Jahn, T., Carter, A., Huan, Q., Kallis, G., Martínez Alier, J., Riva, G., Satgar, V., Teran Mantovani, E., Williams, M., Wissen, M. and Görg, C. (2021), 'From Planetary to Societal Boundaries: An Argument for Collectively Defined Self-Limitation', *Sustainability: Science, Practice and Policy*, 17(1): 264–91. https://doi.org/10.1080/15487733.2021.1940754.

Braun, R., and Randell, R. (2021), 'The Vermin of the Street: The Politics of Violence and the *Nomos* of Automobility', *Mobilities*, 17(1): 53–68.

Buber, M. (1937 [1923]), *I and Thou*, trans. R. G. Smith, Edinburgh: T&T Clark.

Buber, M. (1961 [1929]). 'Dialogue', in M. Buber, *Between Man and Man*, trans. R. G. Smith, 1–38, London: Fontana.

Bull, M. (2000) *Sounding Out the City; Personal Stereos and the Management of Everyday Life*, Oxford: Berg.

Bull, M. (2004), 'Automobility and the Power of Sound', *Theory, Culture & Society*, 21(4/5): 243–59.

Caimotto, M. C. (2020), *Discourses of Cycling, Road Use and Sustainability: And Ecolinguistic Investigation*, Chaim: Palgrave Macmillan.

Carpenter, E. (1896), *Towards Democracy*. Complete edition in four parts, Manchester: Labour Press.

Cass, N., and Manderscheid, K. (2018), 'The Autonomobility System: Mobility Justice and Freedom under Sustainability', in *Mobilities, Mobility Justice and Social Justice*, edited by N. Cook and D. Butz, 101–15, London: Taylor and Francis.

Cayley, D. (2005), *The Rivers North of the Future. The Testament of Ivan Illich*, Toronto: Anansi Press.

Cebrat, G., Cox, P. and Gustavsson, T. (2009), 'New Driver Assistance Systems: Improving Perceived Safety and Breaking the Vicious Circle of Safety Related Weight Gain', *Technology*, 2(10): 1–10.

CCC (2020), *The Sixth Carbon Budget: Sector Summary: surface transport Surface Transport*, https://www.theccc.org.uk/wp-content/uploads/2020/12/Sector-summ ary-Surface-transport.pdf.

CCC (2022), *CCC Monitoring Framework: Assessing UK Progress in Reducing Emissions*, https://www.theccc.org.uk/publication/ccc-monitoring-framework/.

Chakrabarty, D. (2009), 'The Climate of History. Four Theses', *Critical Inquiry* 35(2): 197–222.

Chakrabarty, D. (2018), 'Anthropocene Time', *History and Theory*, 57: 5–32.

Chester, M., and Allenby, B. (2021), 'Transportation for the Anthropocene', *Transfers Magazine* issue #7.

Chesters, G., and Smith, D. (2001), 'The Neglected Art of Hitch-Hiking: Risk, Trust and Sustainability', *Sociological Research Online* 6(3): 63–71. Doi: 10.5153/sro.605.

Clayton, W., and Musselwhite, C. (2013), Exploring Changes to Cycle Infrastructure to Improve the Experience of Cycling for Families', *Journal of Transport Geography*, 33: 54–61.

Clement, F., Harcourt, W. J., Joshi, D. and Sato, C. (2019), 'Feminist Political Ecologies of the Commons and Commoning', *International Journal of the Commons*, 13(1): 1–15.

Cohen, T. and Colebrook, C. (2016), 'Preface', in T. Cohen C. Colebrook and J. H. Miller (eds), *Twilight of the Anthropocene Idols*, 7–19, Ann Arbor, MI: Open Humanities Press.

Colebrook, C. (2002), *Gilles Deleuze*, London: Routledge.

Colebrook, C. (2016), 'What Is the Anthropo-Political?', in T. Cohen, C. Colebrook and J. H. Miller (eds), *Twilight of the Anthropocene Idols*, 81–125, Ann Arbor, MI: Open Humanities Press.

Colebrook, C. (2020), 'The Future Is Already Deterritorialized', in R. Harrison and C. Sterling (eds), *Deterritorializing the Future: Heritage in, of and after the Anthropocene*, 346–83, Ann Arbor, MI: Open Humanities Press.

Collings, D. A. (2014), *Stolen Future, Broken Present: The Human Significance of Climate Change*, Ann Arbor, MI: Open Humanities Press.

Conley, J., and McLaren A. T. eds. (2009), *Car Troubles: Critical Studies of Automobility and Auto-Mobility*, London: Routledge.

Connolly, W. E. (2010), 'Materialities of Experience', in D. Coole, and S. Frost (eds), *New Materialisms: Ontology, Agency, and Politics*, 178–200, Durham, NC: Duke University Press.

Cook, S. (2017), 'Rushing, Dashing, Scrambling: The Role of the Train Station in Producing the Reluctant Runner', in J. Spinney, S. Reimer, and P. Pinch (eds), *Mobilising Design, Designing Mobilities: Intersections, Affordances, Relations*, 62–75, Abingdon: Routledge.

Corrêa, D. S., Peters, G. and Tziminadis, J. L. (2021), 'Human beings are first and foremost resonant beings'. Interview with Professor Hartmut Rosa. *Civitas* 21(1): 120–9.

Cox, P. (2007), 'The Politics of Pedalling: Representation and Advocacy', in *Conference Proceedings: Velo-City 2007, June 12–15, Munich*, Munich: Federal Ministry of Transport, Buildings and Urban Affairs.

Cox, P. (2010), *Moving People: Sustainable Transport Development*, London: Zed.

Cox, P. (2018), 'Senses Matter: A Sensory Ethnography of Urban Velomobility', in K. Hartmann-Petersen, E. L. Perez Fjalland and M. Freudendal-Pedersen (eds), *Networked Urban Mobilities Volume 2: Experiencing*, 101–5, Abingdon: Routledge.

Cox, P. (2019), *Cycling: A Sociology of Vélomobility*, Abingdon: Routledge.

Cox, P., and Koglin, T. eds (2020) *The Politics of Cycling Infrastructure: Spaces and (in)equality*. Bristol: Policy.

Cox, P. (2020b), 'Reading Historical Film through Sensory Ethnography', in D. Turner (ed.), *Transport and Its Place in History: Making the Connections*, 153–68, Abingdon: Routledge.

Cox, P. (2020c), 'Theorising Infrastructure: A Politics of Spaces and Edges', in P. Cox and T. Koglin (eds), *The Politics of Cycling Infrastructure: Spaces and (in)equality*, 15–34, Bristol: Policy.

Cox, P. (2023), Vélomobility Is to Degrowth as Automobility Is to Growth: Prefigurative Cycling Imaginaries', *Applied Mobilities*, 8(1): 265–85.

Cox, P. (2024), *Cycling Activism. Bike Politics and Social Movements*, Abingdon: Routledge.

Cox, P. (forthcoming 2025), *Rethinking Emancipation*. DPS Working Paper, University of Kassel.

Cox, P., and Van de Walle, F. (2007), 'Bicycles Don't Evolve: Velomobiles and the modelling of transport technologies', in D. Horton, P. Rosen and P. Cox (eds), Cycling and Society, 113–32, Abingdon: Routledge.

Cresswell, T. (2010), 'Towards a Politics of Mobility', *Environment and Planning D: Society and Space*, 28(1): 17–31. https://doi.org/10.1068/d11407.

Crutzen, P. J., and Stoermer, E. F. (2000), 'The "Anthropocene"', *Global Change Newsletter*, 41: 17–18.

Culver, L., Egner, H., Gallini, S., Kneitz, A., Lousley, C., Lübken, U., Mincyte, D., Mom, G. and Winder, G. (2011), 'Revisiting Risk Society: A Conversation with Ulrich Beck'. *RCC Perspectives* 2011/6.

Curtin, D. W. (1999), *Chinnagounder's Challenge: The question of Ecological Citizenship*, Bloomington: Indiana University Press.

Curtin, D. (2022), 'Compassion and Being Human', in C. J. Adams and L. Gruen *Ecofeminisms: Feminist Intersections with Other Animals and the Earth*, 2nd edn, 69–87, London: Bloomsbury.

Cwerner, S. (2008), 'Introducing Aeromobilities', in S. Cwerner, S. Kesselring and J. Urry (eds), *Aeromobilities*, 1–21, Abingdon: Routledge.

Cwerner, S. Kesselring, S. and Urry, J. eds. (2008), *Aeromobilities*, Abingdon: Routledge.

Dant, T. (2004), 'The Driver-car', *Theory, Culture and Society*, 21 (4–5): 61–79.

Dedeoglu, C., and Ekmekcioglu, C. (2020). 'Information Infrastructures and the Future of Ecological Citizenship in the Anthropocene', *Social Sciences (Basel)*, 9(1): 3. https://doi.org/10.3390/socsci9010003.

Delaney, H. Parkhurst, G. and Melia, S. (2017), 'Walking and Cycling on Shared-Use Paths: The User Perspective', *Proceedings of the ICE – Municipal Engineer*, 170(3): 175–84.

Demart, S. (2022), 'Afro-Belgian Activist Resistances to research Procedures: Reflections on Epistemic Extractivism and Decolonial Interventions in Sociological Research', *Current Sociology*, 72(3): 581–98.

Deutsches Museum Verkehrscentrum (2023), *Future Mobilities*, Sustainable Urban travel exhibition.

Dialynas, G., Happee, R., and Schwab, A. L. (2019), 'Design and Hardware Selection for a Bicycle Simulator', *Mechanical Sciences*, 10(1): 1–10.

Disch, L., van de Sande, M. and Urbinati, N. eds (2019), *The Constructivist Turn in Political Representation*, Edinburgh: Edinburgh University Press.

Dobson, A. (2003), *Citizenship and the Environment*, Oxford: Oxford University Press.

Dobson, J. (2021), 'Wellbeing and Blue-Green Space in Post-Pandemic Cities: Drivers, Debates and Departures', *Geography Compass*, 15(10): e12593. https://doi.org/10.1111/gec3.12593

Douthwaite, R. (1992), *The Growth Illusion*, Bideford: Resurgence.

Dunlap, R., Jose, J., Standridge, S. H. and Pruitt, C. (2020), Experiences of Urban Cycling: Emotional Geographies of People and Place', *Leisure Studies*, 40(1): 82–95.

Dryzek, J. S. (2013), *The Politics of the Earth*, 3rd edn, Oxford: Oxford University Press.

Dzwonkowska, D. (2021), 'Global Citizenship as a Virtue for the Anthropocene: Philosophical and Educational Perspective', *Globalisation, Societies and Education*, 20(5): 695–704.

Edgerton, D. (2006), *The Shock of the Old: Technology and Global History Since 1900*, London: Profile.

Egan, R., and Caulfield, B. (2024), 'Driving as Essential, Cycling as Conditional: How Automobility Is Politically Sustained in Discourses of Everyday Mobility'. *Mobilities*. (Online first) 10.1080/17450101.2024.2325370.

Eisenstadt, N. (2013), 'Non-Domination, Governmentality and the Care of the Self', in M. Lopes de Souza, R. J. White and S. Springer (eds), *Theories of Resistance: Anarchism, Geography, and the Spirit of Revolt*, 27–50, London: Rowman & Littlefield.

Escobar, A. (2007), ' "Post-Development" as Concept and Social Practice', in A. Ziai (ed.), *Exploring Post-Development: Theory and Practice, Problems and Perspectives*, 18–32, Abingdon: Routledge.

Escobar, A. (2020), *Pluriversal Politics: The real and the possible*, Durham, NC: Duke University Press.

Esteva, G. (2023), *A Critique of Development and Other Essays*, Abingdon: Routledge.

Esteva, G., Babones, S. J. and Babicky, P. (2013), *The Future of Development: A Radical Manifesto*, Bristol: Policy.

Euler, J. (2018), 'Conceptualizing the Commons: Moving Beyond the Goods-based Definition by Introducing the Social Practices of Commoning as Vital Determinant', *Ecological Economics*, 143: 10–16.

Featherstone, M., Thrift, N. and Urry, J. eds. (2005), *Automobilities*, London: Sage.

Feddes, F., and de Lange, M. (2019), *Bike City Amsterdam: How Amsterdam Became the Cycling Capital of the World*, Amsterdam: uitg. Bas Lubberhuizen.

Fox, N. and Alldred, P. (2019), 'Sustainability, Feminist Posthumanism and the Unusual Capacities of (Post)humans', *Environmental Sociology*, 6(2): 121–31.

Fraser, N. (1990), 'Rethinking the Public Sphere: A Contribution to the Critique of Actually Existing Democracy', *Social Text*, 25/26: 56–80.

Fraser, N. (2022), *Cannibal Capitalism: How our System Is Devouring Democracy, Care, and the Planet – and What We Can Do about It*, London: Verso.

Fredengren, C. and Åsberg, C. (2020), 'Checking in with Deep Time: Intragenerational Care in Registers of Feminist Posthumanities, the Case of Gärstadsverken', in R. Harrison and C. Sterling (eds), *Deterritorializing the Future: Heritage in, of and after the Anthropocene*, 56–95, Ann Arbor, MI: Open Humanities Press.

Friends of the Earth (1972), *The Stockholm Conference: Only One Earth. An Introduction to the Politics of Survival*, London: Earth Island.

Fremaux A. (2017), *After the Anthropocene: Green Republicanism in a Post-Capitalist World*, London: Palgrave Macmillan.

Galbraith, J. K. (1958), *The Affluent Society*, London: Penguin.

Galeano, E. (2000 [1998]), *Upside Down*, trans. M. Fried, London: Picador.

García-López, G., Lang, U. and Singh, N. (2021), 'Commons, Commoning and Co-Becoming: Nurturing Life-in-Common and Post-Capitalist Futures', *Environment and Planning E: Nature and Space*, 4(4): 1199–1216.

Gehl, J. (2010), *Cities for People*, Washington, DC: Island Press.

Gilmore, r. W. (2022), *Abolition Geography: Essays Towards Liberation*, London: Verso.

Goodley, D., and Runswick-Cole, K. (2013). 'The Body as Disability and Possability: Theorizing the "Leaking, Lacking and Excessive" Bodies of Disabled Children', *Scandinavian Journal of Disability Research*, 15(1): 1–19.

Goodman, A. (2018), *Gathering Ecologies: Thinking Beyond Interactivity*, Ann Arbor, MI: Open Humanities Press.

Gorringe, T. (1999), *Fair Shares: Ethics and the Global Economy*, London: Thames and Hudson.

Gorz, A. (1980 [1975]). *Ecology as Politics*. London: Pluto [originally *Écologie et politique*, Editions Galilée].

Gotby, A. (2023), *They Call It Love: The Politics of Emotional Life*, London: Verso.

Gret, M., and Sintomer, Y. (2005), *The Porto Alegre Experiment: Learning Lessons for Better Democracy*, London: Zed.

Gros, F. (2023), *A Philosophy of Walking*, 2nd edn, trans. J. Howe and A. Bliss, London: Verso.

Gunn S. (2011), 'The Buchanan Report, Environment and the Problem of Traffic in 1960s Britain', *Twentieth Century British History*, 22(4): 521–42.

Gunn, S. (2018), 'Ring Road: Birmingham and the Collapse of the Motor City Ideal in 1970s Britain', *The Historical Journal*, 61(1): 227–48.

Gupta, J. et al. (2024), A Just World on a Safe Planet: A Lancet Planetary Health–Earth Commission Report on Earth-system Boundaries, Translations, and Transformations', *The Lancet Planetary Health* [online first https://doi.org/10.1016/S2542-5196(24)00042-1].

Häkli, J. (2018), 'The Subject of Citizenship – Can There Be a Posthuman Civil Society?', *Political Geography*, 67: 166–75. https://doi.org/10.1016/j.polgeo.2017.08.006.

Hamilton, C. (2020), 'Towards a Fifth Ontology for the Anthropocene', *Angelaki*, 25(4): 110–19, https://doi.org/10.1080/0969725X.2020.1790839.

Hamilton, C., Bonneuil, C. and Gemenne, F. (2015), 'Thinking the Anthropocene', in C. Hamilton, C. Bonneuil and F. Gemenne (eds), *The Anthropocene and the Global Environmental Crisis: Rethinking Modernity in a New Epoch*, 1–18, London: Routledge.

Hanish, C. (1970), 'The Personal Is Political', in S. Firestone and A. Koedt (eds), *Notes from the Second Year: Women's Liberation: Major Writers of the Radical Feminists*, 76–8, New York: New York Radical Feminists.

Haraway, D. (2016), *Staying with the Trouble: Making Kin in the Chthulucene*, Durham, NC: Duke University Press.

Head, L. (2015), 'The Anthropoceneans', *Geographical Research*, 53(3): 313–20.

Head, L. (2018), *Hope and Grief in the Anthropocene: Re-conceptualising Human-Nature Relations*, Abingdon: Routledge.

Hedenström, A., and Åkesson, S. (2016), 'Ecology of Tern Flight in Relation to Wind, Topography and Aerodynamic Theory', *Philosophical Transactions of the Royal Society B*, 371: 20150396. https://doi.org/10.1098/rstb.2015.0396.

Hempsall, C. (2022), Is the Theory of Wild Pedagogies Precisely the Utopian Philosophy the Anthropocene Needs?, *Canadian Journal of Environmental Education*, 25: 222–36.

Herlihy, D. V. (2004), *Bicycle: The History*. New Haven, CT: Yale University Press.

Hickman, T., Partzsch, L., Pattberg, P. and Welland, S. eds (2019), *The Anthropocene Debate and Political Science*, Abingdon: Routledge.

Houghton, J. (1994), *Global Warming: The Complete Briefing*, Eastbourne: Lion Books.

Illich, I. (1973), *Tools for Conviviality*, London: Calder and Boyars.

Illich, I. (1974), *Energy and Equity*, London: Calder and Boyars.

Ingold, T. (2000), *The Perception of the Environment: Essays on Livelihood, Dwelling and Skill*, Abingdon Routledge.

Ingold, T. (2021), 'The Seat and the Saddle: How Slow Is Quick and Fast Is Stuck', in P. Pileri and R. Moscarelli (eds), *Cycling and Walking for regional Development*, 17–21, Chaim: Springer Nature.

James, C. L. R. (2022 [1938]), *The Black Jacobins: Toussaint L'Ouverture and the San Domingo Revolution*, London: Penguin.

Jaramillo, P. S. Kahn Ribeiro, P. Newman, S. Dhar, O. E. Diemuodeke, T. Kajino, D.S. Lee, S. B. Nugroho, X. Ou, A. Hammer Strømman, J. Whitehead (2022), 'Transport', in IPCC (2022), *Climate Change 2022: Mitigation of Climate Change. Contribution of Working Group III to the Sixth Assessment Report of the Intergovernmental Panel on Climate Change* [P. R. Shukla, J. Skea, R. Slade, A. Al Khourdajie, R. van Diemen, D. McCollum, M. Pathak, S. Some, P. Vyas, R. Fradera, M. Belkacemi, A. Hasija, G. Lisboa, S. Luz, J. Malley (eds)], Cambridge: Cambridge University Press. doi: 10.1017/9781009157926.012.

Jickling, b., Blenkinsop, S., Timmerman, N. and De Danann, M. eds (2018) *Wild Pedagogies: Touchstones for Re-Negotiating Education and the Environment in the Anthropocene*, Cham: Palgrave Macmillam.

Jungnickel, K., and Aldred, R. (2014), 'Cycling's Sensory Strategies: How Cyclists Mediate their Exposure to the Urban Environment', *Mobilities*, 9(2): 238–55.

Khan, M., Bell, S. and Wood, J. (2021), *Place, Pedagogy and Play: Participation, Design and Research with Children*, Abingdon: Routledge.

Kanji, A. (2017), 'Colonial Animality: Constituting Canadian Settler Colonialism through the Human-Animal Relationship', in M. Woons and S. Weier (eds), *Critical Epistemologies of global politics*, 63–78, Bristol: E-International Relations.

Karndacharuk, A., Wilson, D. and Dunn, R. (2014), 'A Review of the Evolution of Shared (Street) Space Concept in Urban Environments', *Transport Reviews*, 34(2): 190–220.

Kern, L. (2019), *Feminist City: Claiming Space in a Man-Made World*, Toronto: Between the Lines.

Kidder, J. L. (2012), 'Parkour, The Affective Appropriation of Urban Space, and the Real/Virtual Dialectic', *City & Community*, 11(3): 229–53.

Kinna, R., and Prichard, A. (2019), 'Anarchism and Non-Domination', *Journal of Political Ideologies*, 24(3): 221–40.

Klein, N. (2014), *This Changes Everything: Capitalism vs. the Climate*, London: Penguin.

Knoflacher, H. (2009), *Virus Auto: Die Geschichte einer Zerstörung*, Berlin: Ueberreuter.

Koglin, T. (2020), 'Spatial Dimensions of the Marginalisation of Cycling – Marginalisation through Rationalisation?', in P. Cox and T. Koglin (eds), *The Politics of Cycling Infrastructure*, 55–71, Bristol: Policy Press.

Kokkola, M., Nikolaeva, A. and Brömmelstroet, M. t. (2023), 'Missed Connections? Everyday Mobility Experiences and the Sociability of Public Transport in Amsterdam during COVID-19', *Social & Cultural Geography*, 24(10): 1693–1712.

Kompridis, N. (2014), 'Introduction. Turning and Returning: The Aesthetic Turn in Political Thought', in N. Kompridis (ed.), *The Aesthetic Turn in Political Thought*, xiv–xxxviii, London: Bloomsbury.

Kothari, A., Salleh, A., Escobar, A., Federico, D. and Acosta, A. eds. (2019), *Pluriverse: A Post-Development Dictionary*, Chennai: Tulika.

Koukal, D. R. (2020), 'Detroit Bike City and the Reconstruction of Community', *Open Philosophy*, 3: 1 716–29.

Krarup, T.M. and Blok, A. (2011), 'Unfolding the social: quasi-actants, virtual theory, and the new empiricism of Bruno Latour', *The Sociological Review*, 59(1): 42–63.

Laastad, S.G. (2020), 'Nature as a Subject of Rights? National Discourses on Ecuador's Constitutional Rights of Nature', *Forum for Development Studies*, 47(3): 401–25.

Laing, M., and Willson, J. eds. (2020), *Revisiting the Gaze: The Fashioned Body and the Politics of Looking*, London: Bloomsbury.

Latouche, S. (2018), The Misadventures of the Good Life between Modernity and Degrowth: From Happiness to GDP to Buen Vivir', in H. Rosa and C. Henning (eds), *The Good Life beyond Growth: New Perspectives*, 17–28, Abingdon: Routledge.

Latour, B. (1999), *The Politics of Nature: How to Bring the Sciences into Democracy*, Cambridge: Polity.

Latour, B. (2022), *After Lockdown: A Metamorphosis*, trans. J. Rose, Cambridge: Polity.

Leblanc, R. M. (1999) *Bicycle Citizens: The Political World of the Japanese Housewife*, Berkeley: University of California Press.

Lefebvre, H. (2014 [1961]), *Critique of Everyday Life*, London: Verso.

Leinfelder, R. (2013), 'Assuming Responsibility for the Anthropocene: Challenges and Opportunities in Education', in H. Trischler (ed.), *Anthropocene – Envisioning the Future of the Age of Human. RCC-Perspectives*, 2/2013, Munich: Rachel Carson Center.

Lessenich, S. (2019), *Living Well at Others' Expense*, Cambridge: Polity.

Linebaugh, P. (2014), *Stop, Thief! The Commons, Enclosures, and Resistance*, Oakland: PM Press.

Locke, P. (2017), 'Elephants as Persons, Affective Apprenticeship, and Fieldwork with Nonhuman Informants in Nepal', *Hau. Journal of Ethnographic Theory*, 7(1): 353–76.

Longhurst, J. (2015), *Bike Battles: A History of Sharing the American Road*, Seattle: Washington University Press.

Loo, W. B., and Bunnell, T. (2018), 'Landscaping Selves through Parkour: Reinterpreting the Urban Environment of Singapore', *Space and Culture*, 21(2): 145–58.

Lou, L. (2019), 'Freedom as Ethical Practices: On the Possibility of Freedom through Freeganism and Freecycling in Hong Kong', *Asian Anthropology*, 8(4): 249–65.

Lou, L. I. T. (2022). 'The art of unnoticing: Risk perception and contrived ignorance in China', *American Ethnologist*, 49(4), 580–94. https://doi.org/10.1111/amet.13099.

Löwy, M. (2018), 'Pessimisme révolutionnaire. Le marxisme romantique de Walter Benjamin', *Cités*, 74: 91–104.

Lummis, C. D. (1996), *Radical Democracy*, Ithaca: Cornell University Press.

Lynch, K. (2022), *Care and Capitalism*, Cambridge: Polity.

Maas, W. (ed.) (2013), *Multilevel Citizenship*, Philadelphia: University of Pennsylvania Press.

MacCormack, P. (2020), *The Ahuman Manifesto: Activism for the End of the Anthropocene*, London: Bloomsbury.

Macey, J. (1991), *World as Lover, World as Self*, Berkeley, CA: Parallax Press.

Mackay, F. (2015), *Radical Feminism: Feminist Activism in Movement*, London: Palgrave Macmillan.

Maller, C. (2018), *Healthy Urban Environments: More-Than-Human Theories*, Abingdon: Routledge.

Maller, C. (2021), 'Re-Orienting Nature-Based Solutions with More-Than-Human Thinking', *Cities*, 113: 103155.

Manderscheid, K. and Cass, N. (2023), 'A Socio-Ecologically Sustainable Mobility Regime: Can We Move Beyond the Car?', *Applied Mobilities*, 8(3): 187–200.

Matveev, J. (2018), 'From Martin Buber's I and Thou to Mikhail Bakhtin's Concept of "Polyphony"', in P. Mendes-Flohr (ed.), *Dialogue as a Trans-Disciplinary Concept*, 21–48, Berlin: De Gruyter.

Mauch, C. (2019), 'Slow Hope: Rethinking Ecologies of Crisis and Fear', *RCC Perspectives*, 1: 1–43.

Mauch, C., and Zeller, T. eds (2008), *The World beyond the Windshield: Roads and Landscapes in the United States and Europe*, Stuttgart: Franz Steiner Verlag.

Mazzei, L. A. (2013), A Voice without Organs: Interviewing in Posthumanist Research', *International Journal of Qualitative Studies in Education*, 26(6): 732–40.

McQueen, M., Abou-Zeid, G., MacArthur, J. and Clifton, K. (2021), 'Transportation Transformation: Is Micromobility Making a Macro Impact on Sustainability?', *Journal of Planning Literature*, 36(1): 46–61.

Melucci, A. (1995), 'The Process of Collective Identity', in H. Johnston and B. Klandermans (eds), *Social Movements and Culture*, 41–63, Minneapolis: University of Minnesota Press.

Melucci, A. (1996), *The Playing Self: Person and Meaning in the Planetary Society*, Cambridge: Polity.

Mendes-Flohr, P., ed. (2018), *Dialogue as a Trans-Disciplinary Concept*, Berlin: De Gruyter.

Merriman, P. (2007), *Driving Spaces: A Cultural-historical Geography of England's M1 Motorway*, Oxford: Blackwell.

Mies, M. (1986), *Patriarchy and Capital Accumulation on a World Scale: Women in the International Division of Labour*, London: Verso.

Mies, M., and Shiva, V. (1993), *Ecofeminism*, London: Zed.

Mignolo, W. (2017), 'Interview with Walter D. Mignolo', in M. Woons and S. Weier (eds), *Critical Epistemologies of global politics*, 11–25, Bristol: E-International Relations.

Miller, D. ed. (2001) *Car Cultures*, London: Routledge.

Mohanty, C. T. (1995), 'Feminist Encounters: Locating the Politics of Experience', in L. Nicholson and S. Seidman, Steven (eds), *Social Postmodernism*, 68–86, Cambridge: Cambridge University Press.

Moreno, C. (2024), *The 15-Minute City: A Solution to Saving Our Time and Our Planet*, London: Wiley.

Möllers, N. and Crutzen, P. (2014), ' "A Huge Variety of Possibilities": Interview with Nobel Laureate Paul Crutzen on His Life, His Career in Research, and His Views on the Anthropocene Idea', in T. Möllers, C. Schwägerl and H. Trischler (eds), *Welcome to the Anthropocene: The Earth in Our Hands*, Munich: Deutsches Museum/ Rachel Carson Center.

Möllers, T., Schwägerl, C. and Trischler, H. eds (2014), *Welcome to the Anthropocene: The Earth in Our Hands*. Munich Deutsches Museum/ Rachel Carson Center.

Moraglio, M. (2017), *Driving Modernity: Technology, Experts, Politics, and Fascist Motorways, (1922–1943)*, Oxford: Berghahn.

Morse, M., Jickling, B. and Quay, J. (2018), 'Rethinking Relationships through Education: Wild Pedagogies in Practice', *Journal of Outdoor and Environmental Education*, 21: 241–54.

Naess, A. (1973), 'The Shallow and the Deep, Long Range Ecology Movement – Summary', *Inquiry*, 16(1): 95–100.

Nandy, A. (1983), *The Intimate Enemy: Loss and Recovery of Self under Colonialism*, New Delhi: Oxford India.

Nayar, P. K. (2012), 'A New Biological Citizenship: Posthumanism in Octavia Butler's *Fledgling*', *Modern Fiction Studies*, 58(4): 796–817.

Neal, Z. (2010), 'Seeking common ground: Three perspectives on public space', *Urban Design and Planning*, 163(2): 59–66.

Nieuwenhuijsen, M. J. and Khreis, H. (2016), 'Car Free Cities: Pathway to Healthy Urban Living', *Environment International*, 94: 251–62.

Nikolaeva, A., Adey, P., Cresswell, T., Lee, J. L., Nóvoa, A. and Temenos, C. (2019), 'Commoning Mobility: Towards a New Politics of Mobility Transitions', *Transactions of the Institute of British Geographers*, 2019: 1–15.

Nightingale, A. J. (2019), 'Commoning for inclusion? Political Communities, Commons, Exclusion, Property and Socio-Natural Becomings', *International Journal of the Commons*, 13(1): 16–35.

Nixon, D. (2014), 'Speeding Capsules of Alienation? Social (Dis)Connections amongst Drivers, Cyclists and Pedestrians in Vancouver, BC', *Geoforum*, 54: 91–102.

Norton, P. (2011), *Fighting Traffic: The Dawn of the Motor Age*, Cambridge, MA: MIT Press.

O'Brien, J. (2020), 'A Path to the Future, or Ambivalent Payoffs: Tragic Complexity, or a Foundation for Good Order?', *Journal of Political Power*, 13(3): 382–96.

Odyssee-mure.eu (2024), Sectoral Profile Transport (https://www.odyssee-mure.eu/ publications/efficiency-by-sector/transport/transport-eu.pdf).

Ogden, C. and Cox, P. (2009), 'The Compulsory Passenger: Mobility, Impairment and Empowerment', *paper presented at RGS-IGB conference, Manchester 26–28 August*.

O'Hern, S. and Estgfaeller, N. (2020), 'A Scientometric Review of Powered Micromobility', *Sustainability*, 12(22): 9505.

Olsen, B., and Pétursdóttir, þ. (2014), 'Unruly Heritage: Trading Legacies in the Anthropocene', *Arkæologisk Forum*, 35: 38–45.

O'Regan, M. (2012), 'Alternative Mobility Cultures and the Resurgence of Hitch-Hiking', in S. Fullagar, K. Markwell and E. Wilson (eds), *Slow Tourism: Experiences and Mobilities*, 128–42, Bristol: Channel View.

Packer, J. (2008), *Mobility without Mayhem; Safety, Cars, Citizenship*, Durham, NC: Duke University Press.

Paterson, M. (2007), *Automobile Politics: Ecology and Cultural Political Economy*, Cambridge: Cambridge University Press.

Paulsen, M., jagodzinski, j and Hawke, S. eds (2022), *Pedagogy in the Anthropocene: Re-Wilding Education for a New* Earth, Cham: Palgrave Macmillan.

PEP (2021), *The Pan European Masterplan for Cycling Promotion*, Vienna: Federal Ministry for Climate Action, Environment, Energy, Mobility, Innovation and Technology, https://thepep.unece.org/sites/default/files/2021-06/MASTERPLAN_2021-05-20-II_BF%203%20June_0.pdf.

Pooley, C., Jones, T., Tight, M., Horton, D., Scheldeman, G., Jopson, A. and Strano, E. (2013), *Promoting Walking and Cycling: New Perspectives on Sustainable Travel*, Bristol: Policy Press.

Popan, C. (2019), *Bicycle Utopias: Imagining Fast and Slow Cycling Futures*, Abingdon: Routledge.

Popan, C. (2020), 'Beyond Utilitarian Mobilities: Cycling Senses and the Subversion of the Car System', *Applied Mobilities*, 5(3): 289–305.

Pope Francis. (2015), *Laudato Si: On Care for Our Common Home* [Encyclical].

Presner, T. (2007), *Mobile Modernity: Germans, Jews, Trains*, New York: Columbia University Press.

Puig de la Bellacasa, M. (2011), 'Matters of care in technoscience: Assembling neglected things', *Social Studies of Science*, 41(1): 85–106.

Puig de la Bellacasa, M. (2012) 'Nothing comes without its world': Thinking with care', *The Sociological Review*, 60(2): 197–216.

Puig de la Bellacasa, M. (2017) *Matters of Care: Speculative Ethics in More Than Human Worlds* Minneapolis: University of Minnesota Press.

Pullinger, D. J., ed. (1989), *With Scorching Heat and Drought? A Report on the Greenhouse Effect*, Edinburgh: SRT Project, Church of Scotland Department of Ministry and Mission.

Purdey, J. (2015), *After Nature: A Politics for the Anthropocene*, Cambridge, MA: Harvard University Press.

Radkau, J. (2009) *Max Weber: A Biography*, Cambridge: Polity.

Read, H. (1937), *Art and Society*, London: Windmill Press.

Read, H. (1961), *Education through Art*, London: Faber and Faber.

Renn J. (2018), 'The Evolution of Knowledge: Rethinking Science in the Anthropocene', *HoST – Journal of History of Science and Technology*, 12: 1–22.

Renshaw, P.D. (2021), 'Feeling for the Anthropocene: Placestories of Living Justice', *The Australian Educational Researcher*, 48: 1–21.

Rérat, P., and Orthar, N. (2024), *Cycling through the Pandemic: Tactical Urbanism and the Implementation of Pop-Up Bike Lanes in the Time of COVID-19*, Cham: Springer.

Rérat, P., Haldiman, L. and Widmar, H. (2022), 'Cycling in the Era of Covid-19: The Effects of the Pandemic and Pop-Up Bike Lanes on Cycling Practices', *Transportation Research Interdisciplinary Perspectives*, 15(1):100677.

Ristau, J. (2011), What Is Commoning, Anyway? Posted 3 March, https://www.onthe commons.org/work/what-commoning-anyway.

Ritzer, G. (1993), *The McDonaldization of Society*, Los Angeles: Pine Forge Press.

Ritzer, G. (2021), *The McDonaldization of Society: Into the Digital Age*, London: Sage.

Rivers, P. (1972), *Restless Generation: A Crisis in Mobility*, London: HarperCollins.

Robinson, F. (2011), *The Ethics of Care A Feminist Approach to Human Security*, Philadelphia: Temple University Press.

Rocheleau, D., Thomas-Slayter, B. and Wangari, E. (1996), 'Gender and Environment: A Feminist Political Ecology Perspective', in D. Rocheleau, B.Thomas-Slayter and E. Wangari (eds), *Feminist Political Ecology: Global Issues and Local Experiences*, 3–26, London: Routledge.

Rosa, H. (2013), *Social Acceleration: A New Theory of Modernity*. New York: Colombia University Press.

Rosa, H. (2019), *Resonance: A Sociology of Our Relationship to the World*, Cambridge: Polity.

Rosa, H. (2020), *The Uncontrollability of the World*, Cambridge: Polity.

Rosa, H. (2020b. 'Beethoven, the Sailor, the Boy and the Nazi. A Reply to My Critics', *Journal of Political Power*, 13(3): 397–414.

Rose, N., and Novas, C. (2005), 'Biological Citizenship', in A. Ong and S. J. Collier (eds), *Global Assemblages: Technology, Politics, and Ethics as Anthropological Problems*, 439–64, Oxford: Blackwell.

Rubin, M. and Parker, A. (2023), 'Many Ways to Care: Mobility, Gender and Gauteng's Geography', *Gender, Place and Culture: A Journal of Feminist Geography*, 30(5): 714–37.

Runnymede Trust. Commission on the Future of Multi-Ethnic Britain (2000), *The Future of Multi-Ethnic Britain: The Parekh Report*, London: Profile Books.

Ryan, A.B. (2013), 'The Transformative Capacity of the Commons and Commoning', *Irish Journal of Sociology*, 21(2): 90–102.

Sachs, W. (1984), *For the Love of the Automobile: Looking Back into the History of Our Desires*, Berkeley: University of California Press.

Salleh, A. (2017 [1997]), *Ecofeminism as Politics: Nature, Marx and the Postmodern* 2nd edn, London: Zed.

Sánchez de Madariaga, I. (2013a), 'Mobility of Care: Introducing New Concepts in Urban Transport', in I. Sánchez de Madariaga and M. Roberts (eds), *Fair Shared Cities: The Impact of Gender Planning in Europe*, 33–48, Abingdon: Routledge.

Sánchez de Madariaga, I. (2013b), 'From Women in Transport to Gender in Transport: Challenging Conceptual Frameworks for Improved Policymaking', *Journal of International Affairs*, 67(1): 43–65.

Santos, B. de Sousa and Avritzar, L. (2007), 'Introduction: Opening up the canon of democracy', in B. de Sousa Santos (ed.), *Democratizing Democracy: Beyond the Liberal Democratic Canon*, xxxiv–lxxiv, London: Verso.

Santos, B. de Sousa and Meneses, M. P. eds (2019), *Knowledges Born in the Struggle: Constructing the Epistemologies of the Global South*, Abingdon: Routledge.

Santos, B. de Sousa, ed. (2007), *Democratizing Democracy: Beyond the Liberal Democratic Canon*, London: Verso.

Santos, B. de Sousa (2006), *The Rise of the Global Left: The World Social Forum and Beyond*, London: Zed.

Santos, B. de Sousa (2018), *The End of the Cognitive Empire: The Coming of Age of Epistemologies of the South*, Durham: NC: Duke University Press.

Schiffner, I., and Srinivasan, M. V. (2016), 'Budgerigar Flight in a Varying Environment: Flight at Distinct Speeds?', *Biology Letters*, 12(6): 20160221. http://doi. org/10.1098/rsbl.2016.0221

Schivelbusch, W. (1977), *Geschichte der Eisenbahnreise: Zur Industrialisierung von Raum und Zeit im 19. Jahrhundert*, München/Wien: Hanser.

Schmelzer, M., Vetter, A. and Vansintjan, A. (2022), *The Future Is Degrowth: A Guide to a World beyond Capitalism*, London: Verso.

Schmid, C. (2022), *Henri Lefebvre and the Theory of the Production of Space*, London: Verso.

Seiler, C. (2008), *Republic of Drivers: A Cultural History of Automobility in America.* Chicago: University of Chicago Press.

Sen, J., Anand, A., Escobar A. and Waterman P. eds (2004), *World Social Forum: Challenging Empires*, New Delhi: Process/The Viveka Foundation.

Sendra, P., and Sennet, R. (2022), *Designing Disorder: Experiments and Disruptions in the City*, London: Verso.

Sennet, R. (2021 [1970]), *The Uses of Disorder: Personal Identity and City Life*, London: Verso.

Sevilla-Buitrago, A. (2015), 'Capitalist Formations of Enclosure: Space and the Extinction of the Commons' *Antipode*, 47:4, 999–1020.

Sheller. M. (2018), *Mobility Justice: The Politics of Movement in an Age of Extremes*, London: Verso.

Sheller, M. (2021), *Advanced Introduction to Mobilities*, Cheltenham: Edward Elgar.

Sheller, M. (2022), 'The End of Flying: Coronavirus Confinement, Academic (Im) mobilities and Me', in K. Bjørkdahl, and A. S. Franco Duharte (eds), *Academic Flying and the Means of Communication*, 53–77, Singapore: Palgrave Macmillan. https:// doi.org/10.1007/978-981-16-4911-0_3

Sheller, M. (2023), 'Mobility Justive after Climate coloniality: Mobile commoning as a relational ethics of care', *Australian Geographer* 54(4): 433–47.

Sheridan, J. (2002), 'My Name Is Walker: An Environmental Resistance Exodus', *Canadian Journal of Environmental Education*, 7: 192–205.

Shilliam, R. (2021), *Decolonizing Politics: An Introduction*, Cambridge: Polity.

Shilling, C. (1993), *The Body and Social Theory*, London: Sage.

Shiva, V. (1988), 'Reductionist Science as Epistemological Violence', in A. Nandy (ed.), *Science, Hegemony and Violence: A Requiem for Modernity*, Delhi: Oxford University Press. https://archive.unu.edu/unupress/unupbooks/uu05se/uu05se0i.htm.

Shiva, V. (1991), *The Violence of the Green Revolution: Third World Agriculture, Ecology and Politics*, London: Zed.

Shove, E. Pantzar, M. and Watson, M. (2012), *The Dynamics of Social Practice: Everyday Life and How It Changes*, London: Sage.

Sliwinska, B. (2019), 'Cathy Wilkes' Care-Full Matter-Scapes: Female Affects of Care, Feminist Materiality and Vibrant Things', *Journal of Visual Art Practice*, 18(4): 285–304.

Smith, K. K. (2003), *Wendell Berry and the Agrarian Tradition*, Lawrence: University Press of Kansas.

Smith, M. (2001), *An Ethics of Place: Radical Ecology, Postmodernity, and Social Theory*, Albany: State University of New York Press.

Sölle, D. (1976), 'Christians for Socialism', *CrossCurrents*, 24(6): 419–34.

Sölle, D. (2001), *The Silent Cry: Mysticism and Resistance*, Minneapolis: Fortress.

Sölle, D. with Cloyes, S. A. (1984), *To Work and to Love: A Theology of Creation*, Minneapolis: Fortress.

Soper, K. (2020), *Post-Growth Living: For an Alternative Hedonism*, London: Verso.

Soron, D. (2009), 'Driven to Drive: Cars and the Problem of "Compulsory Consumption"', in J. Conley and A. T. McLaren (eds), *Car Troubles: Critical Studies of Automobility and Auto-Mobility*, 181–98, London: Routledge.

Sperling, D., and Gordon, D. (2009), *Two Billion Cars: Driving toward Sustainability*, Oxford: Oxford University Press.

Spinney, J. (2006), 'A Place of Sense: A Kinaesthetic Ethnography of Cyclists on Mont Ventoux', *Environment and Planning. D, Society & Space*, 24(5): 709–32.

Spinney, J. (2021), *Understanding Urban Cycling: Exploring the Relationship between Mobility, Sustainability and Capital*, Abingdon: Routledge.

St. John, A. (1912), 'Modifications in Prison Regime and Conditional Release', in *National Conference on the Prevention of Destitution 1912. Report of the Proceedings*, 517–22, London: P.S. King & Son.

Steffen, W., Broadgate, W., Deutsch, L., Gaffney, O. and Ludwig, C. (2015), 'The Trajectory of the Anthropocene: The Great Acceleration', *The Anthropocene Review*, 2(1): 81–98.

Steffen, W., Rockström, J. Richardson, K. Lenton, T. M. Folke, C. Liverman, D. Summerhayes, C. P. Barnosky, A. D. Cornell, S. E. Crucifix, M. Donges, J. F. Fetzer, I. Lade, S. J. Scheffer, M. Winkelmann, R. and Schellnhuber, H. J. (2016), 'Stratigraphic and Earth System Approaches to Defining the Anthropocene', *Earth's Future*, 4(8): 324–45.

Sträuli, L. (2023), 'Negotiating Difference on Public Transport: How Practices and Experiences of Deviance Shape Public Space', *Urban Planning*, 8(4): 89–98.

Sullivan, S. (2021), 'I'm Sian, and I'm a Fossil Fuel Addict: On Paradox, Disavowal and (Im)Possibility in Changing Climate Change', in S. Böhm and S. Sullivan (eds), *Negotiating Climate Change in Crisis*, 139–52, Cambridge: Open Book.

Susen, S. (2020), 'The Resonance of Resonance: Critical Theory as a Sociology of World-Relations?', *International Journal of Politics, Culture, and Society*, 33(3): 309–44.

Symons, J. and Karlsson, R. (2018), 'Ecomodernist citizenship: Rethinking Political Obligations in a Climate-Changed World', *Citizenship Studies*, 22(7): 685–704.

Tabios Hillebrecht, A. L, and Berros, M. V. eds (2017), 'Can Nature Have Rights? Legal and Political Insights', *RCC Perspectives: Transformations in Environment and Society*, 6, doi.org/10.5282/rcc/8164.

Tănăsescu, M. (2022), *Understanding the Rights of Nature: A Critical Introduction*, Bielefeld: Transcript.

Taylor, C. (2005), 'Lévinasian ethics and feminist ethics of care', *Symposium – Canadian Society for Hermeneutics and Postmodern Thought*, 9(2): 217–40.

Taylor, S. (2022), 'Interdependent Animals: A Feminist Disability Ethics of Care', in C. J. Adams and L. Gruen (eds), *Ecofeminisms: Feminist Intersections with Other Animals and the Earth*, 2nd edn, London. Bloomsbury.

Thirlby, D. (2002), *Minimal Motoring: From Cyclecar to Microcar*, Stroud: Tempus.

Topp, H., and Pharoah, T. (1994), 'Car-Free City Centres', *Transportation*, 21(3): 231–47.

Treibl, F. (2018), *Hitchhiking as an alternative form of mobility: The perception of hitchhiking in Czech Republic and Austria as an alternative form of mobility used nowadays by young people.* MA Thesis, Department of Geography and Regional Science, University of Graz.

Trischler, H. (2016), 'The Anthropocene. A Challenge for the History of Science, Technology, and the Environment', *NTM Zeitschrift für Geschichte der Wissenschaften, Technik und Medizin*, 24 (3): 309–35.

Tuvikene, T., Kębłowski, W., Weicker, T., Finch, J., Sgibnev, W., Sträuli, L., Laine, S., Dobruszkes, F. and Ianchenko, A. (2023), *Public transport as public space in European cities*, Leipzig: Leibniz-Institut für Länderkunde e.V. (IfL).

UNEP (2024) https://www.unep.org/news-and-stories/story/what-are-energy-transition-minerals-and-how-can-they-unlock-clean-energy-age.

Urbaniti, N. (2019), 'Representative Constructivism's Conundrum', in L. Disch, M.v.d. Sande and N. Urbinati (eds), *The Constructivist Turn in Political Representation*, Edinburgh: Edinburgh University Press.

Urry, J. (1990), *The Tourist Gaze*, London: Sage.

Urry, J. (1995), *Consuming Places*, Abingdon: Routledge.

Urry, J. (2004), The 'System' of Automobility, *Theory, Culture & Society*, 21(4/5): 25–39.

Urry, J. (2011), *Climate Change and Society*, Cambridge: Polity.

Urry, J. (2014), *Offshoring*, Cambridge: Polity Press.

Urry, J. and Larsen, J. (2011), *The Tourist Gaze 3.0*, London: Sage.

Vannini, P., Waskul, D. and Gottschalk, S. (2012), *The Senses in Self, Society and Culture*, Abingdon: Routledge.

Velicu, I., and García-López, G. (2018), 'Thinking the Commons through Ostrom and Butler', *Theory, Culture and Society*, 35(6): 55–73.

Verkade, T., and te Brömmelstroet, M. (2022), *Movement: How to Take Back Our Streets and Transform Our Lives*, London: Scribe Publications.

Villamayor-Tomas, S., and García-López, G. (2021), 'Commons Movements: Old and New Trends in Rural and Urban Contexts', *Annual Review of Environment and Resources*, 46: 511–43.

Ward, B., and Dubos, R. (1972), *Only One Earth: The Care and Maintenance of a Small Planet*, London: Penguin.

Watson, M. (2012), 'How Theories of Practice Can Inform Transition to a Decarbonised Transport System', *Journal of Transport Geography*, 24: 488–96.

Weeks, K. (2023), 'Abolition of The Family: The Most Infamous Feminist Proposal', *Feminist Theory*, 24(3): 433–53.

Wells, C. (2012), *Car Country: An Environmental History*, Seattle: University of Washington Press.

Weil, S. (2021 [1951]), *Waiting for God*, Abingdon: Routledge.

Whitehead A. N. (1978), *Process and Reality*, New York: Free Press.

Whitelegg, J. (1997), *Critical Mass: Transport, Environment and Society in the Twenty-first Century*, London: Pluto.

Whitelegg, J. (2016), *Mobility*, Shrewsbury: Creativespace Independent Publishing.

Wickham, J. (2006), *Gridlock: Dublin's Transport Crisis and the Future of the City*, Dublin: New Island Books.

Williams, R. (2022), *Culture and Politics: Class, Writing, Socialism*, London: Verso.

Winstanley, G. (1989 [1649]), *Selected writings*, ed. A. Hopton, London: Aporia Press.

Wood, E. M. (2012), *Liberty and Property: A Social History of Western Political Thought from the Renaissance to Enlightenment*, London: Verso.

Wright, C. L. (1992), *Fast Wheels, Slow Traffic: Urban Transport Choices*, Philadelphia, PA: Temple University Press.

Zeller, T. (2006), *Driving Germany: The landscape of the German Autobahn (1930–1970*, Oxford: Berghahn.

Ziai, A. (2023), *Theorising Postdevelopment*. DPS Working Paper Series No.16, Department for Development and Postcolonial Studies, University of Kassel.

Index

acceleration
  economic modernity 3, 6, 25, 33, 62,
    64, 83–4
  velocity 112, 128, 145
accumulation 12–13, 15, 17, 33–4, 42, 72,
    74–5, 105, 125, 133, 139–40, 170
activism 14, 28, 36, 46, 48, 69, 84–6,
    89–90, 152, 170
aeromobilities 66, 158–9, 171,
    see also air travel
aesthetics 26, 47, 49, 98, 100–1, 119, 122,
    139, *see also* kineasthetics
affect sociological concept 60–1,
    67–8, 71, 74, 80, 91, 96–7,
    112–13, 115–6, 121–2, 131, 156,
    see also emotions
agency 5, 10, 17, 25, 28, 30, 40, 49, 58–9,
    68, 71–2, 85, 103, *see also* control
  collective 17, 82
  human 39, 49, 147–8
  individual 21, 58, 146
  more-than-human 25–6, 45, 49, 53,
    90, 101
  technological 91, 147
air quality 10, 105, 127, 168, *see also*
    pollution
air travel 104, 109, 143, 145–6, 153,
    158–9, *see also* aeromobilities
alienation 3, 21, 23, 44, 59, 61–2, 64, 82,
    131–3, 152, 158, 163
ambling 114, 125, 128, 135
animals
  interaction with 79, 93, 111–12, 114,
    118, 122, 131, 134
  rights 30, 50–1, 71, 134
  traction 20, 22, 109, 134, 143
Anthropocene
  concept 34–43, 45, 47, 57, 62, 65, 68, 73,
    85, 87, 89, 99, 145, 150, 158, 162, 175
  era 1–2, 11, 16–17, 28, 30, 33–8, 45–6,
    48, 53, 55, 63, 69, 73, 84, 95, 136,
    138, 163

mobility practices 37, 40, 73, 94–5,
    138, 144, 147, 152, 158–9,
    164–70, 172–4
anticapitalism 72, 87, 140
assemblage 91, 95–6, 112, 115, 144
assisted power travel, *see* augmented
    power travel
attunement 53, 94, 96, 102, 118
augmentated power travel 21, 107–9,
    112–14, 134–5, 143
automobility 2, 6, 15, 31, 79–80, 95,
    104–6, 134, 136, 140, 159, 162,
    164–8, 170
aviation *see* aeromobilities

balance 97–8, 101, 109, 123, 128,
    145, 160
being-in-the-world 3, 4–6, 14–15, 50, 59,
    62, 63, 67, 74, 89–91, 93, 115, 128,
    146, 156, 163
belonging 35, 40, 42, 44, 46, 63,
    73, 175
bicycles, *see* cycle technologies
bodies 19–22, 27, 54–5, 79, 91–2, 94–9,
    101–2, 109, 111, 113–17, 122,
    128–131, 134, 160
bodily
  competencies, skills 20, 23
  energy, work 5, 22–3, 111–13,
    129, 136–8
  experience, sensation 54, 98,
    102–3, 111
  interaction 2, 6, 68, 101, 115
  movement 19–23, 95, 101, 103,
    130, 135
boundaries
  conceptual 14, 34, 35, 37, 40, 59, 74, 76,
    78, 84, 134
  earth-system 1–2, 12–13, 17, 136, 169
  territorial 35, 42, 44, 47, 81, 84, 175
bus travel 5, 25, 92, 109, 117, 119, 134,
    143, 145, 146, 150, 153–4, 167, 173

capacity
  human 4, 13, 17–19, 26, 38–9, 45,
    47–50, 53, 57, 62, 70–2, 84, 90, 116,
    122, 146
  of physical body 96, 99, 114, 118, 148,
    see also bodily energy, experience
  planetary 33
  technological 61, 84, 96, 107, 135
capital, capitalism 6, 12, 15, 17, 27, 35,
  38–9, 42, 62, 65, 71–5, 78–9, 83, 84,
  87, 149, *see also* accumulation
  carbon 31, 70, 80
car dependency 10, 72, 125, 137, 144, 163,
  168, 171, 174
car-free and non-car life 6, 2, 8, 48,
  79, 87, 104, 117, 125, 127, 164,
  171, 174
car travel 21–2, 31, 105, 125, 144, 158,
  163–4, 168–9, 171, *see also* driving,
  passengers
car travellers 6, 126, *see also* drivers,
  passengers
care and caring 4, 11, 21, 24, 29–30, 47–9,
  51–3, 57, 64–72, 74, 76, 78–9, 84–7,
  91, 93–4, 109, 105, 119–23, 135, 145–
  6, 148–52, 157–8, 160, 171–3, *see also*
  ethics of care
  for the commons 89, 165, 170,
    173
care-fulness 24, 48, 131
care mobilities 148, 149
cargo bikes *see* cycle technologies
children 118, 123, 146, 172
cities 105, 113, 118, 120, 123, 125–7,
  147–8, 169,
    see also fifteen-minute cities
citizenship 10–13, 18, 27–8, 30, 32–50,
  53–55, 72, 146, 151, 154, 160–3,
  166, 175
  Anthropocene 2–3, 6, 11, 13, 24–6, 28,
    30–1, 33–37, 39, 42, 44–50, 52, 55,
    61, 64, 66, 68, 77, 84–7, 90, 94–7, 109,
    112, 136, 139, 149, 152–3, 162, 168,
    171, 174
  automotive 159–61, 174
class
  carbon 18
  mobility 27–8, 137
  social 18, 26, 29, 73, 124, 134, 136–8,
    152–4, 157–8, 162–3

climate breakdown 1–4, 9, 11, 15–19, 24,
  30, 33, 35, 38–9, 42, 62, 71, 82, 85–7,
  90, 105, 109, 117, 119–20, 163, 169
clothing 91, 119, 132
cognition 19, 21, 23, 55, 98–9, 102, 122,
  128–9, 131, 145
comfort 129, 154, *see also* discomfort
commodification 10, 78, 100, 129,
  133, 139–40
commodities 17, 27, 62, 81, 133–4, 160
commoning 4, 11, 13, 21, 30, 49, 57,
  73–80, 82, 85, 87–9, 93, 109, 115, 135,
  151, 166
commons 11, 27, 73–80, 89, 91, 123,
  130, 135, 139, 145, 150–1, 162, 166,
  170, 173
commute, commuting 118, 120, 138, 168
consumption
  material 1–2, 13, 15, 18, 61–2, 81, 95,
    100, 104, 107, 162
  spatial 2, 62, 128
conviviality 133, 151
creation 36, 50, 69, 86
cycle technologies 97, 100, 108, 112–14,
  133–5, 137, 144, 159, 163
cycle travel 5–6, 11–12, 19–20, 22–4, 28,
  48, 92–5, 117, 124, 126–9, 132–3,
  148, 157, 167, 172, 174–5
cycling 1–2, 68, 80, 87, 91–5, 97–8, 101,
  104, 106, 113–17, 119, 128–33,
  135–6, 139–40, 164
cyclists 25, 27, 106, 114, 127–8, 131,
  135–6, 153, 161, 164

degrowth 13, 48, 57, 75, 80, 95,
  138–9, 168
democracy 7, 18, 26–8, 41, 50–2, 61, 63,
  77, 107, 136, 151
dialogue 14, 27, 58–9, 62, 64, 67, 83, 91,
  93–4, 101, 161
digital media 23, 54, 114, 129, 131
digitalization 23, 100, 131
discomfort 113, 128–9, 131, 157, 171
domination 4, 6, 27, 66–7, 87, 106, 123,
  130, 134, *see also* non-domination
drivers 11, 25, 54, 91, 96–7, 108–9, 137,
  143–7, 161–3, *see also* driving
driving 10, 48, 79, 87, 91–2, 96–8, 101,
  104–9, 126, 134, 145, 152–3, 158–64,
  169–70, *see also* car dependency

e-bikes 108, 113, *see also* augmented
    power travel
ecojustice 36–7, 67, 69, 86, 159, 170
education, *see* learning, pedagogy
efficiency
   economic 149, 161
   energy 9–10, 95, 106–7, 114
   travel 22, 94, 117, 124, 127,
     164, 166
effort *see* bodily energy, work
electric vehicles 1, 16, 105–9, 113,
    126, 140, 143–4, 165, 168, 172,
    see also e-bikes
emancipatory politics 40–1, 63,
    see also liberation
emissions 9–12, 105, 144, 158, 169
emotions 2, 5, 25, 47–8, 53–4,
    60–1, 68, 71, 74, 91, 96, 131, 156,
    see also affect
employment 10, 79, 117, 138, 169
enclosed travel 5, 21, 68, 97, 103, 112,
    131, 141, 146, 172
enclosure of the commons 27, 41, 73–81,
    110, 123, 128, 162
encounter 6, 11, 15, 20–22, 25–6, 53,
    58, 60, 64, 67–8, 70, 90–1, 99,
    101–3, 111, 118–22, 124, 126–30,
    134–5, 141, 151–3, 156–8, 161,
    172–3, 175
equity *see* fair share
ethics
   of care 13, 47–8, 51, 53, 55, 65–9, 71,
    78–9, 151–2, 171–2
   environmental 29, 48, 50, 66–7, 71
   posthuman 46–7, 68
everyday travel 2, 20, 24, 31, 38, 48, 58,
    66–7, 90, 92–3, 95, 105, 108, 111–13,
    117, 120, 127, 129–32, 135, 139, 151,
    158, 167, 171–2
exclusion 10, 18, 26–8, 35, 41, 44, 47–9,
    51, 73–4, 76–82, 105, 110, 123, 136,
    148, 161, 164, 171, 173
exercise 22–3, 94, 117,
    see also bodily work
experience 2–5, 10, 11, 21, 28–30, 53–5,
    57–61, 68, 74, 80, 82–3, 90–7, 100–6,
    108, 111, 115, 121, 125, 127, 129–32,
    138–40, 143–7, 153, 156–61,
    168–72
exposure 5, 97, 109, 112, 117

extractivism 5, 15–17, 28, 33, 38, 41, 50,
    63, 73–4, 77, 80, 143

fair share 1, 13, 81, 169, 171
family 61, 106–7, 121, 146, 149–50,
    153–4, 168–9
fatigue 98, 112, 120, 129, 131, *see also*
    bodily energy, work
feeling (sensation) 45, 54, 59, 66, 96,
    98–9, 101–3, 113, 127, 147, 151, 156,
    175, *see also* emotion, perception
feminism 11, 30, 45–6, 52, 54, 65, 67, 71,
    75, 123
fifteen-minute city 20, 24, 82, 106, 148
flying *see* aeromobilities
fossil fuels 1–3, 16, 38, 66, 85, 112,
    162–3, 168

gaze 21, 49, 100, 156, 160–2, 164
'good life' 14, 57, 62, 65, 88

habits
   physical 28, 96, 116
   travel 6, 9, 11, 16, 19, 24, 30, 55, 64,
    66–7, 96, 109, 163, 167, 172
health 10, 94, 113, 125, 130, 138
hearing 25, 50, 102–3, 116, 121, 124, 150,
    164, *see also* listening, sound
high energy
   society 1, 9, 13, 18, 170, 175
   travel 2, 5, 10, 13, 15–16, 24, 49, 66, 79,
    136, 143, 168
high speed travel 10, 24, 68, 79, 103,
    168, 174
housing 10, 79, 105, 117, 148, 168–9
human scale
   human rights, *see* rights
   speed 112–15, 128, 164
   travel 111–15, 117, 123, 132, 134, 136,
    140, 145, 149, 164, 169
humanism 35, 38, 44–6, 51

I-it relations *see* relationality
I-Thou relations *see* relationality
imperialism 33, 41, 73, 130, 133–4, 165
individualism 2, 4, 43, 52–4, 74–5, 81, 95,
    162, 165, 168
inequality 2, 13, 15, 17–18, 27–9, 35, 41,
    48, 66, 78, 81, 87, 105, 110, 124, 150,
    168, 170

infrastructure 6, 9, 19, 21–2, 25, 58, 71,
　　79, 81, 90, 92, 103–5, 108, 111–12,
　　118, 120, 123, 128, 135–6, 147, 149,
　　151, 165, 167, 173–4
interiors (of vehicles) 68, 117, 146,
　　154, 156
interdependence 41, 67, 71–2, 79

joy 25, 102, 118, 155, 160
justice, *see also* ecojustice
　　earth-system 13, 67, 169
　　mobility 3, 36, 148, 158
　　social 67, 161

kineaesthetics 98, 100, 131–2, 145

landscapes 21, 62, 90, 100, 102–4, 116–17,
　　121–2, 134–5, 155
learning 20, 30, 64, 83, 87, 89–92, 95,
　　97–8, 102, 109, 117–19, 139, 168
leisure 10, 23, 58, 105, 118, 124–5, 137–9,
　　148, 168
liberal
　　democracy 27, 40–1
　　subjectivity 37, 43–4, 46, 50, 53, 70–2
liberation 26, 41, 95, 133, 145, 170,
　　see also emancipation
limits 4, 5, 12, 20, 22, 40–1, 73, 78, 80–1,
　　112, 135–6, 146, 150, 172–3, *see also*
　　boundaries
listening 53, 63, 121, *see also*
　　hearing, sound
living less destructively 2, 3, 9, 12, 14–15,
　　19, 35, 42, 93, 164, 175
long distance travel 23–4, 106, 125, 143,
　　153, 174
low carbon futures 15, 105, 143, 162–
　　3, 172
luxury 18, 139, 153

mass transit *see* public transport, *see also*
　　buses, trains
mobility aids
mobility impairment 16, 120, 123,
　　147–50, 160, 172
mobility transition 2, 105, 108, 143, 164,
　　167–8, 170
modernity 4, 17, 35, 41, 43, 50, 61–3, 83,
　　86, 134
mode of production 15, 78

modes of perception 97–100, 102, 122,
　　128, 131
modes of travel 10–11, 20–2, 25, 31, 45,
　　64, 72, 79, 96, 100, 103–4, 109, 112,
　　114–15, 121, 137, 144–5, 166, 169
more-than-human 4–5, 11, 13–15, 20–1,
　　24–6, 36, 45–6, 49–53, 61, 66–70, 76,
　　78–9, 90, 93, 97, 99, 112, 114, 131,
　　135, 139, 145, 150, 156, 158, 165,
　　171, 175
motivation, *see* desire
motor vehicles 10, 27, 97, 106, 108, 121,
　　124, 126–7, 137, 144, 159–60
motoring 10, 13, 95, 103–10, 125, 133,
　　144, 147, 152, 160–6, 169–71, 174,
　　see also car travel, driving

nation-state 35, 41–4, 47, 52
nature 4, 15, 25, 29, 37–40, 50, 54, 61, 64,
　　67, 71, 76, 98, 129, 156
　　see also rights of nature
nature-culture 34, 48, 74
neoliberalism 65, 74, 78–9
non-domination 52–3, 66, 68–70

othering 44, 54, 152, 165
'the other' 14, 58, 65–6, 69, 71, 78, 101, 121,
　　152, 157–8, 173 *see also* strangers

parking 10, 125–6, 145, 154
particulates *see* pollution
passengering 5, 101, 105–6, 109, 141
passenger transport 5, 144, 150, 158, 166
passengers 5–6, 11, 21, 25, 97, 101–4, 108–
　　9, 113, 126–41, 144–50, 154–61, 171
pausing 83, 124, 128
pedagogy 24, 26, 64, 88–90, 93–5, 98, 111,
　　139, 144, *see also* learning
pedestrianism *see* walking
perceptions 5–6, 19, 29–30, 54–5, 64, 67,
　　94, 97–103, 109, 111, 113, 115–17,
　　119, 122, 128–9, 131, 134, 139–40,
　　156–8, 167, 171–2, *see also* modes of
　　perception
physical work *see* bodily labour
planetary boundaries, *see* boundaries,
　　earth system
plastic senses 98–9, 101, 119
pluriverse, pluriversal politics 29, 57,
　　63, 87, 95

policy 1–3, 6, 19, 45, 69, 106, 162, 172

pollution 10, 13, 16, 33, 42, 105–6, 127, 162, 168–9, *see also* air quality

posthumanism 45–7, 49–50

power
   energy 5–6, 21–2, 68, 93, 106–9, 111–13, 129, 131, 133–4, 137, 143–4, 168, 170–3
   socio-political 2, 17–18, 25–30, 39, 46, 49, 53–4, 58, 65–7, 70–3, 76–7, 83, 88, 102, 115, 121, 123–4, 130, 134, 136, 140, 148, 156

power-over, *see* domination

power-to, *see* capacity

predictability 4, 17, 23, 37, 60, 82–5, 108, 131, 156, 158, 172

private
   motoring 6, 10, 31, 105–6, 147, 153, 160–1, 168, 169–70
   property 5, 73–4, 147
   spaces 43, 120, 150, 161

privilege 2, 17, 18, 31, 35, 38, 41–2, 46–8, 80–1, 87, 95, 105, 117, 124, 138–40, 147, 161–2, 168–72, 174–5

productivism 12, 15, 33, 72, 74, 76–7, 83, 94, 138–9

progressivism 17, 40, 63, 94, 125, 130

public matters 12, 43

public transport 1, 11, 105, 114, 117, 120, 131, 136, 141–5, 147–51, 154–8

public spaces 19, 28, 140, 150–1, 157

rail travel 21–2, 25, 92, 103–4, 109, 112, 120, 138, 144–6, 150, 153–5, 173

rain, *see also* weather 101, 119, 131, 134

relationality 3–4, 11, 14–15, 21, 29, 43, 51, 58–61, 65, 67, 70–3, 78–81, 88, 91, 111–12, 152, 167, 175

relational self 41, 51, 55, 57, 61, 65, 70

repetition, *see also* habit 92, 118, 123, 131–2

resilience 4, 17, 24, 38, 84, 119

resistance 21, 66
   to motion 127, 143
   political 54, 57, 71, 85–8

resonance 3–4, 12, 14, 21, 57, 59–64, 67–70, 82–3, 85, 88–9, 91, 93, 95–9, 101, 110, 127, 132–3, 139, 152, 156, 172

respons-*a*bility *see* responsive citizenship

responsible living 3, 9, 11, 13, 19, 21, 24–5, 29–30, 175

responsive citizenship 4, 6, 42, 47, 57–8, 61, 68–9, 84, 90, 95, 166, 173

riding, *see* cycling

rights 26, 28, 30, 36, 37, 43, 46, 48, 50, 63, 69–71, 77–8, 81, 87, 136, 162–3
   human 6, 12, 174
   of nature 28, 30, 50–1, 53, 71

scarcity 49, 72, 80–2, 136, 138

scooters 108, 113, 124, 127

seasons 116, 119, 122, 172

seeing, sight 15, 20–2, 50, 94, 98–100, 102–3, 122, 124, 150, 156, 164

senses *see* modes of perception

sensory experience, *see* experience

shopping 107, 120, 123, 125, 148, 168

skills 2, 6, 20, 22–3, 64, 84, 93, 100, 109, 118–19, 147, 171

smell 96, 98–9, 126, 134, 164

social interaction 101, 122

social reproduction 41, 70, 72, 78, 125, 149, 168

sociality 55, 58, 61, 64, 79, 92, 124, 154

sound 98, 102–3, 116, 121–2, 126–7, 134, 161, *see also* hearing

soundscapes 121, 126

speed, *see* high speed travel, human scale speed

stations 117, 120, 153

strangers 119, 146, 150–1, *see also* 'the other'

sufficiency 13, 31, 81–2, 86, 108, 114, 119, 135, 166, 168–9, 173

sustainability 3, 10, 19, 28, 95, 127, 165

sustainable transport 3, 12, 19, 23, 82, 105, 114, 144, 167, 170

symbolic dimensions of life 22, 53, 132, 153, 174

taxis 109, 146, 159

temperature 16, 98, 116, 119, 122

terrain 22, 100–2, 104, 106, 130, 133

time 5, 10, 20, 22–5, 27, 34–37, 40, 43, 49, 69, 94, 114, 117, 122, 132, 134–8, 145, 154

tiredness *see* fatigue

trains *see* rail travel

transformation 60–2, 65–9, 83, 85, 96, 153, 158
transformative politics 46–7, 52, 59, 77, 86–7, 89, 155, 170–2
travel experience *see* experience
travel spaces 10, 23, 27, 77, 79–80, 92, 94, 99, 115, 127, 136, 145, 151, 157, 173–4
travel
    mundane 11, 19–20, 31, 48, 80, 92–3, 130, 139, *see also* everyday travel
tricycles *see* cycle technologies
trust 79, 84, 94, 109, 135, 137, 144, 146–7, 152

uncertainty 3–4, 17, 48, 84, 87, 150
uncontrollability 4, 12, 14, 21, 30, 52, 57, 61, 82–90, 93, 95, 103, 109, 147, 157
unnoticing 65–6
unpredictability *see* predictability
unsustainability 1, 3, 11, 15, 88, 105, 159, 164, 170
utility function 19, 23, 52, 67, 70, 72, 85, 94, 138–40, 147, 154–5

vehicles, *see by individual type*
violence 2, 27, 74, 85, 106
virtue 42–3, 52, 65, 85, 88, 136, 161, 172
visual sense, *see also* seeing 68, 96–101, 131, 134, 150, 155
voice 26, 28, 50–53, 58, 61, 65, 69, 71, 121, 156

waiting spaces 5, 101, 120, 145–6, 154–5, 157
walking 1–2, 5–6, 11–12, 20, 23–4, 28, 48, 68, 80, 89–95, 97, 101–6, 111, 115–30, 135–6, 138–40, 145, 152, 157, 164, 172, 175
waste products *see* pollution
weather 33, 71, 90, 116, 119, 121–2, 131, 172, *see also* rain, wind
weather search also elements
wheelchairs 108–9, 123–4, 127–8, 150
wheeling 5–6, 20, 101, 104, 106, 109, 111, 115, 124–5, 127–8, 135, 140, 155, 175
wind 20, 93, 97, 114, 131, *see also* weather
work, jobs, *see* employment
work, physical *see* bodily labour